BUGS, SLUGS & OTHER THUGS

BUGS, SLUGS & OTHER THUGS

Controlling Garden Pests Organically

Rhonda Massingham Hart

A Down-to-Earth Book
from Storey Publishing

Storey Communications, Inc.
Pownal, Vermont 05261

Cover illustration by Patti Delmonte

Chapter opening illustrations by Patti Delmonte; animal and insect illustrations by Judy Eliason; how-to illustrations by Alison Kolesar

Cover design by Cindy McFarland

Text design and production by Wanda Harper

Edited by Kimberley Foster

Printed in the United States by Book Press
Fifth Printing, February 1993

Library of Congress Cataloging-in-Publication Data

Hart, Rhonda Massingham, 1959-
Bugs, slugs & other thugs : controlling garden pests organically / Rhonda Massingham Hart.
p. cm. — (A Down-to-earth book)
Includes bibliographical references (p.) and index.
ISBN 0-88266-665-7 (hc) — ISBN 0-88266-664-9 (pb)
1. Garden pests—Control. 2. Organic gardening. 3. Plants, Protection of. I. Title. II. Title: Bugs, slugs, and other thugs. III. Series.
SB974.H37 1991
632'.96—dc20

90-50607
CIP

Dedication

With everlasting love and abiding
respect to my grandmothers,
Ocea Mae Rosencrans Cole
and
Marie Massingham,
for all they have taught me about
gardening, and growing.

❧

Acknowledgements

It is with sincere appreciation that I would like to thank the many contributors to this book. Representatives from Cooperative Extension Services throughout the country sent invaluable information, and offered their own time and expertise. Among them I would like to thank the folks at Kansas State University; the University of Tennessee; Washington State University, especially Dr. Roger Akre for his insight into yellow jackets; Cornell University; Mississippi State; Dave W. Bradshaw at Clemson University; and Albert E. Bivings from Arkansas. Also, many of the Agricultural Research Stations throughout the country responded to my requests for new information; I would especially like to thank the Imported Fire Ant Station in Alabama.

I would also like to thank my four- to eleven-month-old daughter, Kailah, for taking her naps, and Bugs Bunny, et. al, for entertaining my three- to four-year-old son, Lance. Without these priceless contributions, none of the information provided would have ever been put to use!

Contents

Introduction **1**

Chapter 1 **Bad Birds** **5**

Blackbirds 6
Crows 11
Starlings 14
General Berry-eaters 17

Chapter 2 **Rodent Warriors** **19**

Gophers 19
Moles 26
Porcupines 30
Rats, Mice, and Voles 31
Squirrels 35
Woodchucks 38

Chapter 3 **Big Game** **43**

Bears 43
Coyotes 46
Deer 49
Opossums 56
Rabbits 58
Raccoons 62
Skunks 65

Chapter 4 **Friends and Neighbors** **69**

Dogs and Cats 69
Farm Animals 72
Kids 72

Chapter 5 **Lowlifes** **75**

Slugs and Snails 75
Turtles 81

Chapter 6 **What Bugs You?** **85**

Plant Health 85
Soil Health 86
Soil Solarization 89
Crop Rotation 91
Timed Planting 91
Companion Planting 92
Resistant Varieties 92
Plant Coverings 92
Ultrasonic Devices 94
Sprays and Dusts 94
Know thy Enemy 100
Aphids 102
Beetles: Flea Beetles 105, Colorado Potato Beetles 107, Cucumber Beetles 109, Japanese Beetles 110, Mexican Bean Beetles 113
Borers: Squash Vine Borers 115
Bugs: Harlequin Bugs 117, Squash Bugs 118
Caterpillars: Cabbage Loopers and Imported Cabbageworms 119, Corn Earworms 121, Cutworms 123, Tomato Hornworms 126
Earwigs 127
Fire Ants 129
Flies: Carrot Rust Flies 133
Grasshoppers/Locusts 134
Leafhoppers 136
Leaf Miners 138
Mites: Spider Mites 139
Nematodes 144

Root Maggots 143
Thrips 144
Wasps: Yellow Jackets 146
Weevils 149
Whiteflies 151
Wireworms 152

Chapter 7 **Getting Help: Acquiring and Managing Beneficials** **155**
Birds 156
Fowl 166
Bats 167
Dogs, Cats, and Ferrets 169
Snakes, Turtles, Toads, and Decollate Snails 172
Beneficial Insects 177

Appendix 1 **Plants and Their Pests** **191**

Appendix 2 **About Traps** **197**

Appendix 3 **Live Traps for Mammals** **199**

Appendix 4 **Mail-Order Suppliers** **203**

Further Reading **207**

Index **209**

Introduction

Welcome to a new era! Today everything old is new again. No longer is it casually accepted practice to grab a spray can of pesticide in response to every bug seen crawling across the potato patch. Instead, watchwords such as "organic," "least toxic pest management," "sustainable agriculture," and "Integrated Pest Management (IPM)" dictate more environmentally conscious and responsible behavior. Age-old garden practices such as composting and planting by the signs of the season are being adopted by the mainstream

The ghost of pesticides past has left us with a legacy of poison and irony. The effects of widespread applications of chemicals may not be fully understood for generations, if ever. Some of the highlights, however, include increased cancer risks, tainted groundwater, depleted topsoil, erosion, and the evolution of designer pests who rode out the toxic storms to emerge stronger than ever.

Forced to adapt in the face of chemical attacks, insects mutated and survived. They developed resistance to pesticides, making it necessary to apply more and stronger chemicals, with ever more severe consequences. With their natural enemies exterminated, insects that had rarely caused problems in the past suddenly reached outbreak proportions. In the face of death, scant numbers of pests survive, adapt, and reproduce to remind us of nature's unbounded will to perpetuate each of her intricately designed species. Resurgence, the population explosions of insects following what had initially appeared to be mass annihilation, proved that you can't keep a good (or bad) bug down. Clearly, it's time to seek alternatives to pesticides.

Identifying the Problem

The first step toward solving any problem is to identify it correctly. Pest control is no different, but given the similarities of many types of plant damage, it offers many complex challenges. How do we identify garden raiders?

Studying the damage done to plants will help solve the mystery. Is it riddled with tiny holes, snipped off at ground level, assaulted from beneath and dragged underground? When does the damage occur? Was everything just fine yesterday afternoon, but ragged by morning?

Sometimes the offender will leave behind additional evidence. Culprits from insects to bears may leave their calling cards in the form of droppings. Though not the most pleasant of detective work, analyzing these will help narrow your suspects. Other signs may include eggs, pupae, or tracks. If you suspect animal rather than insect damage, lay a track trap. Prepare a 6-foot circle by raking the ground smooth, sifting flour over the entire are, and leaving several kinds of bait in the center. At least one should appeal to your intruder. Leave this undisturbed overnight and check it for tracks in the morning.

Often plant pests can be identified by astute observation. Check the plant roots, the base of the plant, and along stems and leaves. Turn the leaves over and look at the bottom sides. If damage occurs at night, visit the garden after hours, flashlight in hand, and you may catch your culprit. If no bugs or beasts are evident, set an appropriate trap.

Trapping leads to the ultimate form of criminal identification — catching them in the act!

Solving the Problem

How will you handle the invasions? The best plan of attack is to start with the least drastic methods and work up to more serious measures if necessary. Cultural methods to try first are removing the pest's habitat (keeping weeds down), planting to avoid insect emergence times, planting varieties that are resistant to pests or less vulnerable to damage, varying planting times, and interplanting. Erecting barriers or trying repellent or scare tactics are often the next step. So are botanical insecticides (those derived from plants), which are safer than chemical equivalents and just as available.

Some of the most exciting weapons in the war on garden pests are biological controls — predators, parasites, and pathogens (viruses, bacteria, and other disease-producing organisms).

Biological control is certainly not new. Nature kept herself in balance quite nicely well before man took notice of her methods. Finally, in the late 1800s careful observation led to the rescue of the California citrus industry. A fuzzy foe, the cottony-cushion scale, had brought that fledgling industry to its knees. This pest, an immigrant to the land of the groves it was destroying, found the pickings far too easy. Having no natural enemies, it raged unchecked to epidemic proportions.

Enter USDA entomologists, who traveled to the opposite side of the earth to find something with which to fight the infestations. Imagine the elation of that first scientist, as he stood in a grove of trees somewhere in the rough and wild continent of old Australia and gazed upon a miracle of hope. A bright red bedalia beetle, similar to the familiar ladybug, devoured one after another of the vile scale. Insatiable. Unstoppable. Salvation! Within two years those little beetles had the scales at their mercy, and they continue to keep them under control to this day.

More and more success stories are heard as new techniques, in cultural as well as biological control, are developed. Sometimes the solutions seem too simple: spraying soapy water on broccoli halts aphids. Often they seem a little farfetched: spraying a solution of rotten eggs will ward off deer damage. And very often the ideas aren't new at all, but rather old folk cures, the mysteries of which are solved under the light of scientific scrutiny.

How this Book Can Help

In this book we will offer the best of the old and the new methods of natural, environmentally nontoxic pest controls. Unfortunately, there are no quick fixes or easy answers to every pest problem. It can be frustrating to try something that worked wonders for one gardener only to find that this approach seems useless in your circumstances. But such is the nature of dealing with nature. It is a constantly ongoing experiment. Nature is constantly changing to meet both her own and our challenge, and considering her track record, it's safe to say she probably still has a few tricks left.

Whether you have already identified the perpetrator or are still pondering "who dun it," this book can help. Likewise, whether you are gearing up for prevention or are already in the heat of the battle, solutions are offered for you here. If you are plagued with gophers, for instance, turn to that section and read it. You will learn more about these rodents and will find many ways to put this newfound knowledge to work. From preventive tactics to methods of catching or evicting troublemakers, each section outlines successful methods of defense, starting with the simplest, least intensive, and building up to more drastic measures. Chances are excellent that you will find the best solution to your problem.

If something has been pestering your plants, but you aren't sure who or what is responsible, check Appendix 1. Common garden plants and their most frequent pests are listed. If, for example, your corn is torn, look up the list of suspects, then turn to the individual headings under each for more information. The sections on Damage and Signs were developed to help you identify garden criminals, even when you can't catch them in the act. Finally, turn to the Deterrents sections for proven ideas on solving your particular pest problem.

What failed you once may work wonders under different circumstances. The only mysteries lie in understanding what was different in these cases. Critical observation, detailed record-keeping, and a measure of good luck may eventually reveal the variables that account for success or failure. Or they may not. The best we can do is to respect nature in all her sometimes frustrating glory and stick to our principles of gardening *with* her rather than against her. When the season is over and the harvest is in, we will have the satisfaction of knowing we have done no harm.

Chapter 1

Bad Birds

Blackbirds • Crows • Starlings
General Berry-eaters

As certain as the coming of spring is the arrival of birds migrating from their winter homes. And while songbirds may bring joy to your winter-weary bones and fill your heart with their carefree singing, others bring less cheerful tidings. To the gardener who has replanted the corn three times because of hungry blackbirds or crows, or the poor soul who loses an entire blueberry crop to one descending horde of starlings, birds are the enemy.

Before taking any measure against feathered guests, be sure you have a problem. The mere presence of birds, even such undesirables as crows, does not necessarily spell impending damage. Many birds feed heavily on garden insects, especially during their summer nesting seasons when they hunt to feed their young as well as themselves. Most migratory birds are raising their babies when you are raising a garden, and they may be doing some good out there. If you find damage, the next step is to determine just who is responsible. Many crops that draw birds also interest raccoons, squirrels, and even neighborhood kids, or may fall to the forces of wind and weather.

Justifying your actions against birds is important not only to spare innocents, but to avoid wasting time and resources against a problem that doesn't exist. Also, migratory birds are protected by federal law. The Federal Migratory Bird Treaty Act is a formal contract between the United States, Canada, and Mexico, agreeing not to

interfere with the free migrations of native birds. It states that such birds can only be killed when "committing, or about to commit, depredations upon . . . crops . . . or when concentrated in such numbers as to constitute a health hazard or other nuisance." In other words, you have to catch them in the act to be justified in using lethal controls.

Because some birds, most notoriously blackbirds and starlings, travel and roost in flocks numbering up to the millions, controls very often are necessary. Even so, try to accept some damage philosophically, while doing what you can to prevent intolerable levels.

Blackbirds

(Family Icteridae)

"Blackbirds" include twenty-two species of migratory birds. Among them are the abundant red-winged blackbird, the common grackle, cowbird, Brewer's blackbird, and others. Though they receive the most attention as "bad birds," they make some beneficial contributions. With roosting congregations numbering anywhere from a handful to a million, their overwhelming presence may exaggerate any damage they may do.

Physical Description

Male blackbirds are medium-sized (7 to 10 inches) iridescent black birds, while females are smaller and colored dull gray or brown.

The red-winged blackbird *(Agelaius phoeniceus)* male is about 9 inches long. He is true black with bright red patches trimmed in yellow on his shoulders. Females are smaller, plain brown birds, heavily stippled with darker brown. Looking more like oversized sparrows, they bear no resemblance to the flashy males.

The common grackle *(Quiscalus quiscula)* is much larger, about a foot long. From a distance the grackle appears jet black, but a closer look reveals iridescent shades of blue, purple, and green. The grackle has startling bright yellow eyes and a long, wedge-shaped tail.

The brown-headed cowbird *(Molothrus ater)* is the smallest of the blackbirds, less than 7 inches long. Males are shiny black with a dull brown head. Females are gray and have a short, finch-like beak, unlike other blackbirds, which have a stout beak.

The male Brewer's blackbird *(Euphagus cyanocephalus)* seems plain black from afar, but sports an iridescent greenish body and purplish head, with bright yellow eyes. The females are much less conspicuous, with dull gray bodies and dark eyes.

Life Cycle

All blackbirds are migratory, spending their nesting season in the northern part of their range and moving south for the cold months. In late winter and early spring, as the daylight hours increase, nature stimulates hormonal and behavioral changes that command the now-restless birds to begin their journey. As the annual migration to northern breeding grounds begins, the males usually arrive first and establish their territories to await the females. Their unusual "songs," rather like small import car horns or multitudes of squeaky gates, fill the air.

Those songs proclaim their territory to the world and call out for female companionship. When the ladies arrive they are courted, and the birds pair off to get down to the business of nesting. Except for those opportunistic cowbirds who spend their energy searching for occupied nests to exploit, nest building comes under the heading of "women's work." The male may follow his industrious mate around and try to look busy, but she does all the work.

Blackbirds usually lay between four and six eggs a season, and due to such natural disasters as predators and accidents, usually only two to four of the young make it out of pinfeathers. If the nests are destroyed, the pair will often start over again. The young remain in the nest for about two weeks as the parents scurry to bring them food and keep them warm. Many fledglings continue to depend on their parents for food after leaving the nest.

In the early fall, the shortening daylight hours trigger the birds first to molt (shed feathers), then to gather in flocks and head south. Many blackbird species winter within the southern United States.

If birds hatched during the summer survive through their first year, they have a good chance at living out a life span as long as five years.

Range and Habitat

Blackbirds are found throughout most of the United States. Most are country folk, though they are making themselves at home more and more in suburban areas.

Red-winged blackbirds are common in wetlands, fields, and parklike areas. They prefer nesting among old cattails.

Grackles inhabit wetlands as well as open areas in town and country. Evergreens provide favored nesting sites.

Cowbirds range from farms, fields, and woods to city yards and parks. They have no nesting preferences, for they build no nests. Instead, they lay their eggs in the nests of other, more family-oriented birds, abandoning them to foster parents.

The Brewer's blackbird prefers open areas: farms, fields, lawns, and alongside waterways.

Habits

Blackbirds can be entertaining to watch. Male red-winged blackbirds, who so fiercely defend their territories around their nests, will peacefully share supper at a bird feeder. Out of the nesting season they gather nightly to roost in massive groups.

Grackles occasionally develop the nasty habit of driving off or even killing smaller birds. They sometimes soak their food before eating it or feeding it to their young.

Somehow cowbirds, raised by parents of different species, always follow the instinctive behavior of their own kind. They manage to join each other in time for the fall migrations, and to leave their eggs for unsuspecting foster parents.

Garden Targets

The most common blackbird damage is to corn just before harvest time, and to sunflower heads. Grackles will also pull up and devour sprouting corn as well as enjoy the ripe ears. They also like cherries and blackberries. Brewer's blackbirds are fond of fruit.

Blackbirds also help the gardener. Nearly 30 percent of the diet of most blackbirds is insects, especially during the nesting season. Red-winged blackbirds take home beetles, weevils, and grasshoppers. Brewer's blackbirds eat cutworm larvae and pupae, corn earworms, and codling moths. Not too finicky, grackles devour just about every insect pest found in the home garden.

Damage and Signs

When blackbirds have raided the corn patch, the husks will be split or shredded and the soft insides of the kernels pecked out, leaving the kernel skin. Other parts of the stalk are unmolested.

Other damage may include pulled or scratched-up seed and devoured cherries or berries with little or no damage to branches or leaves, and ripe fruit with gashes eaten out. Ripe sunflower heads may be stripped of seeds, while the rest of the plant is left intact. Many small grain crops are devastated as the birds bend and break the grasses while feasting on the seed heads.

Deterrents

Cultural Practices. Begin your blackbird control program by eliminating weeds around the garden area. These often attract the birds before the garden does, since the birds prefer wild fruits and grains to most cultivated ones. However, once drawn to an area by these natural delicacies, most birds have few reservations against sampling your garden goodies.

Try to plant vulnerable crops away from known roosting areas. If you have serious blackbird problems, eliminate roosting sites by thinning out trees to reduce cover.

Coordinate planting with neighbors if blackbirds have been a problem. Unusually early or late crops will draw more attention from the birds than those that are maturing at the same time.

Don't till around maturing crops once harvesting begins. Leave the residue of early crops as food. When planting, take care not to leave exposed seed. Birds that find seed on the ground quickly discover there's more where that came from.

Sunflowers that are spaced 18 to 24 inches apart grow larger heads that can sustain more damage without becoming a total loss. Plant large fields of sunflowers in north/south rows. This will prevent the birds from using adjacent plants as perches from which to feed on nearby heads, since these giant flowers tend to face east or west.

Scare Tactics. Some of the most familiar and most outrageous garden antics ever conceived have been developed to frighten blackbirds.

Those folksy scarecrows add a picturesque touch to the gardenscape, and not much else. Such an oddity may frighten wary birds briefly, but even those that boast such fashions as floppy hats or scarves that flutter in the breeze are soon recognized as harmless by the avian population. Birds may even roost on that handy perch in the middle of the garden. However, battery- or propane-powered versions of these rustic relics that flail streamers, wave, bounce, or boom can make the feathers fly.

Other visual scare tactics include placing silhouettes of hawks, great horned owl decoys, or large fake snakes throughout the garden. These phony predators may help to keep birds at bay. To be effective, they must be rearranged frequently. Do this at night so the birds don't see you.

For many visual deterrents, motion is the key factor to success. Try stringing aluminum pie plates or strips of foil from twine stretched across susceptible plants. Cut long plastic strips from garbage bags and staple three or four of them around the rims of paper cups. Set these on stakes at varying heights throughout the garden. A slight breeze will keep all of these in motion.

Bird Scare Reflecting Tape is an elastic silver-coated film available in several colors. It is .025 mm thick and 11 mm wide, and is sold in either 82- or 1000-meter length rolls.

Twist the tape as you stretch it over the crops. Now it will move in the breeze, reflecting sudden flashes of

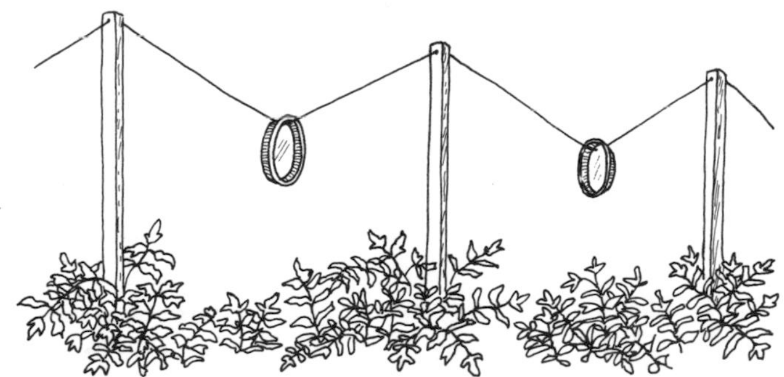

Aluminum pie plates blowing in the breeze may scare off birds.

bright sunlight from its silver surface and producing eerie humming or booming sounds. All of these frighten the birds.

As with other scare tactics, some birds will eventually brave the strangeness, but even if it is effective for only a few days, that's enough to get germinating seeds past the critical point or to save a corn crop ready to harvest.

Manufactured in Japan, this tape has been tested around the world. Damage by birds, including red-winged blackbirds, was reduced in all cases as soon as the tape went up.

Large balloons with exaggerated eyes come in three colors that the manufacturers recommend alternating every few days. Tied to trees or poles at crop height, the balloons bob and bounce, their "eyes" spooking away most birds.

Noise is effective against marauding birds. Recordings of bird distress calls played over a tape recorder or larger sound system will keep birds from feeding on your produce and discourage them from roosting nearby. People have had similar success playing back everything from tractor or lawn mower noise to rock and roll music.

Even more drastic appliances in this audio arsenal include cannons powered by gas, batteries, or propane that can be programmed to go off with a thunderous BOOM! These, however, upset more than just the local feathered community. If you use such methods in a populated area, your neighbors may find you more of a nuisance than the blackbirds. Follow directions carefully and check local ordinances before proceeding with these methods.

Scare tactics can be fun. Consider the gardener who combined his love of the tranquil pursuit of cultivation with his passion for flying. Model airplanes, that is. He found radio-controlled airplanes can do almost anything the birds could do in the air, and the buzzing intruders drove off even the brassiest birds.

Success with scare tactics depends on two things: timing and consistent change. Begin your harassment as soon as you discover blackbird damage, and continue to alter your program throughout the season. Remember that unless you have a serious damage problem actually attributable to the birds, scaring them away may do more harm than good. Blackbirds are among the more aggressive birds, and any methods that scare them from the garden will also drive away any beneficial birds.

Exclusion. Exclusion refers to barriers or other techniques that stand between the bird and the crop. Nylon netting made specifically to exclude birds works well on fruit crops and berries. Protect seedlings by placing a cage over them. Small plastic berry baskets are handy for this. Protect corn ears from damage by placing brown paper bags or the feet of nylon stockings over and securing the bag or feet with strings or rubber bands once the corn has been pollinated and the silks have turned brown (see p. 13). Since blackbirds do their worst damage on corn just before harvest, this is one good way to save the choicest ears.

Other forms of exclusion border on being scare tactics in that they cause the birds to avoid the protected plants rather than physically barring them. Drive a stake at either end of each freshly planted row of seeds. String monofilament (fishing line) or strong, dark brown thread about 2 inches above the ground, directly over the rows from stake to stake. Brown thread blends with the soil color, and transparent fishing line is just as difficult for them to see. Next weave a line or two zigzag across the rows. This "gotcha line" spooks birds as soon as they land to sample seeds or seedlings. They feel an invisible "something" grabbing at their feet and take flight.

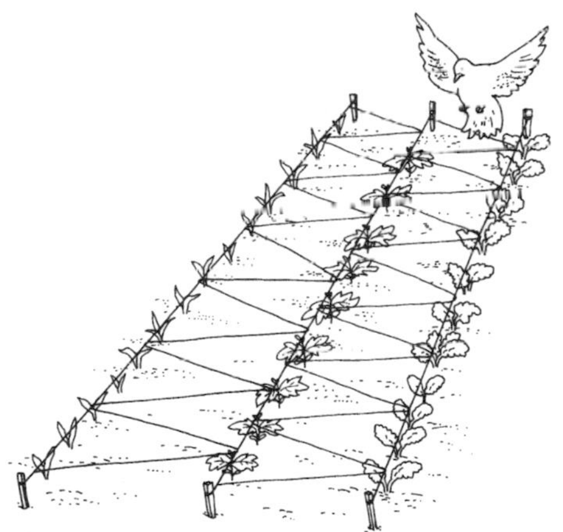

"Gotcha lines" keep birds away.

Crows

(Corvus brachyrhynchos)

Heckle and Jeckle, perched in a tree, survey the farmer's corn patch below. Determined not to be pestered by the crows, the farmer diligently assembles the fiercest, most lifelike scarecrow ever and positions it strategically in his garden. Moments later Heckle swoops down to try on the contraption's floppy hat while Jeckle borrows its corncob pipe! Eyes brimming with mischief, they hop down from their newfound perch to help themselves to the beckoning sweet corn.

The fact that one of the original bird-scaring devices was named after the crow suggess that historically they have made themselves a major pest. Fortunately, recent years have shown fewer complaints lodged against them. Though there are still as many crows around as ever, they have adapted so much to humans and their habitats that they have managed to make their presence and damage less conspicuous.

Physical Description

Crows are large, stocky, jet black birds, from 17 to 22 inches in length. They have dark beaks and eyes and

short, fan-shaped tails, easily identifiable in flight. Ravens, often confused with crows, are larger birds with wedge-shaped tails. The crows' "caw caw caw" gives them away even at considerable distances.

Life Cycle

Crows pair up in early spring. They build their nests of twigs and line them with soft grasses and feathers in densely foliaged trees from 18 to 60 feet high. They are very secretive around the nest, and the casual observer may never know the nest is there. Females lay from four to six eggs in what is usually only a single clutch (batch) for the season. These hatch in about eighteen days, and by the time the hatchlings are five weeks old they join their parents on feeding forays. As the daylight hours shorten and the fall migrations near, the birds' behavior becomes more restless, until finally they begin their journey south.

In the wild, crows commonly live to four to six years of age, but individuals as old as fourteen have been documented. Pet birds have lived as long as twenty years or more.

Habits

Though not quite as jaunty and jovial as Heckle and Jeckle, wild crows have some remarkable qualities. They are very intelligent, able to solve puzzles and problems, and even count to three or four. They are accomplished mimics, copying a number of other bird calls and other sounds, including, for those kept in captivity, the human voice.

Unlike their bold cartoon counterparts, crows are ever watchful for danger and wary when feeding. Often one or more birds remain perched in a tree or off to the side as sentinels, ready to warn of any approaching danger.

Crows are notorious thieves, always snatching some soft thing with which to line their nests, or something sparkly or shiny that fascinates them.

Hawks or owls may be annoyed by the efforts of crows to harass and drive them away. A few crows cawing and diving into the branches of a tall tree may expose a bird of prey you wouldn't have noticed otherwise.

During the fall and winter, crows congregate and roost in large numbers, much like blackbirds or starlings. Unlike these other birds, a roost of several hundred crows will become so quiet after the birds have arrived that you may not know they are there. Crows will fly in from as far away as 50

Range and Habitat

Crows are found throughout most of the United States, except for the extreme desert Southwest. They live best where there are dense trees for nesting or roosting, but are common around wooded areas, farms, parks, and suburban areas, especially near waterways.

miles to roost in their favorite place. A stand of evergreens or other dense trees is often their choice.

Garden Targets

Though crows may feed on maturing corn, they are just as likely to damage the crop by pulling up the seed corn as it sprouts. Studies have shown that crows will eat at least 600 different foods, including watermelon, fruit, grains, bugs, small snakes, trash, and road kills.

Damage and Signs

Due to such factors as weather, crop production and harvest, and the availability of other food sources, damage to garden crops varies from one year to the next. When feeding on corn, crows may pull the seeds from the ground, or strip clean the maturing ears. They will also peck large holes in melons and then clean out the insides.

Deterrents

Many of the methods listed for other problem birds apply in varying degrees to crows. One simple solution is to provide the crows with an alternative source of food. Scattering whole corn that has been soaked in water will divert the hungry birds from newly planted corn. There is always a risk that this may attract crows.

Scare Tactics. Scare tactics such as those previously described are effective in driving crows from their roosts or from crops. Recorded distress calls, explosions, alarms, and other noisemakers, as well as flashing lights, reflective tape, pie pans, or aluminum streamers will shoo crows away. The floating Scare Eye balloons are also effective. As for other pest birds, a combination of scare tactics, constantly altered as to what, where, and when, will produce a much more lasting effect than any one method. Any static device, such as Heckle and Jeckle's sorry scarecrow, is soon ignored.

Exclusion. Barriers are effective against crows in the home garden. Netting over crops offers excellent protection. Row cages built of framing and either netting or chicken wire can be placed over freshly planted corn and removed once the seedlings are well established. Paper cups or bags can be placed over the developing ears, but only after the silks have turned brown.

Protect corn ears with paper bag covers.

Fishing line or fine wire strung across the tops of maturing corn stalks 6 to 8 feet high stops crows. They will avoid flying near these unseen obstacles after a few encounters. Strung across the ground three or four inches high, it will also discourage those seed pullers.

Starlings

(Sturnus vulgaris)

"I'll have a starling shall be taught to speak nothing but 'Mortimer,' and give it him."

Henry IV
William Shakespeare

It was through this obscure reference in a single Shakespearean play that one of the most prolific public nuisances of North America came to be. Between 1890 and 1891, 100 pairs of these birds were imported from their native Europe to Central Park in New York City. A small group of romantically misguided Shakespearean devotees tried to introduce into the United States every type of bird ever mentioned by the Bard. With starling populations now estimated at well over 140 million birds, this attempt at cultural enlightenment has resulted in crop damage, noise and sidewalk pollution, public health risks, and the disruption and decline of native bird species.

Physical Description

The starling's plumage varies so much with the season that between one extreme and the other, it looks like two entirely separate species. Most of us are more familiar with this bird's summer garb of black purplish and green iridescence and bright yellow bill. However, after the fall molt the new feathers are dull and tipped with V-shaped white spots, or "stars." Even the bright bill fades to dark.

They are chunky, medium-sized birds with short, choppy tails.

Life Cycle

Some starlings migrate south for the winter, while others maintain their northern homes year-round. Most of the migrators tend to be the youngest, and may fly up to several hundred miles south. They begin building nests in the spring in any old hole or cavity. Starlings bully many cherished songbirds from their bird houses.

Males help the females build the nest, incubate the eggs, and feed the young. The females lay between four and seven eggs per clutch (batch) and will usually produce two batches each season. Three weeks after hatching, the babies are out of the nest and learning to fend for themselves.

Range and Habitat

Starlings are found throughout the United States and southern Canada.

Habits

When not nesting, starlings are infamous for their mass gatherings and roosts. Large, noisy flocks of thousands of these dirty birds descend to feed or just congregate anywhere they can find sufficient cover from wind and weather. They leave abundant calling cards in the form of caustic droppings that corrode paint finishes, contaminate livestock feed, and harbor such human transmittable diseases as histoplasmosis (comparable to tuberculosis).

Individual birds can be as exasperating as an entire flock. They are extremely aggressive and find their way into buildings, bird houses and feeders, and stored grains. Their nastiness drives native birds from their nests, resulting in displacement and impaired reproduction of the more desirable species.

Starlings are talented mimics, capable of reproducing the calls and songs of many other birds and even animals. The range of sounds they can imitate rivals that of the mockingbird.

Garden Targets

Starlings eat fruits and seeds of many cultivated plants. They delight in grapes, blueberries, and cherries, as well as strawberries, peaches, and other tree fruit. Occasionally, they pull up sprouting grains.

When nesting, they devour an impressive share of insects and other garden pests, including cutworms, Japanese beetle larvae, and grasshoppers.

Damage and Signs

Flocks may descend on planted fields, orchards, and berry patches and greedily consume the entire harvest in minutes.

Deterrents

A number of cultural, scare, exclusion, and other tactics will help to get rid of starlings. Roosting can be discouraged as described for blackbirds and also by eliminating potential roosting sites along building ledges. Insert boards at a 45-degree angle along ledges or install metal or wire prongs on ledges to make them unroostable. Sticky products, such as Roost No More and Bird Tanglefoot, smeared along prospective roosts, will turn the birds away. Birds can be kept from roosting indoors by hanging PVC strips in open doorways or nailing netting underneath rafters. Unfortunately, preventing roosting may do little to reduce plant damage, as starlings fly 10 to 15 miles from their nightly roosts in their daily hunt for food.

Starlings are attracted to livestock areas by feed and water. Any livestock feed should be covered and kept swept

A board propped at a 45° angle along a ledge will discourage birds from nesting there.

up. Watering troughs should be kept half full. This prevents the birds from perching on the edges to drink from the top, but the water is too deep to let them stand on the bottom and create a birdbath.

Scare Tactics. Scare tactics will disperse roosting and feeding starlings from their chosen haunts. Just as for blackbirds, recorded distress calls or other noise is effective, as are explosive devices. Bright lights will discourage them from roosting for the night, and light flashes, such as those from reflective tape or silvery spinning pinwheels, startle them from feeding.

Scare Eye balloons are very effective against starlings. If these are raised before birds get a taste of what you have to offer, you can expect to avoid any damage. Even in tests where the birds were first allowed to feed, the starlings did not return once the balloons were in place.

Exclusion. For the home gardener, often the most practical way of dealing with starlings and many other birds is to use bird netting. Nylon netting with ½-inch mesh lasts indefinitely if handled with care and keeps even these persistent pests from plundering your precious produce. It can be draped over fruit trees and tied around the trunk with twine to prevent any sneak invasions. It can be hung over berry bushes or better yet attached to a frame around the entire berry patch. The frames can be made of anything from PVC pipe to scrap lumber or poles. Frames make working with the netting much easier, as it eagerly snags on bush branches (or nearly anything else it touches). Enclose berry bushes so that the sides of the cage are at least a foot from the bushes. This keeps the birds from reaching in and gives humans a little room to maneuver inside the netting.

Net or chicken-wire cages can be built from panels that fasten together around and over the berries each year. This cuts down the work and frustration. To harvest your berries, either roll up draped netting, take down the panels, or design space enough in the enclosure to allow you to work inside.

Strawberries and freshly planted seeds can be protected by laying netting or row cover material over the beds. The birds avoid anything that tangles at their feet. Hoops for row covers lift the netting away from the plants, putting them even further out of reach of greedy beaks. These can

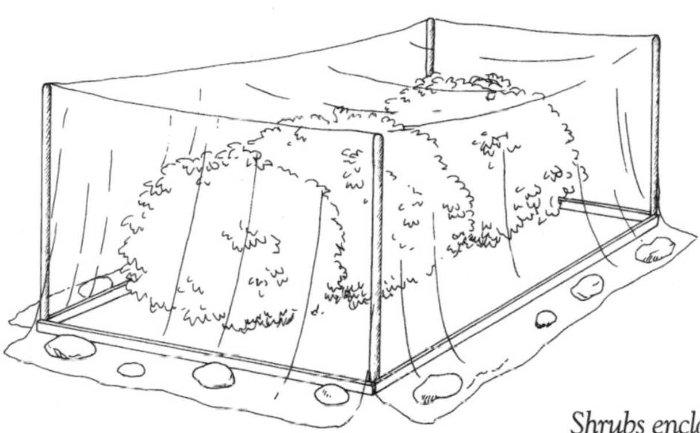

Shrubs enclosed in a cage of nylon netting.

be purchased in garden stores or fashioned from bending PVC pipe or strips of bender board. Drive stakes into the ground along each side of the row and fit the pipe over them to hold it in place.

Seed-stealing starlings can be frustrated using the "gotcha lines" suggested for blackbird thieves.

General Berry-eaters

From time to time your garden will be visited by numerous beneficial birds that eat harmful insects and other garden pests without damaging the plants you tend so carefully. On occasion beloved songbirds will frequent your garden patch, possibly to relieve you of a few caterpillars or weed seeds. Versatile little darlings that they are, they may eventually make inappropriate overtures towards your sprouting lettuce or corn, or glance with more than a mere leering eye toward your berry bushes. Suddenly they are no more appreciated than the blackbirds, starlings, or crows!

Unless birds cause an intolerable amount of damage, don't concern yourself with their presence and occasional pilferings. Live and let live is one of the cardinal rules of organic gardening. Within reason. No one expects you to forfeit the entire blueberry harvest to feathered thieves, but perhaps you may consider sharing just one bush.

Some of the normally welcome garden guests that may tend to stretch your ability to play host graciously may surprise you. Goldfinches *(Carduelis tristis)* may discover your sunflowers and eagerly help themselves. Robins *(Turdus migratorius)* will feast on your grapes or cherries as well as that blueberry bush, and on any precious earthworms they can pluck from the soil. Thrashers *(Toxostoma* spp.*)* partake of corn and berries, such as currants or raspberries. Cardinals *(Cardinalis cardinalis)* may sample tender greens or seeds. Pheasants *(Phasianus colchicus)* and other game birds are especially fond of pulling up sprouting seed corn, for which crows and others

often get the blame. Migrating flocks of ducks and geese have been known to pick newly planted fields clean on their stopovers. Blue jays will stake their claims to a variety of cultivated fruits as well as corn. You can still enthusiastically welcome and enjoy these and other visiting birds, but you should keep an eye on their eating habits.

Deterrents

Scare Tactics. Most of the tactics for deterring blackbirds, starlings, or crows apply to other unwanted birds. Scare tactics that incorporate movement, flashing lights, and/or noise are very effective in frightening wary wild birds. Rigged moving scarecrows, reflecting tape, aluminum pie tins hung on stakes or on wire or fishing line strung between stakes, or even just on the plants themselves, will frighten away birds. Flashy children's pinwheels, foil or plastic streamers, strips of plastic garbage bags or surveyors tape, automatic sprinklers set to go off for a few minutes at random intervals, tethered Scare Eye balloons, decoys of great horned owls, large snakes, or hawk silhouettes will all spook birds. Prowling cats or the noise of taped distress calls, mechanical din, or other sounds are all effective bird-scaring devices. Combining and constantly rearranging a program of these or other tactics should signal to area birds that your garden is off limits.

Exclusion. Should you desire to reap the benefits of allowing or even encouraging beneficial birds in your garden, you can do so with little or no damage by protecting susceptible plants with bird netting or other plant covers. "Gotcha lines" strung at crop level will startle would-be diners back into the air even as they try to land.

Alternative Food. One trick is to plant oats along with seed corn and other crops. The oat seeds sprout quickly, but birds don't like them. As the corn or other crop emerges, the birds generally don't notice it through the oats or else figure it's just more of the same and ignore it. One drawback to this method is that you'll probably have to weed out the oats once the birds have gone away.

Offering alternative food may draw the birds' attention from your crop long enough to protect it during critical periods of germination or harvest. Sunflower seeds, bread crumbs, and soaked seed corn should be scattered away from the garden. Strawberry thieves can be tempted with raisins, also scattered away from the garden. If you're lucky, such peace offerings will fill the birds' crops without sacrificing yours!

Chapter 2

Rodent Warriors

Gophers • Moles • Porcupine
Rats, Mice, and Voles
Squirrels • Woodchucks

Nothing quite brings out the human urge to kill like rodents. Chemical companies produce vast amounts of rodenticides annually, most of which are liberally applied and toxic. Lethal traps abound, and while mass mouse murder seems unfair or unnecessary to many, quick-working traps are infinitely safer and more humane than other lethal alternatives. These small pests can do big damage in a hurry, and effective control usually calls for swift and often drastic action.

In the pages that follow a variety of alternatives to lethal controls are offered. If ultimately, however, you must resort to lethal means, suggestions for successful trapping are also included.

Gophers
(Order Rodentia)

Though less universal in their habitats than birds, gophers seem to turn up just about everywhere. With thirty-three species to challenge them, many gardeners who never thought it could

Range and Habitat

Gophers are most common west of the Mississippi, though they may be found back East as well. Pocket gophers will make the best of it in many types of environments. They can be found in low coastal areas or in high country, 12,000 feet up. They exist in a wide variety of soil types, but flourish in friable, light-textured soil with good drainage and plant production, especially plants with large, healthy roots. Sounds a lot like a well-tended garden, doesn't it?

Soil texture dictates the integrity of the gopher's tunnels. Too sandy and the tunnels may cave in. Thick clay interferes with the free exchange of oxygen and carbon dioxide between the air aboveground and that in the tunnels.

happen to them find themselves faced with the relentless presence of these furry little earth miners. What makes a little ball of fur such an indomitable foe? Well, when you've got them, you know!

Therein lies the most frustrating aspect of dealing with gophers: when you've got 'em, you've got 'em, or more appropriately, they've got you! They are exasperatingly difficult to get rid of, and even after you've waved a fond farewell to one, another often shuffles in to claim the territory.

Physical Description

Some other animals are often confused with gophers due to local common names. Ground squirrels and moles are sometimes mistakenly identified as gophers, and in some southern areas, true gophers are even referred to as salamanders, whom the rest of us picture as slinky amphibians.

Pocket gophers are burrowing rodents named for their fur-lined cheek pockets in which they carry food. Well adapted for their underground dirt-pushing existence, they have stocky front ends, very short, thick necks, and small, flattened heads. Large, yellow incisor teeth account for disastrous gnawing abilities, and great, sturdy claws on the front feet are designed for serious digging. Gophers range in size from only 5 inches to 18 inches long. They bear soft pelts of fine hair in shades from dark brown to dirty white.

Gopher sense organs are modified for their subterranean lifestyles. The eyes and ears are very small, but long, sensitive whiskers and a near-naked tail work overtime as navigational devices, guiding gophers through their dark, silent tunnels

Life Cycle

Gophers are decidedly antisocial critters. They keep to themselves, one to each entire network of burrows, except during those times when boy gopher seeks girl gopher. Eighteen days after a quick courtship, between one and ten young are born, with three to four being an average litter. Though this varies in different climates, litters typically arrive between March and June. Dad sticks around mama's burrow briefly after the babies are born, possibly even helping to care for them. Then he tunnels off in search of new digs and a new love. Though they won't reach full maturity until the following spring, the kids are driven off to establish their own burrows and fend for themselves when they are as young as six weeks of age.

Habits

Tunneling. It's estimated that digging under the ground burns from 360 to 3400 *times* as much energy as moving around on top of it. Which leads to the gopher's other most notable habit: eating. It takes a tremendous amount of food to sustain such a high level of activity. And since gophers do *not* hibernate, as some might hope, they are active continuously.

The burrow systems can be extensive and elaborate. Generally, there is one main tunnel with side trails that are constantly being excavated and then closed. The tunnels may go as deep as 10 feet down, but most often violate only the top 2 feet of soil. Two hundred yards of tunnel per single occupant burrow system are common. Poorer habitats require even more extensive systems to provide adequate foraging. As many as sixty-two gophers, each with its own separate burrow, have been found in a one-acre area. With the average gopher's home territory covering about 700 square yards, sixteen to twenty of the varmints per acre is more likely.

Although gophers lead mostly solitary lives, respecting the territorial boundaries of each individual's burrow, if a burrow is abandoned, claim jumpers are quick to move in. Once established in a home burrow, gophers are staunch defenders of what they feel is rightfully theirs. Other gophers or rodents are met with a characteristically threatening stance, as the defender raises up onto his hind legs, pants, gasps, and thrusts his oversized claws forward. Even gopher-eating predators, including large snakes, get the same fearless welcome, though sometimes the gopher will retreat from snakes and try to block them off by digging an instant wall of dirt. Interestingly, gophers will ignore non-competitive animals such as frogs, salamanders, or lizards in their burrows.

Though they will eat aboveground as well as from underneath, gophers never stray more than a few inches from a tunnel opening. As they tunnel merrily under the soil surface, they devour any roots they find to their liking, and joyously yank tender seedlings into their burrows for a green feast.

One more thing about gophers: they can swim.

Garden Targets

Gophers are fond of alfalfa. Cover crops as well as larger fields of this legume are enthusiastically attacked. Almost any plant with roots qualifies

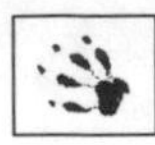

as gopher chow. Those with thick roots or tubers, such as carrots or potatoes, are special favorites. Many flower bulbs, including tulips, are not safe. Gophers have even been known to consume whole garlic bulbs (presumably not during the mating season).

In the spring, when tender green shoots are pushing their way through the soil, salad rates high on the gopher's menu. During the summer growing season, roots are favored. Winter may find them stripping bark from tree roots or low-level parts.

Damage and Signs

Dying or disappearing plants are the most obvious damage. If one day you find nothing but an inch-wide hole where the parsley once was, congratulations! It's a gopher. Trees and ornamentals are often damaged or killed by girdling (stripping away bark) or nibbling on roots, thereby exposing them to air.

Gophers also cause plant casualties as they push up mounds of dirt. These fan-shaped heaps crush or smother what vegetation the gopher's busy teeth leave intact. The exposed soil is vulnerable to erosion. Also, the tunnels themselves can channel water away from crops.

Deterrents

In accordance with Mr. Gopher's high ranking as a garden pest, myriad remedies exist to alleviate the symptoms of "gopheritus." Some are more wishful thinking than practical solutions; others are simply chemical warfare.

Offered here are some of the more successful methods to minimize damage, or eliminate the perpetrators.

Repellents. Believe it or not, there are a few plants that gophers won't eat. In fact there are some known to detour the furry little beasts. The best known of these is the gopher plant or gopher spurge *(Euphorbia lathyrus)*. It is sold under a variety of labels, including Nature's Farewell Seed and Gopher Patrol. As with many nontoxic pest controls, some gardeners swear by this as a wonder cure, while others are just left swearing.

The roots are poisonous to gophers and apparently saturate the soil around them with unpleasant substances. The plants grow to 4 feet high, and the root systems go deep enough to penetrate almost any gopher territory. The most successful use of this, as with many deterrent plants, is to plant a solid wall of the plants around gopher target areas. One plant every 2 to 3 feet is usually sufficient. When the gopher nears this root zone he digs in a different direction. So unless you surround your garden patch with the repellent plants, he will eventually dig around them.

Other plants avoided by gophers include daffodils, squill, and, most effective of all, the castor-oil plant. Dropping a few castor-oil beans into the tunnels will poison any takers. Castor-oil plants are highly poisonous and should not be planted where children may find them. A soil or plant

spray can be made from one tablespoon of castor oil, one tablespoon of liquid soap (to help the spray stick), and a gallon of water.

Using newspaper for mulch may turn back surfacing gophers. Other deterrents can be placed in the tunnel to encourage a hasty retreat. Take advantage of gophers' natural fear of predators by dumping used kitty litter into the burrow. Commercially available ferret scent, placed in the runs, will also turn away any sane gopher. Others to try are human or dog hair and even elderberry cuttings.

Scare Tactics. Many claim it is the racket from whirligigs or large rattling pinwheels that gophers find objectionable. More likely it is the gophers' incredible sensitivity to ground vibrations that makes them avoid such contraptions. Drive the support sticks into or as near as possible to the tunnels, facing the prevailing wind. As the wind spins them, vibrations carry down through the supports and into the ground. The obvious drawback to using wind-activated devices is that unless there is wind, you only have garden decorations.

One popular device is an ultrasonic noise emitter. Sold under such names as Go'pher It, these battery-operated devices release intermittent sounds that are inaudible to humans and most animals. But gophers and other small animals, including ground squirrels, moles, voles, mice, and shrews, can't stand them. They will do whatever is necessary to avoid the annoying vibrations. Most often this involves relocating out of range of the device. Advertised to protect up to 1000 square yards, one or two of these devices should keep most home gardens free of unwanted pets as long as the batteries hold out.

Empty glass (pop) bottles placed in gopher holes, or half-buried with the open end up, produce eerie sounds whenever a breeze passes.

Exclusion. It's almost impossible to fence out gophers on a large scale. But home gardeners willing to work can prepare small beds just for crops that gophers like, such as bulbs and root crops.

It is work. The soil of the bed must be removed, then the bed lined with wire mesh. The protected bed must be deep enough to permit tilling, particularly if you use a rototiller, and for the healthy growth of plant roots.

Gophers, rabbits, and other wildlife may be scared off by the sound made when a breeze passes over empty pop bottles sunk into the ground.

Begin by removing at least 18 to 24 inches of the soil of the bed. Now take a break! The next step is to lay down a gopher-proof material, such as 1-inch mesh chicken wire or better yet ½-inch mesh aviary wire or hardware cloth. Place the wire on the bottom of the bed and line all sides with it. Attach the wire where the edges meet. Overlap these contact points by at least 2 inches and wire them together with medium (20 gauge) steel wire. Now fill in the bed and plant your first gopher-proof carrots.

Knowing that gophers will not normally feed aboveground more than a few inches away from a burrow opening, you should have no nibbling problems as the enticing seedlings emerge. But if you want added insurance, construct cages out of the same material used to line the beds and place them over the plants, rows, or the entire bed. Build these cages like a box with the bottom left out, and place them over vulnerable plants with the edges resting on the soil surface. If using hardware cloth, no frame is necessary — just cut out the sides and the top of the cage and wire them together. Aviary or chicken wire needs to be attached to a frame for shape and support.

The size of your gopher beds depends on your available space, energy, and resources. Many of the materials are sold in rolls of 3-foot, 4-foot, or 6-foot widths in lengths up to 150 feet. You may want to plan accordingly. Vegetable beds 4 feet wide or less are easy to work in without having to step on, and thus compress, the soil. Just reach halfway across the beds from either side.

Trees or other plants can be protected by an underground fence about 2 feet deep.

Another way to gopher-proof

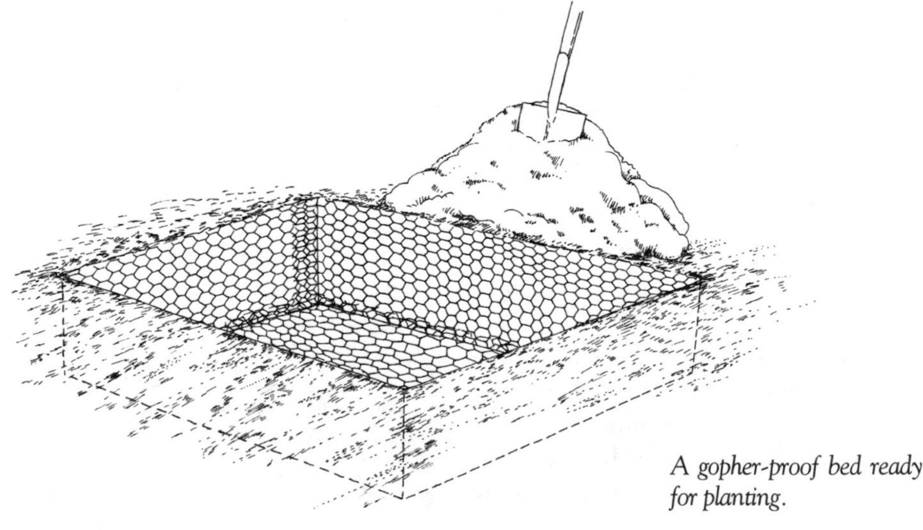

A gopher-proof bed ready for planting.

plants is to transplant them into pots or buckets, then sink the containers into the ground. Large-growing plants, such as cucumbers or other vines, can be planted in 5-gallon buckets with holes drilled into the sides and bottoms, or with the bottoms removed. Leave about 2 inches of lip aboveground to discourage any foragers. Individual flowers can be sunk in pots or coffee cans with drainage holes. Since plants kept this way have little room for root development you must plan a regular feeding program of an organic plant food such as fish emulsion or manure tea.

Flooding. Flooding gophers' tunnels may induce them to seek drier quarters. Unless you can submerge the entire garden, you are not going to flood them out. Remember, gophers can swim. However, soggy soil does not a comfortable burrow make. Digging through the wet stuff is difficult, and it clings to the critter's fur and clogs its digging tools. Water-saturated soil will not diffuse gases in and out of the tunnel systems, causing air supplies to be cut off. If your garden is near an unlimited, free water supply, such as a river or lake, diverting a burrowful into Mr. Gopher's domain may send him down the river.

Predators. Although they can put up an impressive show of defense, gophers fall prey to a number of predators. King snakes or bull snakes (*Pituophis melanoleucus*), also referred to as gopher snakes, will patrol the burrows in pursuit of their prey. It's possible that their mere presence is enough to convince the gopher to look for a new neighborhood. Though even the larger snakes rarely take on mature gophers, the young make easy targets. Any home inhabited by a mortal enemy is not much of a home, even to gophers.

Other predators that follow the gophers underground include members of the weasel family, not the least of which is the ferret. Ferrets can be trained as hunters. Possessing an unmistakable scent, a pet ferret romping through the gopher tunnels will make even the fiercest gopher uncomfortable — possibly enough to change addresses. The scent is sold under the name Ferret Scent and may be all you need to do the trick.

Skunks, badgers, coyotes, foxes, cats, hawks, and many owls, including great horned and barn owls, will take on gophers either underground or while they are on the surface.

Removal. The most common gopher remedies in use are traps. Many different ones are available, including live traps. Live-trapping of gophers, however, is impractical. You will have to dispatch your catch or release it elsewhere, which is generally frowned upon by those who live elsewhere. In some cases it is even illegal.

Lethal traps are designed to be set underground in the tunnel. The first step is to *find* the tunnel. To locate the main run, find one of the dirt mounds created when accumulated dirt is pushed from the tunnel. Mr. Gopher

closes each mound with a plug of dirt. The main tunnel is within a foot and a half of this plug. Dig around until you find it. Side runs will be several inches away from the mound on the same side as the plug. The plugs can be several inches thick, but the tunnels are down there (otherwise the mounds wouldn't be), so keep looking.

Wear gloves when handling the traps to avoid contaminating them with your scent. Before digging up your garden, practice setting the traps according to manufacturer's directions until you are good at it.

First, anchor the trap securely to a stake or fence post, to prevent either caught gophers, or opportunistic predators, from making off with it. Dig into the tunnel, as quickly and quietly as possible, then set the trap, drop it into the tunnel, and close up the tunnel. Place a piece of sod over the exposed area, grass side down.

You may have to suffer through some trial and error. Some gophers seem to be wise to the idea of traps and avoid them. Sometimes it's the time of year or the placement of the trap that is out of sync. Generally spring and fall, when the gophers are the most active, are the most productive trapping times. If a trap hasn't caught a gopher in two or three days, pull it up and reset it elsewhere.

A nontoxic alternative to commercially available gas bombs or capsules is to insert dry ice into the burrows at several intervals. Seal off any leaks (you'll see the "smoke" from the dry ice) with dirt and be prepared to dispatch any gophers retreating from the carbon dioxide gas. The gas suffocates the inhabitants.

The best time to do this is in early spring, when the gophers are active, the dens are easily located, and the young are not yet born. Do it when the soil is moist and the diffusion of gases out of the tunnel is reduced.

Any gopher eradication program should be used as soon as you realize you have gophers. Allowing them time to expand their tunnels is a common mistake of many gardeners who don't realize that even if they eventually get rid of the resident, they are unwittingly inviting a replacement.

Moles

(Order Insectivora, Family Talpidae)

Contrary to what most people think, moles are not rodents. They belong to a group of mammals known as insectivores, meaning insect eaters. While their diets cause no damage to gardens, their habits can make a real mess of things. Even so, they have their following who will tell you that the mole's activities do far more good than harm.

Range and Habitat

Found throughout the United States and southern Canada, moles prefer loose, moist loam like good garden soil and avoid dry, sandy, or heavy clay soils. They are commonly found in or near woodlands, grasslands, weed patches, lawns, or parks, and invariably show up in garden patches.

Physical Description

Moles are odd-looking creatures designed to "swim" underground. They have bare, usually pointy noses, hidden eyes and ears, and velvety, dark fur that offers no resistance in any direction. This kind of coat allows the mole to move about through soil with equal ease in any direction. Large, paddle-like front feet on stout, strong limbs force soil out of the mole's way with every stroke. A mole's body is thick and compact, from 5 to 8 inches long and weighing in at only 3 to 4 ounces. Males are somewhat larger than females

Life Cycle

Moles spend nearly their entire lives underground, coming to the surface mainly by accident. They mate, deliver, and raise their young inside their tunnels. One litter per year, usually born between March and June, produces from three to five young. These mature quickly and live two to three years.

Habits

Moles are active day and night in their constant search for food. The tremendous energy requirements for tunneling keep them ever hungry. They can starve to death in several hours without food.

Moles are not social animals. Usually only one animal occupies a tunnel system, which can be immense. A hungry mole needs a big territory to fulfill his foraging requirements. They have been known to fight to the death in territorial disputes. Under average conditions, no more than two or three moles per acre can coexist.

Garden Targets

Surprise! Moles *do not eat plants*. Although some vegetation may be found upon examining their stomach contents, it is so slight that researchers generally conclude it was ingested by accident as the moles went after their real food — grubs, earthworms, insects, and even an odd snail now and then. They may consume close to their own body weight of this menu every day.

Damage and Signs

Since moles don't eat plants, their damage is limited to that caused by their tunneling. They excavate two different types of tunnels. Those near the surface are dug primarily for hunting and use during mild weather. They may or may not be reused. Tunnels dug about 7 inches deep are the main highways, used to connect nests to

feeding grounds, and are used exclusively during temperature extremes. It is these deeper tunnels that result in mole hills as the worker pushes up excavated soil. The number of hills has little to do with the number of moles present. You could have one very busy mole or a few average workers.

The surface runways often show as a ridge just under your perfect lawn. Tunnels often follow along protected areas such as fencerows and hedgerows, and alongside buildings.

Aside from ruining the looks of lawns and flower beds, moles damage garden plants as the roots are exposed to air. Too, other animals will use the tunnels. Usually they are mice or voles, who nibble at the roots. Seedlings are smothered or smashed by the eruptions of earth.

Deterrents

Before you decide to eliminate every mole in the vicinity, be sure the moles are causing problems. Their diets and roles as soil aerators are very beneficial in the grand scheme of things.

Cultural Practices. Compacting soil with a heavy roller or allowing it to become very dry will make it less appealing to moles. Eliminate white grubs by applying milky spore disease, *Bacillus popilliae*. (See chapter 6 under Japanese beetle deterrents.) This will cut out a large share of their diet and may encourage them to search in other areas. As their food supply dwindles, however, they will have to work even harder. That means dig *more*, to satisfy their appetites, and damage may get worse before they vacate. In addition, moles may survive even without their primary food source as long as other food is available.

Repellents. Some people report good results using windjugs, whirligigs, and whistling pop bottles. (See Gophers.) Given the mole's sensitivity to ground vibrations, these may deter him from a particular area as long as there is a breeze to activate them.

Moles are leery of odd things placed in their burrows. Rather than effectively repelling these critters, such things as broken glass, kerosene, human hair, or thorns placed in their burrows only cause the moles to dig around or under the oddity. Used kitty litter placed in the tunnel is said to convince the moles that a predator is lurking within their runs, causing them to move.

Planting mole plant, *Euphoria lathyrus*, or castor-oil plants may detour moles. Drenching the soil of fresh digs with a castor-oil mixture makes them uninhabitable. Mix two parts castor oil with one part liquid detergent and stir until foamy. Dilute 2 tablespoons of this in a gallon of water and use to saturate the soil inside and around the mound. Castor beans are extremely poisonous, and great care and discretion should be used with both the beans and the entire plant.

Exclusion. In small areas, mole fencing may be feasible. Using hardware cloth, build a fence about 6

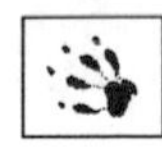

inches high and at least 18 inches deep. Bending the bottom of the buried portion away from the protected area will further hamper any digging attempts.

Predators. Some cats and dogs delight in digging up moles, and other predators including coyotes, badgers, skunks, hawks, and owls will kill them. Because of their peculiar, musky odor, they are often killed but left uneaten.

Removal. The singularly most effective method for mole control is trapping. Since mole populations are usually small, this should be relatively easy, right? Understandably the moles have different ideas, and unless you go about it carefully your traps will be left as unfulfilled as your dreams of a mole-free garden. They are notoriously difficult to catch, possessing an uncanny ability to detect and avoid traps.

First, find a frequently used runway. Moles repair damage to the tunnels they are using. Knowing this, you may be able to find a main thoroughfare just by flattening a spot on a surface tunnel with your foot and checking the next day to see if it has been raised. Runways that go in a straight line or that connect two mounds, or systems of tunnels, are usually main routes. Look for freshly turned soil as a sign of recent activity.

Three types of traps are effective for killing moles. These are the harpoon-type trap, sold as Victor, probably the easiest to use; a scissor-action trap, sold under the name Out O' Sight; and the choker loop Nash trap. Select your trapping sites and dig up a short section of the tunnel. Set the trap according to directions, remembering to keep all parts of the trap away from the inside of the tunnel. Depending on the model used, the trap should be situated above or surrounding the runway, never in it. Replace the soil loosely and leave, making sure not to disturb any other part of the tunnel.

Being very suspicious of changes in their runways, moles will take a detour around any traps they detect. However, having an instinct to reopen what appear to be any cave-ins or naturally occurring plugs of earth, they will dig right into a properly positioned

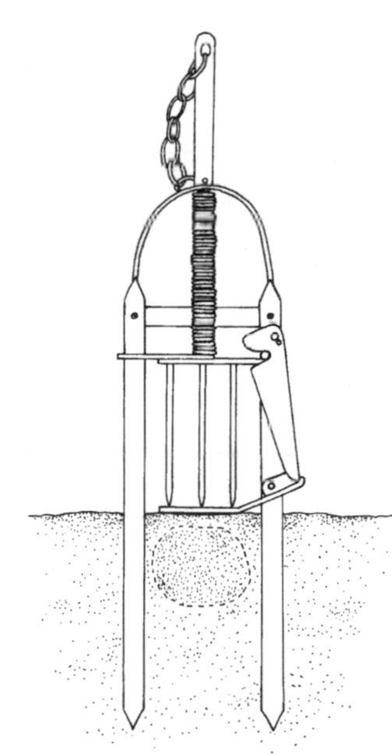

The harpoon-type mole trap is set so the trigger penetrates the runway when disturbed.

trap. Traps that yield no moles after two or three days may signal that the mole has changed his habits, that your carefully selected main runway is not in use, or that the mole discovered the trap. Any of these reasons means you should reset the trap elsewhere.

Moles can dig up to 200 feet of tunnel every day. Their systems are far too extensive to be fumigated effectively, so the poison gas cartridges used on gophers, and even sold for mole control, aren't recommended. Other poisons are not effective because the moles won't eat the bait.

Porcupines

(Erethizon dorsatum)

One of nature's most ingenious exercises in passive defense is the shy, slow porcupine. He makes his strongest points for his own protection.

Physical Description

The porcupine, alias "quill pig," is a large, lumbering rodent covered with approximately 30,000 spiny quills. The quills are barbed at the head, and work their way into the flesh of any molester unlucky enough to come in contact with them. These modified hairs cover the entire body except for the underside and face.

Range and Habitat

Found west of the Rocky Mountains and throughout Canada, the porcupine prefers coniferous forests, but occasionally can be found in areas ranging from prairies to high alpine tundra.

Life Cycle

Porcupines mate in autumn. Usually only one baby is born, seven months later in the spring. The youngster stays with mama throughout the summer, striking out on his own at about four or five months of age.

Habits

The plodding porcupine tries to avoid confrontation, being active mostly at night and climbing trees or scuttling under cover when threatened. But when push comes to shove, a flick of his heavy tail can embed enough of those quills to fend off most any predator.

Garden Targets

Porcupines feed primarily on smooth, thin tree bark, leaves, and buds. They have a sweet tooth and can develop an insatiable taste for any sugary crops, including sweet corn, berries, melons, and fruits, and may

damage berry bushes or trees by stripping the bark from the stems or trunks. At times they crave salt so desperately that they try to lick or chew the traces of it left by human hands on such things as shovel or hoe handles.

Damage and Signs

Heavy overnight damage of sweet crops and tracks accompanied by "swish marks" from his dragging tail implicates the porcupine as the culprit.

Porcupines may also strip trees of their bark, girdling the tree and exposing the wood to birds, insects, and disease. Dogs who never seem to get the point are also common casualties. Veterinarians should treat animals that have a run-in with a porcupine as soon as possible, as the quills may be broken off by amateur doctoring with a pair of pliers, leaving the patient open to serious infection.

Deterrents

Exclusion. Surprisingly able climbers, porcupines aren't slowed from relishing their garden favorites by ordinary fencing. A chicken wire fence at least 2 feet high, topped with an electric wire a few inches above it, will stop most. Sometimes an overhang of the fencing, angled about 65 degrees toward the outside of the garden, will be just as effective (see Woodchucks). A chicken-wire basket around saplings or aluminum flashing wrapped around larger tree trunks will protect them.

Removal. When barriers fail, trapping may be in order. Porcupines are not difficult to trap in a live trap (32"x10"x12") or a homemade box trap. Place the trap, baited with a salt lick or cloth soaked in salt water, near the scene of damage or close to a den entrance. Release any caught porcupines at least 25 miles away in a suitable habitat to give them a fair chance of survival.

Rats, Mice, and Voles

(Order Rodentia)

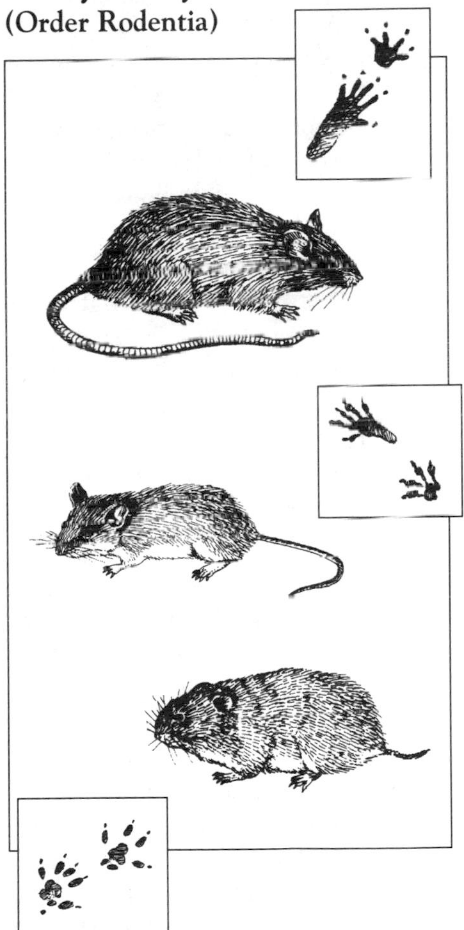

Probably even before dogs or goats were domesticated, rats and mice had made themselves fairly constant, if not desired, companions of humans. Rats in particular seem to flourish when close to their human benefactors.

Physical Description

Rats and mice come in a variety of shapes, sizes, and colors, but all are almost instantly recognizable as unwanted rodents. Norway rats, also known as house rats, sewer rats, or brown rats, are the largest of this group, growing to over a pound, and 18 inches in length when well fed. They have coarse dirty brown or gray fur with a lighter-colored belly. Most rats have small eyes and poor eyesight.

Among the largest of the mice are the meadow mice, or voles; many species commonly grow to a length of 7 inches or more. Most are gray to brown, some with yellow or black markings. House mice, while being among the tiniest of offenders, can easily make up for what they lack in size by sheer numbers and mischief.

Life Cycle

Rats begin breeding at three months of age, producing an average of four to six litters of six to twelve little rats each year. They live only about twelve to eighteen months. Mice can reproduce when only seven to eight weeks old, annually bearing from two to four litters of up to eight young. Voles have been documented to produce up to seventeen litters in one year, in captivity, but in the wild produce from one to five litters of four or five young. These live from only two to sixteen months, with most dying in the first month.

Range and Habitat

Rats, mice, and voles are represented throughout North America. Virtually every habitat of humans has been quickly claimed by these rodents. Any crevice large enough to squeeze into is considered fair game in the rodent housing market.

Habits

One thing most of us learned in biology class is that rats are definitely smarter than they look!

Most rats and mice are active during the night, hiding out in underground burrow or nests or in walls during the day. Voles tend to be active day or night.

All these rodents have excellent senses of taste, smell, hearing, and touch, are good climbers and diggers, and can at least tread water. Any opening ½ inch across or more provides them with free access, as they are good at remodeling such inconspicuous holes into entrances with their chisel-like teeth.

Rats, in particular, are creatures of habit. They tend to reuse the same pathways over and over, commonly along walls or other edgeways.

Garden Targets

Rats and mice may dig up freshly planted seeds, nibble on tender green shoots, or sample fruits or berries. Voles have been known to ruin field crops such as legumes, grains, and potatoes.

Damage and Signs

Even if you don't have a "rat problem," you may have rats or mice. If you see no signs of them, that's good. It could mean you have only a few, or else some new arrivals. Signs such as old droppings as large as ¾ inch long and ¼ inch in diameter, gnawing, and an occasional nighttime sighting indicate there are more rats about than you might think. Finding fresh droppings, tracks, and gnawing, and spotting several rats at night or even during the day, means you have far too many pet pests! In the garden, crop damage may be unnoticeable or disastrous, as with the surface tunneling and heavy feeding of voles. Voles also strip bark off trees in orchards. Mice and rats will dig seeds or nibble a little of anything.

Dust suspected areas for tracks with flour or talcum powder and recheck the next day. In moist areas a thin layer of mud will reveal tracks nicely. Some folks have even left out an open ink pad with some bait, surrounded it with blank paper, and let the perpetrators footprint themselves.

Other evidence of rats or mice includes fresh or dry urine (which fluoresces under ultraviolet light), runs, burrows, oil and dirt smudges that have rubbed off their coats onto walls, rafters, or objects along their regular pathways, and strange noises in your walls. Voles develop surface runways, visible aboveground, that lead between burrows and food sources.

Deterrents

The first step in reducing rat or mouse populations is to remove any apparent sources of food, water, or shelter. This means cleaning up, burning, or deeply burying refuse, properly packaging and "rat-proofing" stored edibles, excluding rodent entry into or under buildings and other likely breeding and nesting sites, and removing weeds, debris, junk piles, and any other sources of shelter.

Rats rarely travel more than 300 feet from their burrows, so cleaning up a limited area can greatly reduce their presence.

Sanitation and old-fashioned good housekeeping are basic requirements for discouraging rodents. Garbage should be kept in metal, rat-proof containers with tight lids. Food should not be left out, and animal feed should be kept on shelving or pallets. Pet food should be taken up as soon as Rover or Puff finishes eating to prevent rats from polishing off the leftovers. Bird feeders should have a lip around them to prevent spilling seeds onto the ground. Making life tougher for rats and mice in and around the house and outbuildings will make their presence in the garden a whole lot less likely.

Cultural Practices. Since sneaky little rodents love to take cover in quiet, dark spaces, hold off on mulching until the end of the season. Weed mats that lie flat on the ground and are covered with a layer of soil to weigh them down will substitute nicely for thick, fluffy mulches that provide hiding places.

Repellents. Sensitive to taste and odors, rats and mice may be swayed by repellents that assault these senses as well as their hearing. They avoid daffodils, hyacinths, and scillia. A sprinkling of ammonia has been recommended. Ferret scent sends rats scooting, as they are instinctively terrified of ferrets.

Scare Tactics. Although they are wary animals, rats and mice soon learn that there is little to fear from most scare tactics, either audible or visual. Voles are more timid and usually stay underground, so they don't notice these. Ultrasound, however, has been shown to provide at least temporary relief from rats and mice in limited areas. So far it has not been proven that ultrasound will drive established rodents from their homes (or ours). Whether it will send your critters scurrying off in a trail of dust depends on many uncontrollable variables such as alternate food or shelter, the sensitivity of particular rodents, and their numbers.

To work at all, ultrasound must be properly used and at least fundamentally understood. Discomforting sound waves, detectable only by critters with high-pitched hearing, are produced from a source in much the same way as radio waves. Unlike sound waves, ultrasound does not travel very far or around obstacles. Outdoors, the waves dissipate quickly. Varmints can avoid the nerve-racking effects by running around a corner or behind a rock. However, if set up and aimed at a specific point of entry, an ultrasonic device should effectively lower the perpetrator's use of that area.

To date the EPA has frowned on the sale of ultrasonic devices, and unsubstantiated claims by some overenthusiastic manufacturers have cast a shadow of doubt on their usefulness. However, that is not to say that they haven't worked. Most likely unrecognized factors contribute to the success or failure of these units, but the use of nontoxic, harmless sound waves may be an idea worth investigating.

Exclusion. In the garden, barriers will help to prevent rats, mice, and other small rodents from nibbling your produce. Solid or hardware cloth fences 18 inches high and buried at least 6 inches deep will stop most mice and all but the most determined rats. Transplants may be set out under cages or in wire baskets where rodents have been a problem. Protect tree trunks by wrapping with foil or plastic strips.

Predators. Some animals make excellent rat and mouse hunters. Cats and some dogs, especially terriers, may help keep rodents away from your house or garden, but seldom reduce the numbers of rats or mice. Ferrets are

rat hunters extraordinaire and will drive entire colonies away.

Other predators include hawks, owls, snakes, coyotes, foxes, bobcats, and bears.

Removal. One alternative to toxic poisons for mice is to mix equal parts of dry cement and cornmeal and leave it in a shallow dish for them to find. Supplying water next to this fatal feast will speed things along. As the mice chow down on the cornmeal mixture, the cement gets moist and turns into an undigestible dead weight.

The most common method of dealing with rats and mice is using traps. Snap traps baited with bits of fresh bacon, hot dog, peanut butter, or nutmeat tied to the trap work best. Place the trap along the rodent's runway with the trigger end against the wall, or in any places where rats or mice have been active. In the garden, set the trap in a coffee can or other small, covered container to prevent pets or children from being harmed. Experts recommend that you feed your varmints a time or two from the traps before setting them, and put out many traps at once. Rats and mice can learn by watching their fallen comrades, so catch them all as quickly as possible.

Live traps work well to catch rats. An alternative to mechanical snap traps is the glue board trap, which works the same way as flypaper. The critter starts across a sticky surface and gets stuck. Along with other traps, glue boards have the advantage over poisons of being less dangerous to use, and also allow you to dispose of your catch rather than having it rot away inside your walls.

Squirrels

(Family Sciuridae)

Bright-eyed and bushy-tailed, scampering along tree limbs, pausing occasionally to scold and chatter at passersby, squirrels are one of the most familiar wild animals. Aside from the common gray squirrels, fox, tassel-eared, pine (red and Douglas), and flying squirrels are found in various areas throughout North America. Their cousins, the chipmunks, are the darlings of many an outdoor picnic in the park, while other relatives, the ground squirrels, are cherished by none.

Physical Description

Tree squirrels are universally recognized by their bushy tails, either twitching with excitement or smartly curved upward in a perpetual salute. They may be as large as a 3-pound, 27-inch-long fox squirrel or as tiny as the 7-inch-long flying squirrel. Colors

Range and Habitat

One species or another may be found throughout North America. Gray squirrels in particular are opportunistic cohabitants with humans. They have made themselves at home in parks, cemeteries, and neighborhood trees. Most tree squirrels prefer woody areas, but homes for chipmunks and ground squirrels range from sagebrush and rock cliffs to golf courses.

range from the grays and silvers of gray squirrels and fox squirrels to the reddish two-toned pine squirrels. Occasionally black squirrels and very rarely albinos are found.

Chipmunks are smaller, reddish brown, with dark and light stripes from the base of their tails to the tip of their perky little noses. Ground squirrels have the same coat color. The smallest is the petite thirteen-lined ground squirrel, often mistaken for his cousin the chipmunk but distinguishable by his clean face, slightly larger size, and habit of carrying his tail held out rather than up. Largest is the 18-inch-long California ground squirrel, which is a ruddy brown to cinnamon color.

Life Cycle

Most squirrels are territorial and antisocial, except during breeding season. They usually mate twice each year, producing babies in the early spring and late summer. An average of three blind, bald, ½ ounce, totally dependent young are born in each litter. They are weaned in about ten weeks. Squirrels are vulnerable to diseases and to internal and external parasites, including bot fly larvae (warbles), fleas, ticks, and mange, as well as predators. In the wild they rarely live past the age of four years, but in captivity they live up to ten. Up to one-half of the population of squirrels perish in any given year. Populations fluctuate due to available food supplies and habitat. Periodically mass overland migrations occur.

Habits

The tale goes something like this: Upon coming to a river a group of migrating squirrels gathered at the bank, unable to cross. Industrious little critters that they are, some dragged pieces of bark and dried wood to the river's edge and climbed aboard. They hoisted their bushy tails to the wind and set sail, safely crossing the deep water. And that explains why squirrels hold their tails the way they do.

Other than relentlessly chastising anyone who violates their territory, squirrels have one other well-known habit, that of burying, or squirreling away, nuts for the winter. Gray squirrels bury theirs one at a time. They can locate them weeks later, apparently by scenting even through several inches of snow. Ground squirrels collect their bounty in their dens.

Ground squirrels dig burrows with small hidden openings. They manage

to leave no evidence of their excavation by filling their cheek pouches as they dig, then scattering the dirt away from the den. At night they close up shop by plugging the entrances with grass or sod.

Both ground squirrels and chipmunks hibernate.

Garden Targets

Being readily adaptable to a variety of foods, gray squirrels will take their toll on berries, fruits, corn, just-planted seeds, tender plants or plant parts, and flower bulbs, as well as their natural diet of mast (wild nuts). They also indulge in mushrooms and even insects.

Chipmunks and ground squirrels excavate seeds of cucumbers, squash, melons, and corn and happily sample vegetables, strawberries, bulbs, flowers, and tomatoes.

Damage and Signs

Chipmunks, ground squirrels, and gray squirrels delight in unearthing buried treasures, from seeds and bulbs to entire plants. They molest cornstalks, nibbling at the topmost ears; peel bark from young trees; and wreak havoc at bird feeders.

Deterrents

Repellents. Repellent borders of dried blood meal protect planting beds.

A spray made from pureed and strained hot peppers, in water with a tablespoon or so of liquid soap, is said to keep squirrels away from plants. Ground hot pepper in mineral oil, applied to the silk end of corn ears, is supposed to protect them. Corn ears, after the tassels have turned brown, may also be covered with paper bags, for protection.

A resident cat prowling the area will greatly cut down on any squirrel visitors. Sometimes just cat or dog hair, either suspended about in pouches or scattered around plants, will keep the furry little beggars at bay.

Ultrasonic noise devices emit unpleasant sound waves within the hearing range of squirrels, as well as most other rodents. They can be effective in repelling squirrels from limited areas.

Exclusion. Squirrels can be frustrated in their digging raids by placing chicken wire or screening over freshly planted seeds, or chicken wire cages over transplants. If the wire is to be removed, do so before the plants grow too large to pass through the mesh. If the mature plants will not be hindered by the wire, leave it in place throughout the season.

You can stop squirrels from climbing by using baffles, metal bands, or tumblers. Baffles can be made from wide strips of aluminum or other lightweight metal flashing wrapped around a tree or pole and flared at the bottom to prevent climbing over or around. Commercial baffles are sold to protect bird feeders, and simple homemade versions can be made by threading the feeder pole through the neck ends of two or more plastic two-

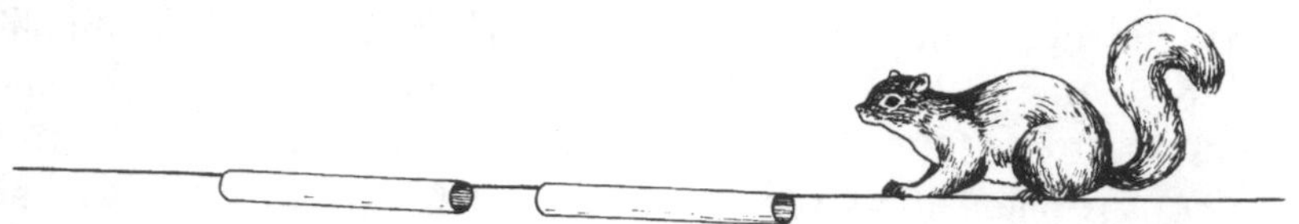

"Tumblers" prevent squirrels from walking across wires in pursuit of a bird feeder.

liter pop bottles with the bottoms cut out. Wide metal bands wrapped around tree trunks and poles deny the critters a foothold. Tumblers are used to keep squirrels from scurrying across wires. Tumblers are short lengths of PVC pipe fitted over wires. They spin whenever a squirrel sets foot on them, tumbling the would-be tightrope walker to the ground. Plastic film cartridges, empty toilet paper rolls, and other household items will serve the same purpose.

Predators. Predators include house cats and wildcats, foxes, hawks, owls, and, for ground squirrels, even snakes.

Removal. Traps baited with oranges, apples, shelled nuts (pecans especially), peanut butter, raisins or other dried fruit, or pumpkin or sunflower seeds can be very effective at catching squirrels. Use a commercial metal live trap if you wish to release your catch elsewhere; those sharp teeth can shred the wood of a box trap quickly. Glue board rat traps will stop smaller squirrels as well.

Ground Squirrel Strategies. Some special tactics to curb ground squirrel damage include soil cultivation to disrupt their burrows and planting as early as possible to avoid seeds and young plants from being available to the emerging hibernators.

If the other squirrel repellents or traps fail you, try flooding the burrows or fumigating with dry ice (see Gophers).

Woodchucks
(a.k.a. Groundhogs and Whistle Pigs)
(Marmota monax)

Although these fat, lazy rodents are major nuisances to countless farmers and gardeners, somehow they have also managed to endear themselves to many of us. A little at least. For none other than the lowly groundhog has its own special day set aside on the human calendar. Every February 2, the famous Punxsutawney Phil emerges from his burrow to check out the weather forecast. And every year

Range and Habitat

The woodchuck is common throughout Canada, and in the United States south and east from Minnesota, except for the extreme Deep South. Woodchucks prefer open farm country, near wooded areas. Burrows are dug in pastures, along fencerows, hedges, or roadsides, near orchard's edge, down brushy slopes, or under wood or brush piles or old stumps. They prefer a slope, but are quite adept at finding a suitable niche wherever the pickings are acceptable.

a crowd gathers in anticipation of his forecast for the coming spring.

Folklore has it that if he is seen on an overcast day, spring comes early that year. But if startled back into his burrow by a dark, ominous creature who mimics his every move — his shadow — six more weeks of winter will follow. Either way, the eventual coming of spring and the inevitable emergence of greedy groundhogs go hand in hand.

Physical Description

The chunky, compact woodchucks have short, sturdy legs; their forefeet are equipped with long, curved claws for digging. Occasionally, white or black individuals are seen, but usually they are a dirty brownish gray color, with furry brown tails, from 4 to 7 inches long. They average 16 to 20 inches in length and 5 to 10 pounds in weight. Their ears, eyes, and nose are all placed at the top of their stout heads, allowing them to peek out of their burrows with the least possible amount of exposure. They have long, white, chisel-like incisor teeth, handy both for gnawing and defense.

Life Cycle

Woodchucks are among the few true hibernating animals. They retire underground with the first killing frosts, and their body temperatures fall to that in the den. Respiration drops to as low as one breath every five minutes. Thus they remain, their bodies drawing all nutrition from stored fat, for the next four and a half to five and a half months. With one exception:

Early in February or March, the woodchucks awaken long enough for the males to dig out of their burrows in search of female companionship. They move in with the first available lady, and soon after mating both fall back into that deep, nearly lifeless sleep. By April or May a litter of two to six young is born, and the parents go their separate ways. Within little more than a month the babies are weaned and sent out to find or dig dens of their own and to get on with that all-important business of putting on enough fat to see them through the coming winter. On average, a wild woodchuck can expect to spend four or five such winters during its natural lifespan.

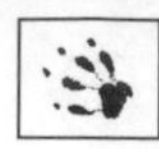

Habits

True, the most notable habits of woodchucks are eating, eating, and digging. They feed aboveground rather than from within the tunnels, usually ranging no more than 50 yards from the den. Except for when foraging, most often in the early morning and evening, woodchucks spend most of their time underground. They are good housekeepers, regularly changing nest linings and maintaining separate areas within the burrow for sleeping and bodily functions. Burrows are from 2 to 5 feet deep and vary considerably in length. The main entrance is characterized by a large mound of earth, but from one to several back doors lead into every den. These are dug from the inside out, leaving no telltale signs, so that a startled woodchuck can disappear down his secret escape hatch.

Abandoned burrows are often quickly resettled, either by another woodchuck or by other wildlife that benefits from the woodchucks' efforts.

Woodchucks can be fun to watch. They often sit up on their haunches to survey the view. When danger approaches, they belt out a sharp whistle to warn other animals. During warm summer days, they sun themselves out in the open, lolling on logs, rocks, or even atop fence posts.

Garden Targets

Being general herbivores, woodchucks will make the most of almost any available greenery. They favor succulent plants, plantains, and some grasses; clovers and legumes are special favorites. They will ravage alfalfa, peas, and beans, and take their toll on carrot tops, lettuce, squash, and some flowers. They adore melons and will even venture far from the safety of the den after fallen tree fruit.

Damage and Signs

Large mounds of earth may be the first signal that you have woodchucks about. These present a hazard to farm machinery, and horses and other ani-

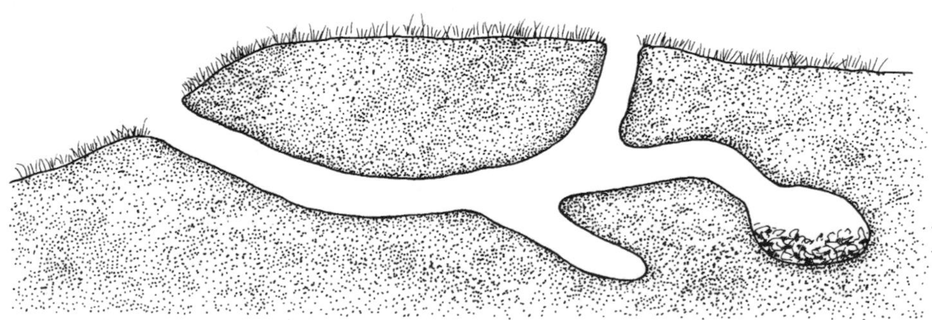

A typical woodchuck burrow.

mals in pastures often suffer broken legs when they step into secret burrow openings.

Look for tracks if you believe this animal is dining in your garden. A light sprinkling of flour may help make them more obvious. Check the area the next day after sprinkling the flour. Just noting which plants are being damaged may help to eliminate other suspects. For instance, while often pulling up entire pea or bean plants, woodchucks will generally ignore corn.

Deterrents

Cultural Practices. Simply removing woodchuck cover, such as tall grass, weeds, woodpiles, or old stumps, may make your garden area less inviting. You may want to try to entice the feasting chucks with a patch of clover, alfalfa, or soybeans planted strategically away from the garden. Or plant repellent onions, garlic, or other alliums near the burrows for the opposite effect.

Repellents. Besides repellent plants, several home remedies have worked. Try sprinkling ground hot peppers or ground black pepper near the burrow openings and near susceptible plants. Dried blood, blood meal, and talcum powder have also been reported to repel woodchucks.

Puree and strain hot peppers and garlic. Mix this with water and enough liquid soap to help the concoction adhere. Sprayed liberally around the garden, this mixture dampens even the hottest woodchuck appetites. A 1 percent solution of rotenone sprayed or dusted on plants also deters them.

Exclusion. Woodchucks are notoriously hard to discourage and are surprisingly nimble climbers, so fencing is of little value unless specifically designed with them in mind. Thoughtfully constructed, however, a fence may be your best and most permanent protection from invading woodchucks. As a bonus, any fence that will bar woodchucks will also exclude many other pests.

Use sturdy fencing material, such as woven or welded wire, and metal fence posts. Build the fence 3 to 4 feet high, leaving the top 12 to 18 inches unattached. Bend this section outward at an angle of about 65 degrees away from the garden, all around the fence. This way, when a chunky woodchuck attempts to scale the fence, his own weight will plop him right back down where he started.

To foil any tunneling into your plot, either bury the fencing material straight down to a depth of at least 18 inches or install a 2-foot-wide wire apron a few inches under the ground outside the fence. Bend the apron back from the bottom of the roll of fence wire if you purchase it in 6-foot widths, or add a separate segment. If you add this segment, secure it to the upright portion of your fence so that there are no gaps large enough for a woodchuck to squeeze through. It may be enough to add the underground segments only in places where woodchucks have already been digging, or

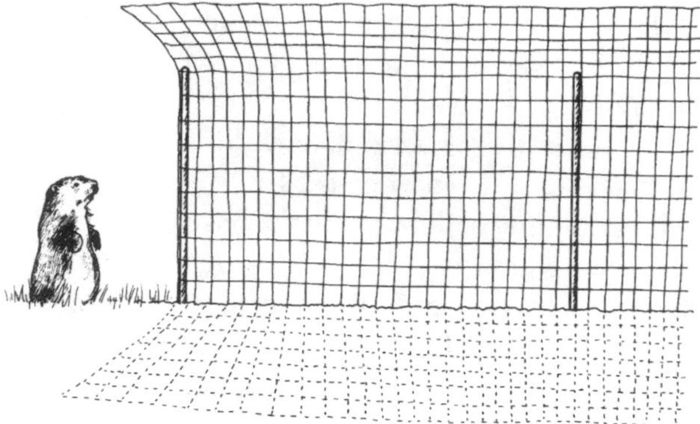

The top part of this fence is left unattached to supports. If the woodchuck tries to scale it, his weight will drop him back to the ground.

you may have to fortify the entire fence line. It all depends on your particular woodchuck.

A strip of black plastic, weighted down along the perimeter so that a few feet extend inside the garden as well as outside, has also discouraged diggers.

A hot wire (electric fence) placed about 4 to 5 inches outside the fence, 4 or 5 inches off the ground, should eliminate attempts to scale the fence or crawl beneath it. Some gardeners use just the hot wire. When using electric fencing, check it regularly for anything that may come in contact with it and cause it to short out.

Garden gates must be sturdy and fit tightly with the rest of the fence. Consider eliminating a gate by using a stile — two sets of steps — so you can walk over the fence. Leave one set on the inside and pull the outside set away from the fence whenever you leave the garden.

Predators. Nature may lend a helping hand, or paw, or talon. Foxes, bobcats, weasels, hawks, and owls, as well as pet or stray dogs, will prey on the hefty pests. Woodchucks are also vulnerable to rabies, which they can transmit to humans.

Removal. If you are truly overrun with woodchucks, you have no choice but to remove the offenders. Trapping with a live trap is a common method. Live traps are easy to set and pose no threat to other wildlife or area pets. Bait the traps with apples or other fresh fruit. Check the traps every morning and evening to reduce stress on the animal. You will have to release him far, far away! Woodchucks should not be trapped and moved just before hibernating or in the spring when they may have babies back at the den.

As a last resort, try fumigating with dry ice. Follow the directions given under Gophers. Do this is early spring when the woodchucks are active, the dens are easily located, and any young are not yet born.

Be certain that the den is *currently* inhabited by woodchucks. Many other animals make use of a woodchuck's former quarters. Check for tracks and try to get a glimpse of the resident.

Chapter 3

Big Game

Bears • Coyotes
Deer • Opossums • Rabbits
Raccoons • Skunks

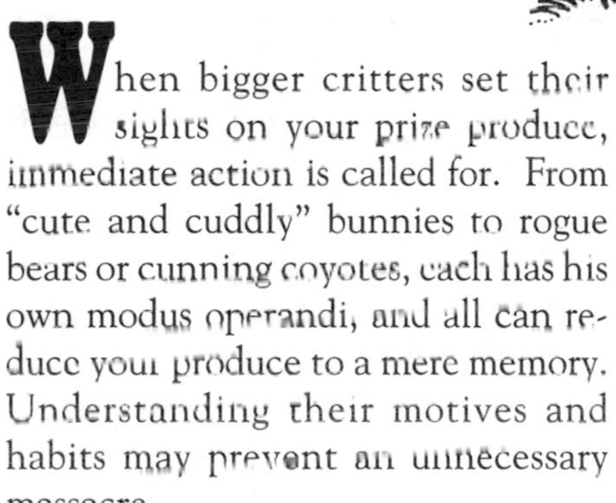

When bigger critters set their sights on your prize produce, immediate action is called for. From "cute and cuddly" bunnies to rogue bears or cunning coyotes, each has his own modus operandi, and all can reduce your produce to a mere memory. Understanding their motives and habits may prevent an unnecessary massacre.

Bears

(Ursus spp.*)*

Slow, lumbering, dimwitted creatures, the few bears left in our national parks certainly pose no threat or annoyance to backyard gardeners. Don't you believe it! Due to ever-increasing habitat encroachment by man, the adaptable bear has found himself quite literally at our doorsteps. In recent years bears have been making more and more brash excursions into city limits in their constant search for food. No longer just a concern of the backwoodsman, the possibility of an ursine visitor is a startling reality for many a rural or even suburban gardener.

Most often the marauder will be a black bear *(Ursus americanus)*, and only rarely the the renowned and dangerous grizzly *(U. horribilis)*.

Physical Description

The smallest of the North American bears, mature black bears range in size from 200 to 400 pounds. (The largest on record was an 800-pound male killed in the late 1800s in Wisconsin.) While jet black black bears are common among the Eastern bruins, the Western varieties run in shades of brown, cinnamon, and dirty blond. In the coastal forests of British Columbia lurks a pure white, blue-eyed version, Kermode's bear.

All have stubby tails, shaggy coats, tremendously powerful bodies, strong jaws, and sharp teeth and claws. Blacks can be distinguished from grizzlies by the lack of a shoulder hump, short, dark claws rather than long, brown claws, relative size (grizzlies may grow to half a ton), and usually by habitat.

Life Cycle

Beginning in their third or fourth year, black bears breed in the summer. Not until the following winter, when the sow (female) is in a hibernation-like state, does the embryo implant and begin to develop. By January or February, more than 200 days after mating, two or three tiny cubs, merely 7 to 12 *ounces*, are born in the den. Mama bear drifts back into her winter's sleep while the cubs wake frequently to nurse and explore their surroundings. When the babies are about sixteen months old, they are mature enough to fend for themselves. But until that time the mother will not mate again, and makes her young her top priority.

Range and Habitat

Bear populations are scattered throughout the Northeast and parts of Minnesota. They are also found in the South — from Missouri down through Arkansas, Louisiana, and into Florida. Bears are also common throughout the Rocky Mountain region and the northwestern regions of the United States and Canada. They live near woody areas or swamps, but may travel into open areas in search of food. Grizzlies, being much less tolerant of humans, prefer remote, subalpine wilderness areas.

Habits

Black bears lead a solitary life, except when mating or raising cubs. They may be active during the day, but are most often night wanderers. They roam vast territories of several square miles or more, depending on available food. Winter finds bears in northern areas falling into a groggy semi-hibernation.

They are omnivorous, eating anything of animal or plant nature. One of their most unpleasant and infuriating eating habits is that of gorging themselves, usually in the garden or orchard, then vomiting great heaps of stuff, only to turn around and go back for more. Pity the beleaguered farmer who finds wasted piles of corn

throughout his demolished patch.

A bear's eyesight is poor. Moving objects are more likely to be spied than still objects. The bear uses keen senses of smell and hearing to make up for what he misses visually.

Though it's rare, black bears have attacked humans. Not all of these cases involved provocation from the victim, and some were even found through gruesomely convincing evidence to have been predaceous.

Bears are inquisitive, bold (make that nearly fearless), immensely strong, determined, and quick to learn despite their somewhat dopey antics. Females with cubs will attack without warning if they even suspect any possibility of a threat. In short, any bear should be considered unpredictable and potentially dangerous.

Garden Targets

Though they may sample everything from the grapevines to the compost pile, most bears prefer corn, melons, or berries, as well as the crops of fruit trees. They are also famous for raiding garbage cans, ransacking empty cabins or campsites, and preying on young livestock, including lambs and calves — even pets. Beehives are also a favorite target.

Damage and Signs

Bears will claw up the bark of trees to mark their territory. This, as well as their large, distinctive tracks and piles of what they're famous for doing in the woods, may be your first warning that bears are about. Their presence in the garden can leave trampled plants; knocked-down fences, trees, berry bushes, or vines; devoured produce; or piles of regurgitated waste.

Deterrents

Because bears are strong, agile, intelligent, and persistent, the absolute best insurance against bear damage is prevention. Once they get your number, they will be back for more. Eliminate any invitations. Don't collect garbage in open pits or piles. Keep tightly covered garbage cans locked up, and dispose of the garbage regularly. Don't leave pet food or sweet horse feed out. Never allow dead animal carcasses to lie out. Be careful as to what you compost, avoiding any fats or other substances that may lure a searching snout.

Scare Tactics. Though not easily intimidated, bears will avoid strange, loud, or apparently threatening situations. Exploding cannons, loud radios, flashing night lights, or scarecrows dressed in your dirty laundry may be enough to send them past your garden. See chapter 1 for more information on those tactics. Constantly changing such gadgets around will help to extend their effectiveness.

Rather than scaring bears away, the sound and scent of dogs often rouses their curiosity or aggravates them. Though Ol' Blue may alert you to a large, hairy visitor, he may also contribute to the bear's discovery of your prize blueberry bushes.

Exclusion. Many of the sturdiest fences have fallen before the push of a mighty bear, but a well-constructed, electrified barrier may turn them away, especially if they have not yet been allowed to establish a habit of raiding your patch. The secret to getting a bear's attention with electric fencing is to surround the entire plot with chicken wire rolled out flat and secured to the ground. Bend coat hangers or other stiff wire in half and push them into the earth to hold the chicken wire in place. The chicken wire provides a substantially more shocking experience than merely touching one charged wire. Keep any vegetation from growing in underneath the chicken wire with weed killer.

The Minnesota Zaps electric fence (see p. 55) may be worth a try in educating bears about the nature of electricity. Currently there is no research about the effectiveness of this type of fence against bears.

Removal. While trapping bears is highly effective in eliminating a rogue intruder, it is not an undertaking for the average zucchini grower. If repeat visits from a trespassing bruin seem inevitable, contact local wildlife authorities. Besides assisting in removal of problem bears, many states pay for damages done by them.

Coyotes
(Canis latrans)

Predator. Opportunist. Survivor. The wily coyote is all of these. In these times when loss of natural habitat is

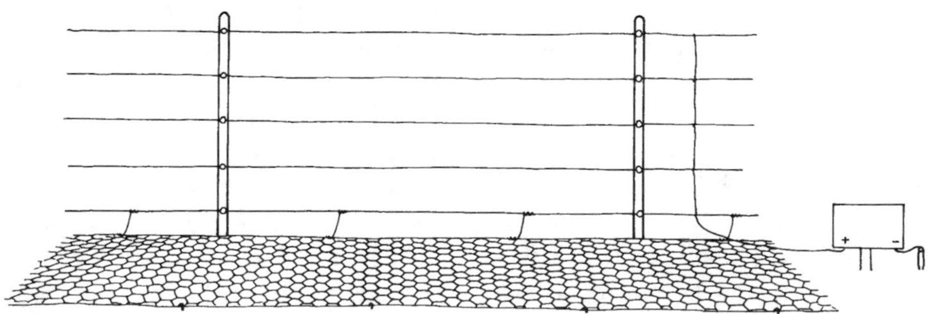

This fence uses electrified chicken wire to prevent enchroachments by bears.

forcing scores of other species out, the coyote adapts and even thrives.

Physical Description

A coyote looks much like a small shepard dog, and little like the savage, wolf-like beast you may have expected. Males are larger than females, standing about 24 inches at the shoulder and averaging about 30 pounds. Coat colors vary from gray to buff with long dark guard hairs casting a more brownish look to the overall color. Color variations range from nearly black to red to whitish.

Coyotes have bushier tails than dogs, alert, pointed ears, relatively long legs, and slender, pointed muzzles.

Life Cycle

Coyote pups start life as one of about five to seven in the litter. From their hidden den they will venture out occasionally around the age of three weeks, and be weaned and learning to hunt in eight to ten weeks. Occasionally the females will breed the first winter, in February or March, and deliver their own litters about nine weeks later. Both mama and papa, who sometimes pair for life, hunt to feed the youngsters. Sometimes more than one mother and litter will share a den and puppy-raising responsibilities. Coyotes will crossbreed with dogs or wolves.

Though in captivity they can live to twenty years or more, the average age in any wild population is around two or three years.

Range and Habitat

Found throughout most of the United States and Canada, coyotes are believed to have inhabited only grassy open areas originally; they can now be found in virtually every type of American habitat from arctic to tropic.

Habits

To understand a coyote is to learn a great deal about canine behavior and ability. When sharing their habitat with humans they will confine much of their activity to the hours when most humans retreat to their own dens. But in wilder areas, they will be active day or night.

Coyotes possess that typically remarkable canine sense of smell as well as good eyesight and hearing. They are clever, persistent, and not terribly finicky eaters. They eat almost anything, but acquire decided preferences.

These are incredibly tough animals with great physical endurance. Superb runners, they have been clocked at speeds of 40 miles per hour and can cover several miles at slower speeds. Unlike pack-oriented wolves or dogs, coyotes are solitary animals, each policing a territory from 5 to 20 square miles.

The most celebrated of coyote habits is their nightly singing. Their howls, yips, chirps, and other indescribable sounds reverberate for miles. Two or more coyotes chiming in can

sound like a chorus of dozens, with an alien or two thrown in for effect.

Garden Targets

Though much of the coyotes' mainstay is rodents, rabbits, and insects, they will happily supplement their diets with pets, young livestock, or garden produce. Plums, pears, mulberries, and especially watermelon and cantaloupe are favored.

Damage and Signs

When your garden has become Wile E. Coyote's hunting ground you will find narrow, doglike tracks, possibly piles of doglike scat, and toothmarks, as well as gaping wounds, in fruit or melons.

Deterrents

Scare Tactics. Since coyotes have become accustomed to man and his often bizarre antics, they are often not easy to scare. Certain dog breeds and individuals have made good guard dogs, especially for livestock; Komondor and Great Pyrenees are among the most recommended. Some stockmen keep donkeys with their flocks, as they will defend their "own" when threatened. Many equines distrust and dislike canines.

The arsenal of loud noises, flashing night lights, and other oddities may make coyotes somewhat leery, for a while at least. For best results combine and constantly rearrange any scare or repellent tactics.

Exclusion. Ordinary sheep fencing can be made coyote-proof by adding an electric wire about 6 inches off the ground and a foot or so toward the outside of the main fence. Since the athletic coyote can clear a 5-foot jump with ease, add two more hot wires, 6 to 18 inches apart, to the top of the wire mesh.

When melons are the target, they can be protected individually with

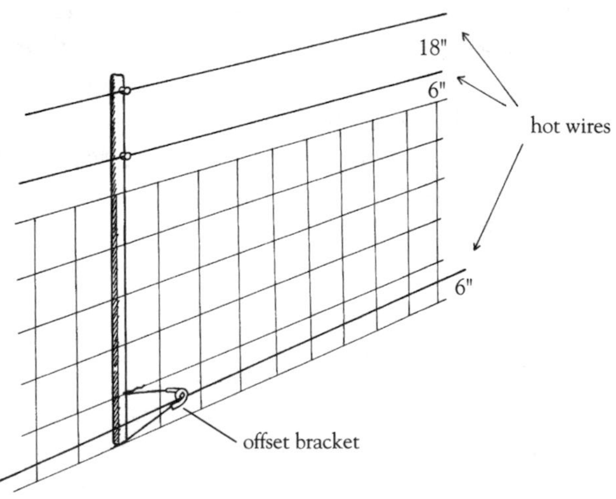

Hot wires added to this 5' sheep fence keep coyotes from digging under or jumping over.

heavy wire mesh cages placed over each ripening fruit and anchored to the ground. Use wire of no larger mesh than 2 inches square to prevent nipping or clawing through it. Though cages for each melon may seem expensive, they should last indefinitely and can be modified to other uses in the garden, from heat-retaining cloches to shade covers.

Deer

(Family Cervidae)

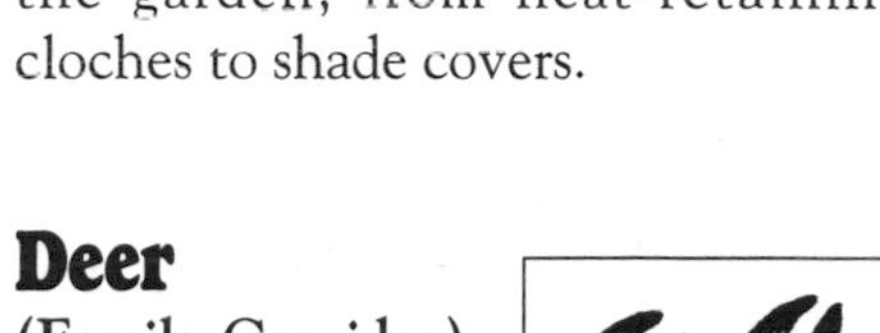

Deer are at once among the most graceful, majestic, and troublesome of wildlife. During hunting seasons, millions of dollars a year are pumped into rural economics, yet deer cost farmers and gardeners obscene amounts of money — and sanity — throughout the year. People are often so enchanted by the movements of deer that they freeze in silence to watch one approach, for fear of frightening it away. Yet during periods of crop damage, it seems nothing we do will drive them off.

Range and Habitat

White-tailed deer can be found throughout most of the United States; mule deer are concentrated in the west. Deer are most at home along the forest's edge. They thrive in rural or subrural areas, as long as there are nearby woods, water, and browsing available.

The most common deer in North America are the white-tailed deer *(Odocoileus virginianus)* and the mule deer *(O. hemionus)*, along with several other species and subspecies. Elk, moose, and caribou also belong to the deer family.

Scientists estimate that fifty million deer roamed the pristine woodlands of North America in the days before white settlement. Current estimates are for between five and twelve million.

Physical Description

The stately deer moves gracefully on dainty two-toed hooves and long, slender legs. Sizes range from tiny 50-pound mature Key deer of southern Florida to over 400-pound trophy mule deer. White-tails average about 36 to 40 inches tall at the withers, and from 150 to 300 pounds.

Deer coats vary with the seasons, from thick, coarse, and grayish in winter to silky reddish brown in summer. Fawns are born rust colored with

white spots to camouflage them in the dappled light of the forest. The spots fade as the fawns mature.

Mule deer have slim, black-tipped tails and large, mule-like ears. White-tailed deer use their broad, flashy namesakes as warning flags.

Only bucks (males) grow antlers. These are shed in midwinter and grow back over the next summer. "Velvet" is the soft outer layer, well supplied with blood vessels, that nourishes the growing antlers. Rack size depends on the animal's age, nutrition, and genetics. Mule deer antlers grow in forks, while those of white-tailed deer grow as single spikes along a central beam.

Deer, like cows, are ruminants. They have multichambered stomachs and lack upper incisor teeth.

Life Cycle

Deer breed from October to January. All but first-time mothers usually produce twins in a little more than 200 days. The youngest does bear single fawns. The fawns weigh only about 7 or 8 pounds at birth. In a few days they are able to walk, but are kept hidden until they are strong enough to run.

Adult size varies with the species and how far north they are found, southerners being the more petite. Bucks grow larger than does by about 25 to 40 percent. Deer continue to grow for five and a half to six and a half years, which means few reach full size. Given adequate forage and left unhunted by man or beast, they can live up to twenty years.

Habits

Deer are most active around dawn and dusk. Though shy by nature, they can become very daring when food is scarce, going into suburban yards in search of a meal. They are prone to reproduce in numbers that make this scene more and more common.

They are browsers, often consuming their total food intake for the day while not stopping long enough to take more than a bite or two from one place. Later, quiet and secret, they will rest to regurgitate their partially digested food and chew their cuds.

Smell is probably the most highly developed of their senses, while taste, hearing, and vision (in that order) are also keen.

Garden Targets

A deer's year-round diet staples include the leaves, stems, and buds of woody plants. The menu, though, is governed mainly by what is available, and they seem eager to try new fare.

Corn, soybeans, small grains, alfalfa, vegetables, and fruit trees are readily demolished. Roses are a special treat. Grasses are generally ignored.

Damage and Signs

Due to their browsing habit and lack of upper incisors, deer leave a jagged edge on the plants they feed on.

Classic signs of visiting deer are small, dark, rounded "pellets" and their distinctive pointy, two-toed tracks.

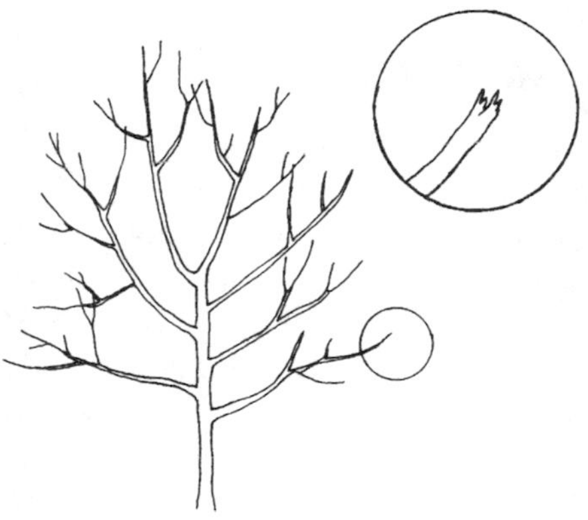

Deer damage to tree branches.

Deterrents

Deer are protected by law in all states where they are found. In return for their game status some states offer to help pay for damages through their wildlife programs, and a few even pay for damages from public funds.

Cultural Practices. While habitat modification is generally out of the question, given a deer's average range of many hundreds of acres, some cultural practices may save you some frustration. Try planting things that deer won't eat. This applies mostly to landscape plants, since they eat most garden vegetables.

Castor-oil plants are not only uneaten, but actively avoided. (They're also poisonous to humans.) Trap crops of corn, soybeans, or alfalfa may lure deer away from the garden.

Repellents. In home gardens repellents can be very effective, and some of the most successful may sound like the least likely. Deer repellents work either by smell or by taste. Check and replenish them if needed after a rain or watering. Don't give up on the usefulness if a particular repellent fails you in one instance. The deer's hunger and lack of alternate food may force him to overlook a deterrent that in another time and place he would avoid.

Human hair, dog hair, or (like we've all got this stuff handy) hair from large wild cats, placed in nylon stockings or fine mesh bags, will frighten deer off. Hang the bags in or near plants needing protection or along fencelines. Rags soaked in kerosene, creosote, or bone tar oil, and bags of mothballs may be used in the same way. Blood meal in pouches or spread on the ground will turn them away.

The smell of people revolts most wild animals, and if leaving your dirty laundry around the garden doesn't turn deer away, hanging bars of deodorant soap at intervals no more than 20 feet apart might. Dial works best. Avoid cocoa-based soap; deer will eat it. Other distasteful odors include a sprinkling of baby powder.

Two or three rotten eggs blended in a gallon of water and sprayed on plants will keep deer at a distance. Decaying fishheads or tankage, the rotting leftovers from slaughterhouses, repels deer almost as much as it repels people but may attract other unwanted animals. Punch holes in the sides of tin cans, place the putrid stuff inside, and hang them 3 to 5 feet high around the garden.

Plants that Deer Won't Eat

Ageratum
Ash
Black-eyed Susan
Black locust
Bleeding-heart
Blue lily-of-the-Nile
Bottle brush
Boxwood
Butterfly bush
Calla lily
Canterberry-bells
Carolina cherry laurel
Chives
Clematis
Columbine
Coreopsis
Daffodil
Daphne
Daylily
Devil's poker
Dogwood
Dusty miller
English ivy
English lavender
Foxglove
Giant reed
Hazelnut
Hellebore
Holly
Iceland poppy
Iris
Japanese rose
Jasmine
Jonquil
Larkspur
Lily
Lupine
Matilja poppy
Myrtle
Narcissus
Nightshade
Oriental poppy
Oxalis
Oleander
Pampas grass
Peony
Persimmon
Pine
Prickly phlox
Peppermint
Red elderberry
Redwood sorrel
Rhododendron (except azalea-leaved)
Rosemary
Scotch broom
Sea buckthorn
She-oak
Snowflake
Soapbark tree
Spearmint
Spruce
Trailing African daisy
Tree pepper
Trillium
Tulip
Wax myrtle
Western spice bush
Wild cucumber
Wild lilac (Blue Jean and Emily B.)
Yarrow
Yucca
Zinnia

Deer have an inborn fear of the smell of their once natural predators. Besides hair, the manure or urine of lions, cougars, and tigers will panic most deer. If you obtain it from the zoo, be sure to store it in a plastic bag to retain moisture and freshness.

Taste repellents ruin the flavor of crops for deer. Hot pepper sauce or a Tabasco sauce solution of 2 tablespoons per gallon of water sprayed onto the foliage will protect plants.

Commercial repellents Big Game Repellent and Hinder repel deer. Hinder is reported safe by the USDA to use on foods to be eaten.

Scare Tactics. Scores of scare tactics have been tried against intruding deer. Gas exploders like those used for birds will scare them off. Be sure to move them every few days and change the firing pattern or the deer will learn to adjust to repetitive sounds. Flashing lights, radios, rattling pie pans, and other noisy contraptions (see chapter 1) may help to turn deer away.

Dogs are frequently used against deer. Take care though. Free-ranging dogs can get into trouble. They kill a great many deer annually. Winter snows bog the deer down, making

them much easier prey for dogs. Dogs tied near the garden may or may not be helpful. The deer soon come to know the dog can't chase them, and the dog may even get used to the deer and not bother to comment.

Exclusion. The surest way to keep Bambi and friends out of your garden is to prevent them from getting in. Erecting deer fencing *before* deer discover your salad bar is the most reliable method. Several designs, both permanent and temporary, are effective. Some even use the added zap of electricity.

1. Eight-foot deer fence. Using hog wire fencing 4 feet wide and 12-foot fence posts, spaced every 20 feet, you can put up a durable, permanent, but expensive deer fence. Sink the posts 3 feet deep, then attach the fencing, keeping it as snug as possible to the ground. Hungry deer think nothing of wriggling through a gap under the fence. Attach a second roll of fencing along the top of the first, and link the two levels together with wire every foot or so. Some deer can clear even an 8-foot fence, so you may want the extra insurance of running a strand of barbed wire 6 to 8 inches above the top of the hog wire.

2. Mystery fence. Deer will not jump over a fence they can't see through. A solid fence 5½ to 6 feet high will keep them out. Some gardeners have had luck hanging sheets, black plastic, or other material over a line to hide the view of their gardens. While such a fence may not be lovely to look at, the results can be. Of course a solid wood privacy fence will also do the job. Don't forget that such fences also shade a fair area of ground, so they should be backed away far enough from the planting area.

3. Seven-wire slant. This fence can be made as an electric or nonelectric barrier. The slanting design takes advantage of deer's lack of desire to hurdle a broad jump.

At 20-foot intervals, sink 8-foot posts to a depth of at least 2 feet. To these supports attach 8-foot lengths of weather-treated 2x6s at a 45-degree angle to the ground so that the highest point of the frame is at least 6 feet high and facing away from the garden. If you want an electric fence, install the wire on insulators. Starting 10 inches from the bottom of the 2x6s, string wire at 12-inch intervals.

Deer walk underneath the slant and try to reach through. With the fence angling over their heads, they don't even think to jump. Be sure to keep the area under the slant cleared so that deer are able to move in underneath and don't try to jump from a distance.

4. Tripod slant. This electric fence works on the same principle as the seven-wire slant, but on a more frugal level. Tie 10-foot or longer poles together at the top in groups of three to form tripods. Space these supports up to 50 feet apart. Attach insulators and run three strands of wire starting at 10 inches high and at 12-inch intervals up the poles.

Deer try to creep under rather than jump this fence and get zapped in the process. They quickly learn to avoid the hot wires.

5. Traditional electric deer fence. Wooden dowels glued into holes in the posts extend electrified wires out from the fence line toward the deer side, as shown in the illustration. Though only 6 feet high, this fence is wide and hot, and very effective at keeping deer out.

Even if an occasional straggler does brave the electric fence and finds himself on the growing side, most often he is so rattled by the shocking encounter that he is too unsettled to eat—shoo him out if you must. Not many contacts with the electric wires are necessary before the deer decide the pickin's are better elsewhere.

6. Penn State five-wire. Going on the tendency of deer to try to go under or through a fence, rather than over, this fence differs from most but has proven to be an extremely effective barrier.

Sink 8-foot pressure-treated posts to a depth of 3 feet and space them 50 to 60 feet apart. Using tube-type insulators and high-tensile smooth steel (New Zealand) wire, run the wires according to exact measurements that follow. Any wider spacing may fail to prevent deer from squeezing through the wires.

The lowest wire must be 10 inches above the ground, no more. Fill in any gaps in uneven ground with rocks or dirt. Run four more strands of wire 12 inches above the last. This makes the resulting fence 58 inches tall. Use a New Zealand energizer to power the fence. These produce high voltage to turn back deer and low impedance to help prevent shorting out.

Though a costly fence to put up if you use the recommended materials, it will last up to forty years with low maintenance costs.

7. New Hampshire three-wire. This temporary fence also uses a deer's lack of confidence in broad jumping. Cut equal numbers of 4-foot and 3-foot stakes from 1x2 wood. Drive the taller stakes in around the garden perimeter 3 feet from the outside edge of the garden. Drive the shorter stakes in around the garden's edge, parallel to the first, leaving 3 feet between each pair of stakes. Each pair may be spaced 20 to 45 feet apart. Attach 18-gauge wire to insulators at 15 inches and 36 inches up on the tall stakes and at 24 inches to 27 inches high on the short ones. This creates a 3-foot-high, 3-foot-wide electrified barrier.

8. Minnesota Zaps. This clever fence teaches deer to avoid it by first tempting them to touch it. Getting zapped on their tender noses or tongues just once convinces the deer to keep away from this fence. Proven effective in many experimental and field situations, this low-cost surprise is simple to build and satisfying in its results.

Attach insulators to 4-foot stakes and drive the stakes in every 50 feet. String wire; 50-pound tension will do.

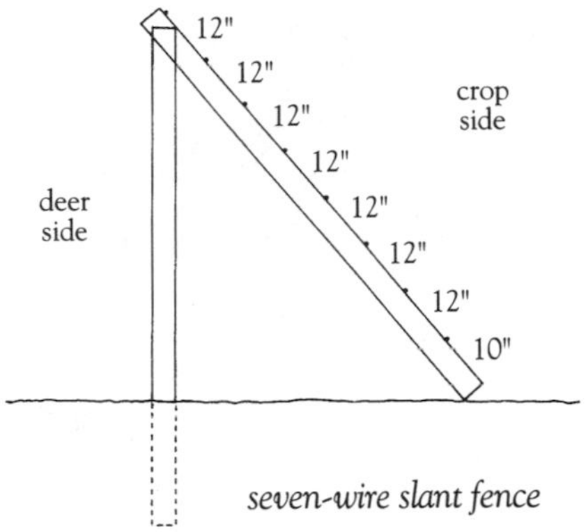

12"
12"
12"
12"
12"
12"
12"
10"
crop side
deer side

seven-wire slant fence

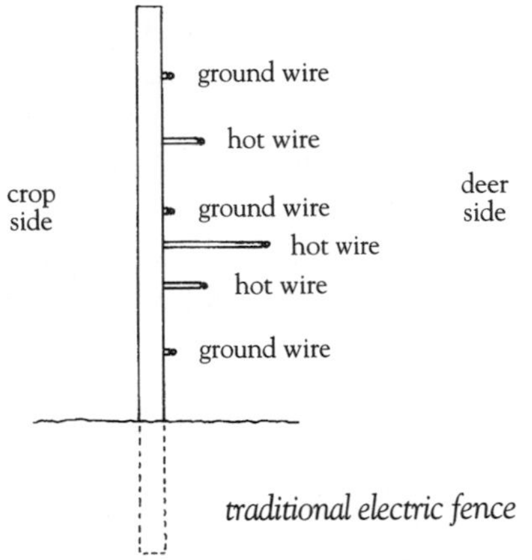

ground wire
hot wire
ground wire
hot wire
hot wire
ground wire
crop side
deer side

traditional electric fence

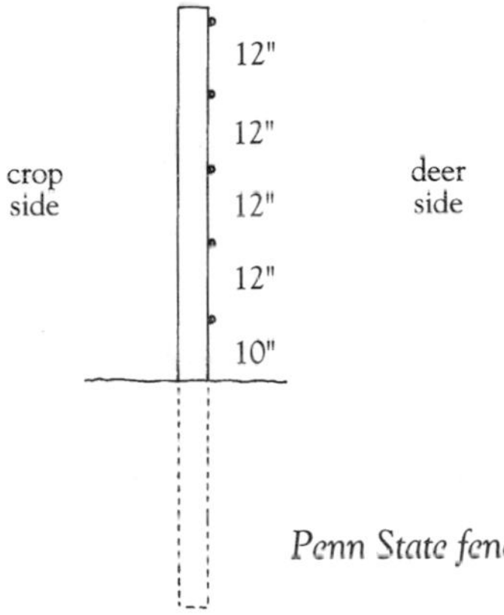

crop side
12"
12"
12"
12"
10"
deer side

Penn State fence

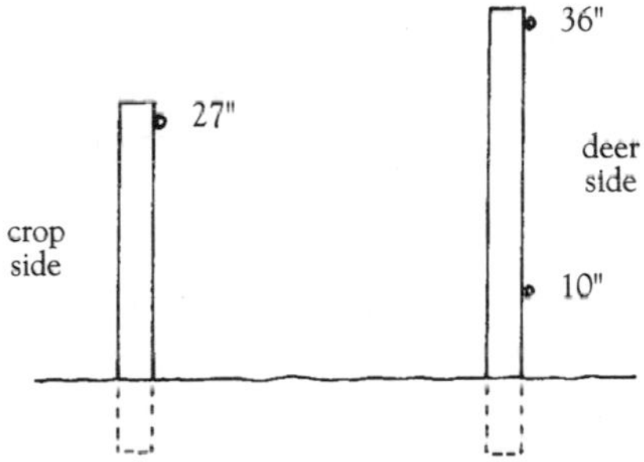

27"
crop side
36"
deer side
10"

New Hampshire 3-wire

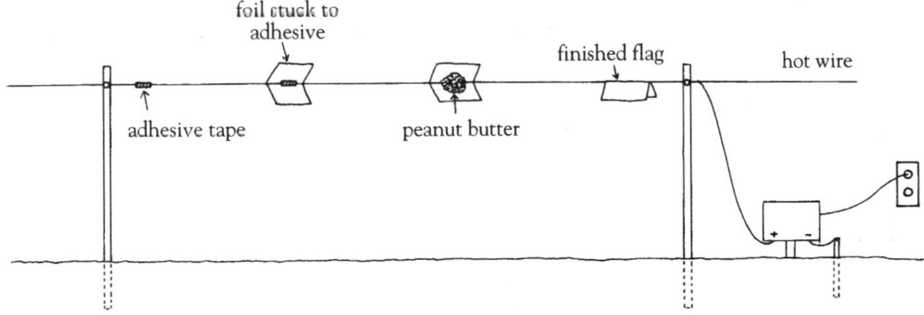

Minnesota Zaps fence

Now comes the clever part. Tear 2-inch pieces of cloth adhesive tape and bend them around the wire every 3 or 4 feet so that the sticky sides are exposed. Stick a 3- by 4-inch piece of aluminum foil on each piece of tape so that the long side folds along the wire and the shiny side is out. Spread a glob of a mixture of peanut butter and peanut oil (about 50/50 makes a spreadable consistency) on the inside of each foil flag, as shown in the illustration. Spread this also on the backing of the tape, then fold the flag closed over it. As soon as deer get a whiff of that yummy-smelling peanut butter they can hardly resist a little taste, but they soon learn to back off.

9. Flat out. While not technically a fence, some gardeners report success by laying out a 4-foot-wide section of wire mesh fencing along the ground surrounding the garden. This uncertain footing makes the deer stay off, and they don't often try to leap over such a wide obstacle.

Protect individual plants with wire mesh cages. Tree trunks or bush stems and limbs can be protected by wrapping them with chicken wire or plastic stripping or by spiraling a strand of wire along the length of vulnerable branches.

Predators. Due to man's extermination of nearly all of the deer's natural predators, such as cougar and wolves, man himself is now the chief predator.

Opossums

(Didelphis virginiana)

Though not the most handsome critter in the forest, the opossum rates as one of the most intelligent. Don't underestimate him.

Physical Description

In a word, unattractive. Possums are house-cat–sized varmints with dense, scraggly, dirty gray fur. They have pointy white heads and long, hairless prehensile tails. Both the front and hind feet resemble little "hands."

Life Cycle

The opossum is the only marsupial native to North America. Mama possum may bear as many as twenty-five underdeveloped ½-inch babies with each litter. The young must then migrate on their own to the safety and nourishment of the pouch, where they will spend the next seven or eight weeks. Rarely will more than seven or eight make it. Babies can sometimes be seen clinging to the tail of the mother by their own prehensile tails or grasping her thick fur to hitch a ride. The young are weaned six to seven

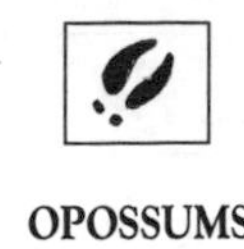

Range and Habitat

Opossums are most common east of the Rocky Mountains and on the West Coast. They generally keep to areas with nearby streams or swamps.

weeks after emerging from the pouch.

Most opossums die during their first year. Those that survive through the winter mate in their first year, and usually twice a year thereafter. The breeding season extends from midwinter through the summer. Babies are born in only thirteen days. Survivors of that first year can expect a lifespan of about seven years.

Habits

Possums are good climbers, but for some reason they can't seem to keep from falling out of trees. They drool a lot and have been aptly described as "dripping from both ends."

As if they know how repulsive they look, possums keep to themselves and are active mostly at night. When cornered, they may either throw a growling, snarling, spitting hissy-fit, complete with release of stinking green goo from the anal glands, or flop over, tongue hanging out, and play, well, possum.

Professional scavengers that they are they patrol roadsides, ever hoping for that favored possum delicacy, road kill. Ironically, or perhaps fittingly, they often provide this for each other.

Although they appear stupid when disturbed during daylight hours, they actually rate (sorry, Lassie) higher than dogs on animal intelligence scales.

Garden Targets

Opossums will eat almost anything, raiding compost piles, tomato plants, and corn patches with equal zeal. They can develop a real craving for fruit. They will raid trash cans and occasionally henhouses.

Damage and Signs

Trenches or holes excavated into working compost piles may be the work of this nocturnal nuisance. Tomato plants may be mauled or lower fruits picked clean. Cornstalks may be bent or damaged as the possum reaches for his ill-gotten goodies.

Deterrents

Be clean. Keep trash picked up and secured inside tightly closed cans. You may have to use a rubber strap to be sure Squire Possum doesn't jimmy off the lid.

Exclusion. Wire mesh fences can be possum-proofed in much the same way as for raccoons (see p. 64) or with an electric wire strung a few inches above the fence, and held about 3 inches out from it. Vulnerable plants can be protected with individual wire mesh cages anchored securely to the ground.

Trapping. Not suspicious of traps, opossums are easily caught in a live trap. You can use just about anything

smelly for bait. If you absolutely must handle the critter, wear gloves. Possums bite and are carriers of rabies. Release them at least a mile from areas where they may become a problem.

A simple but effective trap can be rigged from a garbage can. Put the can next to a porch or other runway, and leave the lid on upside down and at an angle so that if you push down on it, it gives. Leave some bait on the overturned lid. When the possum jumps from his takeoff point and lands on the bait, the lid will give and flip him unceremoniously into the trash can. Relocate the beast at your convenience.

Rabbits

(Family Leporidae)

"Here comes Peter Cottontail, hopping down the bunny trail. . ." The next line in that familiar Easter tune doesn't mention that the bunny trail leads straight to Mr. MacGregor's garden. And though sour old Mr. MacGregor was the closest thing to a villain in the story of Peter Rabbit, many a "harried" gardener has learned to sympathize more with Mr. MacGregor's exasperation than with any cute, furry, plant-nibbling bunnies.

The wild rabbits most often encountered by gardeners are real-life cottontail rabbits and jackrabbits, which are actually hares, close relatives to rabbits.

Physical Description

Cottontails average 12 to 20 inches in length and 2 to 4 pounds in weight. Their soft coats appear gray or brown from a distance, but under close inspection, long black, brown, gray, and white guard hairs are seen growing through a dense, pale undercoat. They sport small, white cottonball tails, for which they are given their common name. Though they shed their coats twice a year, they do not change colors like their kin, the hares.

Hares, including jackrabbits and others, are larger than the cottontails, averaging about 22 inches long and from 5 to 8 pounds. They have a lankier build and longer ears than their cousins. Like rabbits, their hind legs are more powerful than front legs, and their hind feet are much larger than the front. Coat color is gray to brownish in the summer, but is gradually replaced in blotches by snow white fur, with only the tips of the ears and tail showing any color.

Life Cycle

Yes, they breed like rabbits! Hares can produce as many as four litters of up to eight kits annually and rabbits

Range and Habitat

Rabbits and hares are found throughout the United States and southern Canada. Rabbits such as cottontails tend to concentrate in sheltered areas, such as along fencerows or under brush or junk piles. Hares prefer open areas and are found on grassy plains or prairies.

up to six litters of similar numbers. While rabbit babies are born blind and helpless in carefully prepared, fur-lined nests, young hares greet the world in full fur and are able to walk around by the time they are dry. Though no nest is prepared for the new arrivals, the mother keeps them in hiding for a few days after birth.

Though they may live several years in captivity, most wild rabbits and hares survive little over a year, with perhaps only 1 percent making it to a third summer.

Habits

Though rabbits commonly nest in burrows, called warrens, they do not dig their own, relying instead on such hosts as departed woodchucks for their accommodations. They are timid animals, most active in the morning and late afternoon. Their movements are restricted to small territories; they don't venture out into more than a few acres in their entire lifetimes. Occasionally, most often due to lack of feed, they will migrate to new feeding grounds and establish new territories.

Garden Targets

Carrots, peas, beans, lettuce, beets, strawberries, and many flowers, especially tender young tulip shoots, all succumb to the bunnies' buck teeth. Clover, alfalfa, bark from trees or bushes of the rose family (such as apple trees, raspberries, or blackberries), buds, and wild grasses and weeds are also on their menu.

When wild food is scarce, almost any tender garden crop may be tested or clipped off clean to the roots. Among the few crops spared are corn, squash, cucumbers, tomatoes, peppers, and potatoes. Once most plants pass the tender seedling stage, bunnies will ignore them.

Damage and Signs

Tracks are easily identifiable. Foliage is nipped off clean. Trees and berry bushes may be stripped of bark, severely damaging or even destroying them. During snowy weather, rabbits use the snow as a stepladder to reach ever farther up tree trunks.

Deterrents

Cultural Practices. You can encourage rabbits to relocate by removing inviting piles of debris and brush. Since jackrabbits prefer an open atmosphere, allow tall grasses to surround your plot to unnerve them. Avoid planting especially susceptible crops such as alfalfa, lettuce, and new

grapevines if jackrabbit damage seems inevitable.

Some softhearted gardeners try to keep the peace with a bribe crop of alfalfa, clover, or soybeans planted well away from the garden.

Repellents. Gardeners have tried scores of rabbit repellents with tremendously varying degrees of success. Scattering wood ashes, crushed limestone, ground hot peppers, ground black pepper, chili powder, or talcum powder on the soil around plants has worked for many gardeners. Using blood meal around target plants, and human or dog hair mulches were even more effective. Collect the hairy stuff from hairdressers or dog groomers.

Interplanting garlic, onions, Mexican marigold, or dusty miller deters bunnies. A fish spray is recommended to put them off as well. Soak 3 or 4 ounces of chopped garlic in 2 tablespoons of mineral oil for about twenty-four hours. Add 1 teaspoon of fish emulsion dissolved in 2 cups of water. Mix and strain, then store in a glass jar. Dilute 1 tablespoon of this mixture per cup of water and spray around vulnerable plants. At the very least, it makes good plant food.

Scare Tactics. Owing to their timid nature, rabbits can easily be spooked from the garden, temporarily at least. Try burying empty pop bottles (the glass ones) with the tops poking up a few inches aboveground. The eerie wind whistles from these pipes scares the bunnies away (see Gophers, chapter 2). Clear glass jugs, filled with water and set out in the garden, are reported to frighten rabbits due either to light reflections or the bunnies' own distorted likenesses.

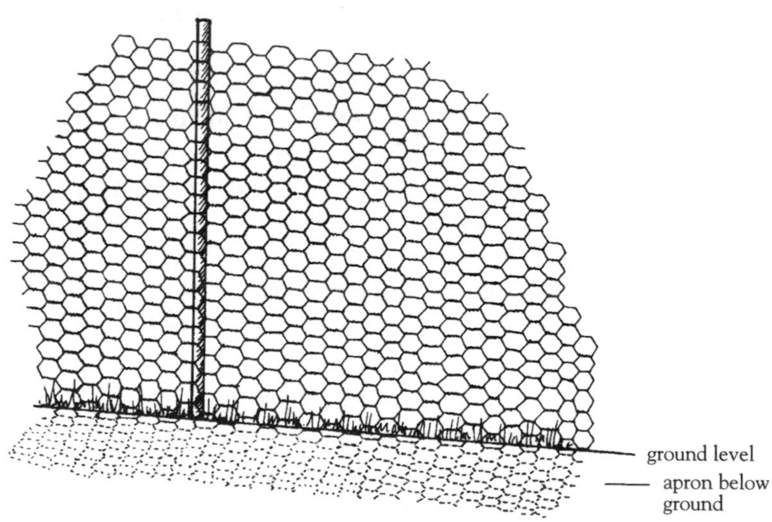

Extend an apron of chicken wire parallel to the ground, buried 6" deep, to keep rabbits out.

Exclusion. Rabbit-proof fencing, plant cages, or row cages will prevent damage on a small scale. Rabbit fence should be constructed of 1-inch chicken wire (or smaller or stronger mesh wire) to a height of at least 2 feet, and buried at least 6 inches deep with an apron of several inches turned outward from the garden before the wire is covered.

Individual plant cages and cages designed to protect several plants to entire rows or beds are variations of this useful idea. Hardware cloth may be used to make the cages even more all-purpose pest-proof; ¼ inch is small enough to bar mice, yet strong enough to stand up to dogs and larger animals.

Frame the cages with 2x1 furring strips or scrap lumber, and staple the wire to it securely. Leave 2 to 3 inches of wire extending from the bottom of the frames, unattached, so that when the cages are put in place this can be sunk into the soil to prevent digging under the cage.

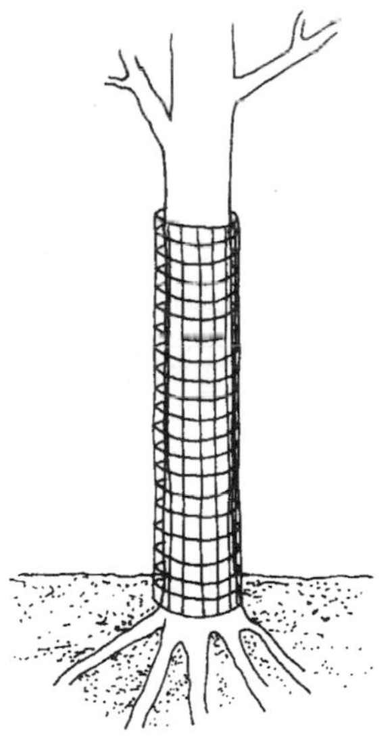

A hardware cloth tree guard.

Tree trunks can be protected by wrapping them with hardware cloth, plastic strips, or foil. The wrap should extend higher than the rabbits can reach, even when standing on a snowbank.

Predators. Fake snakes or owls will keep some rabbits on their own side of the garden gate. Even more effective is a real garden-patrolling dog. For a sure thing that won't squash your squash when lying down on the job, try that ferret. No bunnies in their right mind will come anywhere near a ferret's territory, even if it is harnessed to a tie-out. So strong is their innate fear of these furry little beasties that all you may need is some ferret scent applied here and there to keep the hopping population away.

Other predators may take their share of rabbits but never seem to have much impact on the number of survivors. Hawks, owls, foxes, coyotes, mink, weasels, and snakes may all contribute their appetites to your cause.

Removal. Trapping will remove any offenders, but there will always be a constantly replenishing crop of newcomers to take their places. However, if the new bunnies are not allowed to establish a habit of raiding your garden, removal of the current culprits may be just the head start you need.

Whether using commercial live traps, such as Havahart traps, or a homemade box trap (see Appendix 3 for plans), it is most effective to cover the trap so that Brer Rabbit thinks he is entering a secure hiding place. Apples, carrots, or rolled cabbage leaves are excellent bait for use in warm weather, but can turn mushy after freezing. During cold spells, opt for a handful of clover or alfalfa, corn on the cob, or dried apple pieces. Place traps in areas of rabbit activity, near cover so that the bunnies will feel brave enough to approach them. Captured rabbits can be released into an unpopulated area.

If bunnies are using a single entryway such as a hole in the fence, position the trap near the opening.

Raccoons

(Procyon lotor)

Who was that masked bandit? If he comes as a thief in the night to rob, pillage, and even kill; if he outsmarts you at every turn; if he tries the very limits of your goodwill towards nature — you've got yourself a raccoon!

Physical Description

Instantly recognized by his black mask and ringed tail, the raccoon has grizzled black, brown, and gray fur that has been highly valued as a market pelt. Adult animals are from 24 to 40 inches in length and weigh from 10 to 30 pounds, with rare individuals weighing up to 50 pounds. They have dexterous "hands" that can manipulate intricate items, such as the latch on the garden gate.

Life Cycle

Mating in February or March, mature females produce one litter of about three to five young after a sixty-three-day gestation. The babies stay with mama throughout the semihibernation of their first winter until the following spring. Though a ripe old age of twelve or more is not unheard-of in the wild, it is estimated that as much as three-fourths of any given raccoon population is less than a year old.

Habits

Raccoons are night raiders, pursuing their livelihoods under cover of darkness. They are fairly territorial, generally not sharing dens or territories except during mating or raising of young.

Extremely intelligent, they can be more than a match for any gardener's wits. They can use their paws to open garbage cans and garden gates, spring trap triggers, rob bait, and stuff their furry faces with your hard-earned

Range and Habitat

Raccoons are found throughout the United States and southern Canada. Most often encountered around woods with a natural water source, they have infiltrated many other areas where humans have graciously supplied artificial watering holes, food, and shelter. They prefer dens in the heights of hollow trees or cool refuges under a rocky outcropping.

crops. Those paws also contribute to an excellent climbing ability.

The raccoon diet is well rounded and includes bugs, snails, crayfish, eggs, and mice as well as garden groceries. Much of their food is caught in or near water, and they have a tendency to play with it there. This led to the popular belief that they always wash their food.

Though they are not true hibernators, they undergo periods of inactivity in winter. During this time they will share dens, presumably to conserve body heat. The worst weather may find them napping for several weeks, but days at a time is more the norm. In between naps they emerge to catch up on their eating.

Garden Targets

The raccoon's all-time favorite food is sweet corn, with field corn and melons coming in tied for second. Coons are also known to roll up newly laid sod in search of grubs underneath and to raid the henhouse.

Damage and Signs

Raccoon tracks, like tiny human footprints, are easy to identify in the garden.

When corn is the target, coons will bend down the stalks as they scramble to get at as many ears as possible. Most damage is to lower ears, but at times they take a few bites from a lot of ears. They always seem to know just exactly when corn is at its peak for harvest! Watermelon damage starts with a tiny hole dug into the flesh of the melon and finishes with greedy little hands scooping the sweet insides out.

When chickens are their victims, coons seem to enjoy biting off the heads or pulling apart body parts of more than a few of the poor birds.

Deterrents

Whenever there is a threat of a raccoon beating you to the corn crop, consider the benefits of picking just a little early.

Repellents. Some repellents are very effective because they play on inborn fears. The scent of natural enemies will keep many coons away. Try leaving your dirty clothes in the corn patch, spreading dog droppings, or better yet lion droppings (for those of you who live near a zoo) in the rows, or sprinkling red fox urine lure at the base of plants. For an even more realistic human scent you can always invite friends over for a garden campout!

Other repellents include dusting corn ears and leaves with baby powder. Raccoons detest the stuff. Sprinkling ground hot peppers on corn silks or on vulnerable crops makes them less palatable.

Spreading blood meal has also worked for some people.

Scare Tactics. Many scare tactics have been suggested for raccoons. Moving, flashing, or automatically timed floodlights should send them scampering. However, a constant light source is soon ignored. Leaving a radio tuned to a talk station all night may work. Consider venting your frustrations on tape and putting it on continuous replay in the corn patch. If if doesn't scare them off, at least you can give them a piece of your mind along with a piece of corn.

Rattling pie pans, whistling pop bottles, scarecrows, windmills, plastic streamers, and other devices will contribute to scaring off coons. Though they quickly adjust to any one of these, rotating and combining tactics should keep them guessing long enough to get you through harvest.

Exclusion. A good coon fence may be your best defense. Given the raccoon's superb ability to climb, a *good* coon fence must be designed around his abilities. Chicken wire, or 2- by 4-inch mesh, 3 feet high, will not stop them. However, make that 4 feet or more high, with the top 12 to 18 inches left unattached to any support and bent outward, and you have that good coon fence. As the raccoon attempts to scale it, his own weight pulls the wire down, depositing him right back where he started (see Woodchucks, chapter 2). Acclaimed by some to be even more effective is a 3-foot-high chicken wire fence topped with two strands of electric wire strung 6 inches apart. To make the fence even more critter- proof, bend about a foot of wire away from the garden and bury it to stop any digging underneath.

Make certain that there are no tree branches or other bridges the coons might use to bypass your barrier.

In extreme cases, growers have enclosed the entire patch in a chicken-coop–like fence, complete with chicken wire roof. While this keeps coons as well as virtually every other noninsect pest away from the crop, it is quite an undertaking, and not the easiest place for the gardener to work.

Try draping plants with bird netting and weighing down the edges. Coons don't like the clingy stuff grabbing at their feet. A 3-foot-wide strip of wire mesh, black plastic, newspaper, or other foreign material that might make for nervous footing, laid on the ground surrounding the garden patch, may ward off unwanted advances.

Create a living fence to take advantage of a coon's habit of standing on his hind feet to keep a lookout while he goes about his business. Do this by interplanting vining crops (cucumber, pole beans, squash, pumpkin) with the corn. As the ma-

turing vines tangle up and among the cornstalks, they make it an uneasy place for a watchful coon to sneak a snack.

Individual ears of corn may be saved by covering each with a paper bag or old knee-high stocking and securing these to the stem with a rubber band or string (see p. 13). Don't cover the ears before the silks have turned brown or you will prevent pollination and kernel development.

Predators. Natural enemies are few, but include dogs, coyotes, foxes, weasels, and great horned owls. Most losses to these wild hunters are the very young.

Removal. Trapping may be your best bet for removing repeat offenders. Live trapping, as always, is safest and probably simplest. Use a box trap at least 10"x12"x32", baited with sardines, marshmallows, bread soaked in honey, chicken innards, or sweet corn. Choose an attractive, unusual bait that curious coons can't obtain otherwise. You will find that unless you cover the back end (bait end) of the trap with fine wire mesh or other similar material, your crafty coon may well just snatch your offering from that side without ever venturing into the trap.

Skunks

(Family Mustelidae)

Belonging to the same group as weasels and mink, skunks aren't much trouble to gardeners. In fact, with small animals and insects accounting for over half of their diet, most skunks should be considered beneficial.

Physical Description

Several species exist in North America, most being about the size of a house cat. The common striped skunk *(Mephitis mephitis)*, or civet cat, à la Pepé le Pew, is most likely the one that comes to mind when someone mentions skunks. These squat little animals grow to over 2 feet in length (including their bushy, striped tails) and up to about 8 pounds. Thick, shiny black fur, marked with two distinctive parallel white stripes running along the back from the nape of the neck to tip of the tail, is their instantly recognizable attire.

Life Cycle

Skunks breed at the end of February to produce litters of four to six young, in about nine weeks. The ba-

Range and Habitat

Found throughout most of the United States and Canada, skunks most often occupy open areas that border forests or streams.

bies stay with mama skunk through the summer and sometimes den with her in the winter to share body heat. Though they are not true hibernators, they do retreat to a sleeping state during the worst winter weather. By the next spring the youngsters are mature and ready to bring up little stinkers of their own.

Habits

Skunks will normally claim a home range of from ½ to 1½ square miles. They travel this area throughout the night, as they are primarily nocturnal. Skunks may carry rabies, and the sight of one active in the daytime, especially if aggressive, could mean one sick skunk. Avoid any such animals and report your suspicions to local health officials.

Skunks as a rule are rather mild mannered. They even offer fair warning before blasting away with their best known means of defense — chemical warfare. Before spraying their ammunition, the harassed skunk will curl his tail up and over his back, take aim (which can be all too precise), and stamp his feet. A calm, quiet, though expedient retreat is a good idea.

The smell is sickening to some, and none too appealing to anyone. It can cause temporary blindness, usually lasting no more than ten or fifteen minutes, and a painful burning if it gets into the eyes. Rinse eyes with water to help dilute the spray. Wash clothing or animal fur with diluted vinegar, tomato juice, or neutroleum alpha, a scent-masking agent.

The skunks' stubby legs make them slow, clumsy runners and even worse climbers. They may burrow under buildings, steal eggs, or even kill an occasional chicken.

Garden Targets

Skunks may feed on lower ears of corn, though during the summer months they are more likely to be out searching for insects. If you are none too tactful in dealing with a visiting skunk, his carefully aimed-for target may be you!

Damage and Signs

Lack of odor means absolutely nothing as to whether skunks are in the vicinity. Of course, their presence is well known when you do catch a whiff.

Since grubs make up a good portion of a skunk's summer diet, he may make a nuisance of himself by digging up lawns or even garden soil in search of them. Several 3- to 4-inch holes could be the work of a striped exterminator. Five-toed tracks or droppings containing a good deal of undigested insect parts may be found.

Deterrents

Take pet food dishes in for the evening. Keep garbage can lids on tight. Skunkproof the henhouse by covering any ground-level openings with wire mesh. If a skunk decides to sample your corn patch, chances are he won't do much damage. But if you have no intention of sharing, you can set up a 2-foot-tall wire mesh or picket fence to keep skunks out.

Repellents. Understandably, not much offends the olfactory sensibilities of skunks enough to sway them from a given area. However, cloths soaked in ammonia repel them.

Removal. Skunks are easy to catch in box-type traps. Good baits are fishy-smelling cat food, chicken innards, or peanut butter on bread. Put the prepared trap near the skunks den or where you've seen the skunk. Tie a long cord to the cage door so you can set free any caught skunks from a safe distance.

Check the trap each morning. Some people rig a flag to the trap so that it will move when a skunk is caught and they can see the flag without coming too close.

When you catch a skunk, put on old clothes and goggles — just in case! Working slowly, cover the trap with a tarp or heavy canvas. This gives the skunk a cozy, secure feeling and protects you from getting sprayed. If you are moving a skunk out of your area, slowly and quietly lift the tarp-wrapped cage into the back of a pickup, take it to an area where the skunk won't bother other people, lift the cage out of the truck, and open the cage by pulling that long cord from a distance.

A homemade trap that works well for skunks and other small raiders is the Skunk Drop Trap, similar to that used for opossums. Cover the top of a large (33-gallon or bigger) garbage can with several layers of newspaper. Place a tuna fish or cat food can, half full of

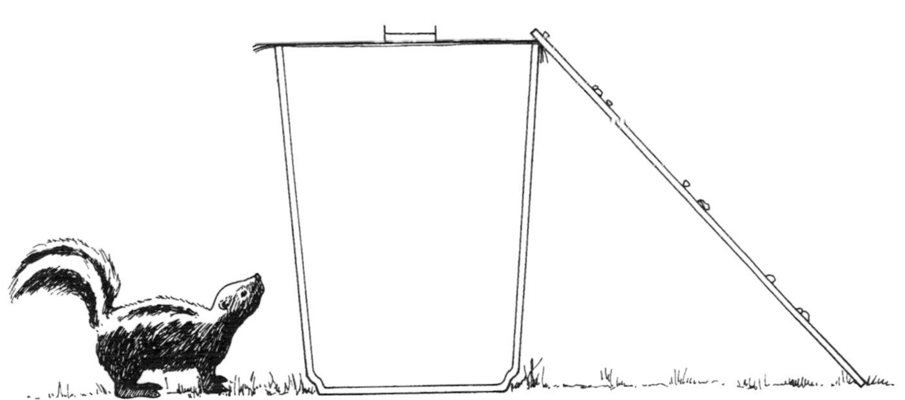

The Skunk Drop Trap

fish or other bait and half full of water, in the center of the newspaper. Lean a plank up to the rim of the can. Nailing strips of 1x2 across the length of it every 6 inches or so will help poor climbers get a toehold.

When a hungry varmint scales the plank and helps himself to the contents of the dish, the water splashes out, weakening the paper, and plop!, down he goes.

Wearing gloves, goggles, and old clothes, approach the canned skunk quietly and slowly place a "stink shield" over the can. An old rug, the can lid, a piece of plastic tarp, or any similar material will serve the purpose. Transport the skunk gently to its release destination. Lay the can on its side and carefully remove the covering. Step away quickly and quietly, with your back toward the skunk.

Chapter 4
Friends and Neighbors

Dogs and Cats
Livestock • Kids

When all of nature is behaving itself nicely and your garden is sprouting, blooming, and just generally growing beautifully, you can always count on your friends, be they human or animal, to keep you humble. Man's best friend will dig and roll, cats will deposit smelly calling cards, livestock will devour, disrupt, or demolish, and at the very least admiring neighbors may borrow a bouquet. Common sense and thoughtful prevention should keep you all living in harmony.

Dogs and Cats

Dogs and cats spell disaster in the garden. Large dogs dashing through your greens can shred them into coleslaw in seconds. Some dogs, especially during hot spells, may take their time, casually sniffing here and there, until they find just the right spot — to dig! And roll around. And dig some more. The cool earth feels so good they just can't stop. Still others, territorial

males in particular, may leave no readily evident damage — until you pick lettuce for a fresh salad and catch an unhappily familiar aroma of ammonia.

Cats often do no better. Though a really good mouser is worth his weight in D-Con, other felines view gardening and mousing purely as spectator sports. Their disinterested observance of all your diligent garden activity is interrupted from time to time by the call of nature. But why bother looking for a private corner, let alone that dinky little litter box, when this giant-sized litter pan is so handy? Later, as you weed through the bean plants, you find some of the seedlings overturned and a surprise waiting for you just under the soil surface. Also, some cats will gleefully demolish catnip transplants in ecstatic fits of appreciation.

Deterrents

When contemplating a solution to pet problems in the potato patch, think about when and why the critters are doing damage. Does Rover lazily stroll across the carefully prepared seedbeds only when you're out there poking around in them? Or does he bolt through the entire garden in hot pursuit of bunnies or cats, trampling everything in his path? Some dogs just pick the wrong place to lie down, while others see you digging around in that sweet-smelling earth and figure, Hey! Then there are the lazy corner-cutters who are just "in the habit" of taking a shortcut across the strawberry patch. Discovering the motive for the crime will help to prevent further violations.

Getting your own protective dog may be enough to chase off vagrant beasts. But when all else fails, and the vandals are not your own, consider setting up live traps to catch them. Consult your local humane society or animal control officials first. Return catches to their owners and explain as tactfully as possible your circumstances. Most people do not want their animals to become public nuisances and at the very least have a vague understanding of the term "liability" when it pertains to legal damages.

Cultural. Cats may be lured away from garden or flower beds with a "trap" planting of catnip as far away as practical. Be sure to cover any catnip transplants you would like to keep, or make sure they are big, healthy specimens before setting them in the ground. These have the best chance of survival.

Repellents. Several homebrewed repellents have enjoyed success in turning dogs and cats away — provided, of course, you are not dealing with free-ranging animals who barrel through your humble plot as if on a dare. Such beasts don't slow down long enough to get a whiff of your carefully prepared repellents. Plodding hounds, those that stop to dig and wallow, or short-legged critters whose anatomy places their keen noses close to the ground, are the most likely

candidates for such concoctions.

Try mixing a tablespoon or two of Lysol disinfectant (the kind in the brown bottle) per gallon of water and sprinkling it on the ground around the garden border or vulnerable plants. Take care to keep it off plants, though, as it will burn the leaves. Various hot pepper, garlic, and onion mixtures, pureed in a blender, strained, and sprayed liberally, are recommended against a host of intruders including pesky pets. One suggestion is to chop finely one garlic bulb, add a tablespoon of cayenne pepper, let sit in a quart of warm water for at least an hour, strain, add a teaspoon of liquid dish soap, and spray away. Take care to avoid getting this, or any hot pepper sprays, into your eyes. Sprinkling ground black pepper or hot peppers around garden perimeters is also frequently recommended.

Rue is especially unpopular with cats. Scatter dried leaves or interplant the herb near vulnerable areas to discourage feline visitors.

Create a home version of commercial dog and cat repellents by distilling the active ingredient, nicotine sulfate. Save up a jar of cigarette butts (or collect them from public ashtrays, maybe while no one is looking), fill with water, and let stand a few days. Strain, add a teaspoon of liquid soap, and apply either as a spray or just by leaving a few drops here and there. Like any nicotine preparation this is poisonous, so use precautions (as noted on p. 98).

Exclusion. Sophisticated as they are, house pets, be they yours or someone else's, can be difficult to keep out of that precious digging site you hopefully refer to as "The Garden." Fencing at least 3 feet high, using nonwooden posts to discourage climbing cats, keeps out most pets. Use a small enough mesh (chicken wire is fine) to exclude cats, but set posts securely to hold back pushy canines. Some dogs may attempt to dig underneath. Bending a foot or two of the wire outwards from the garden and burying it a few inches deep will foil such excavations. For persistent offenders, a hot wire, strung to hit the culprit at mid-chest level, or one about 4 inches high and a second a few inches above it, should stop any gate crashers.

For cats, laying a flat section of chicken wire over newly planted beds will make them less inviting, as the cats don't like the way the wire feels and can't dig through it to bury their "surprises." Be sure to pull the wire up before the plants grow too large to slip through. As plants grow the bed will be less appealing and less vulnerable as a potty site.

Dogs may or may not respect the paths created between raised beds, but cats couldn't care less. Individual plants may be protected with wire cages or by bending stiff wires, such as clothes hangers or even old croquet wickets, over them at right angles to each other.

Farm Animals

From the henhouse to the pigpen to the pasture, bold, curious, and hungry critters are waiting for the opportunity to invade and demolish your garden.

Fowl Play

Although chickens, ducks, geese, and other fowl may devour a fair number of other garden pests, they will cheerfully do more harm than good. What hen can resist a good dust bath, right in the middle of your freshly sown carrot patch? Big birds also cause damage by their incessant scratching, as they hunt and peck for those other garden pests. And they also enjoy a few greens now and then.

The best way to bar birds from the garden is to construct a chicken wire fence, at least 4 feet high (6 is better) with metal posts. (Or attach something to the top of wood fence posts, such as old bedsprings, to make them unperchable.) Otherwise individual plants or rows can be protected with cages. Either way, be sure the barricade is either flush with the ground or partially buried.

Lively Livestock

Barnyard beasts can wreak irreparable havoc before you even know they have escaped. Goats, and occasionally sheep, are browsers, clipping shoots and buds. Horses, being grazers, will pass by many crops but can't resist a nibble of corn, pea vine, or many flowers. In the meantime, their not-so-dainty hooves will crush everything in their paths. Cows prefer pea vines but will also sample other edibles. They are much more likely than horses to lie down on the job, flattening out entire beds. Pigs can do an amazing amount of damage before they taste a thing. Curious snouts will upend and uproot anything that looks interesting. Hooves so sharp they can be used to decapitate large snakes can also put a quick and merciless end to any vegetation in their way.

Because domesticity has dulled many of their natural fears and instincts, farm animals, like pets, can be very tough to frighten off. Your best garden protection lies in proper fencing. Horses and cows will try to reach over and through. Sturdy posts are a must, and use at least four strands of wire. Sheep can melt right through separate-strand wire fences. Keep them in with wire mesh "sheep fence." Goats can climb and, except for pigs, who are strong enough to knock down or root under a surprising percentage of fences, may be the hardest to keep in. You may want to reinforce fence lines that abut the garden area. Often adding a strand or two of electric wire will make all the difference. It can easily be removed or turned off after the growing season.

Kids

Of all the fresh, wonderful little miracles of nature that sprout in our gardens, nothing is as precious, or worthy of more tender nurturing, than a

child's interest in making things grow. Kids belong in the garden. The raw essence of dirt and things growing draws children of all ages to the soil.

Get 'Em Dirty Early!

Youngsters can learn to appreciate much more than the fresh sweetness of just-picked strawberries, though that in itself is a most rewarding lesson. In the garden, they have an opportunity to see nature at work and gain respect and understanding for the natural order of things. They see the results of planning and work, as small, hard seeds transform into lush, living, and ultimately giving things. Like all of us who coax from the earth our own designs, children, especially, wonder at the simple magic of creating the intricate, living work of art that even the smallest gardens represent. As the season comes to an end, and the garden is "put to bed," there are lessons in the reward of the harvest, the reuse of spent plants in compost so that next season's garden may grow ever greener, and the reassurance of the coming of the next spring, the perpetual cycle of life.

Another important aspect of encouraging children to participate in gardening is the relationship between the apprentice and the master. When a child's interest is sparked, the one who guides him becomes a central figure in his or her life. Take advantage of this wonderful opportunity to share your values and deepen your bonds with children who wander into your garden.

Preventing Damage

Notwithstanding the value of involving kids in the garden, there are undeniably times when little hands and feet can damage a lot more than your good intentions. Discipline goes with the territory. Kids must be taught to respect boundaries. Most of us are not apt to sacrifice the entire crop just to show Johnny that "if you play sandbox in the corn patch you won't have any corn on the cob." If you garden in raised beds, start with never allowing anyone to step on the beds once they have been prepared. Don't forget to set a good example!

One of the best ways to get kids to cooperate in the garden is to help them set up their very own patch. Select things that kids like. Bright flowers, strawberries, sweet peas, pumpkins for Halloween, and cherry tomatoes are good. Include a few transplants to satisfy that childish need for instant gratification, and plant some quick-sprouting seeds to reassure them that there really are miracles about to unfold. Radishes are great groundbreakers; lettuce, peas, and marigolds all come up fairly quickly and will do so even faster if the seeds are presprouted. Drop a few seeds into a paper coffee filter, wet it down, and fold it into quarters. Place it inside a plastic sandwich bag and leave it in a windowsill for a couple of days.

When the kids who pose problems in the garden are not your own, things become a little touchier. If you have the time and the inclination, neigh-

bor kids can benefit just as greatly if you share a bit of your plot with them. If this isn't practical for you, and kids are turning your transplants into trash, there are a few little tricks you may want to try.

Groundskeepers from parks, parking lots, and urban centers have found that by planting flowers, vandalism can be significantly reduced. Border your garden with a wide row of cheerful blossoms.

Start a bug bounty. Pay a penny a bug for pests kids collect and squish, and a penny a bug for ladybugs or worms they bring in! Most kids like bugs almost as much as they like dirt, and as they learn about the differences between harmful and beneficial insects you may be able to sneak in a little appreciation for gardening.

Purposeful damage calls for more serious measures. Try talking directly to the child, before confronting parents, and depending on age, explain things in appropriate terms. You may have to stretch a point to win cooperation. Does "We need this food to eat or we might starve" sound too farfetched?

For kids who can read, a sign can be worth a thousand words even if only two or three actually go on it. Rural gardeners can try "Beware of Bull" (especially appropriate if you are bluffing!). "Large Snakes on Duty" is another winner.

If you go to all the trouble of erecting an electric fence (or something that just *looks* like an electric fence) and placing several bright yellow warning signs in conspicuous places, you may never have to go to the extreme of actually throwing the switch. Like bulls or hiding snakes, who wants to chance it? If you ever do, however, take care. Low-shocking pet chargers are available, and though the zap (even from a livestock fence) will do no physical harm, it's a drastic step to take. Some areas even outlaw their use as some people, those with heart problems or wearing pacemakers especially, could suffer serious consequences from an accidental run-in with a charged fence.

The approach you take depends on whether you are dealing with your own children or someone else's, the age and level of understanding of the offenders, the type of damage being done, and their motive for doing it. Greedy little hands stealing a few mouthfuls of strawberries cause little concern compared to the teen next door who continually drives over your flower beds. And don't these both pale by comparison to the troubled child who strikes out to get attention? Before barring even a seemingly destructive child from the garden, consider the possibilities of doing something he probably doesn't expect — welcome him with open arms.

After all, gardeners are like that.

Chapter 5

Lowlifes

Slugs, Snails, and Turtles

Slugs and snails are among the most common garden pests. They seem to find their way into nearly every garden. Traditionally, snails have been looked upon with somewhat less disgust than slugs. They are the "cute" ones with the little spiral shells collected by children. Thanks to their terrific appetites, however, they are definitely on the hit list of many gardeners. Likewise with turtles, who are often beneficial in the garden — when they do damage, they may not be such welcome friends.

Slugs and Snails

(Mollusks, Subclass Pulmonata)

Some claim that slugs are gaining a sort of popularity today. They've been chosen the school mascot by the University of California at Santa Cruz, and are the object of festivals and various retail goodies from T-shirts and postcards to dolls and replicas.

However, any gardener who has ventured out on a morning stroll through the garden only to find that the freshly transplanted marigolds have mysteriously vanished probably feels no affection for the slimy slug at all.

Physical Description

Unlike his close relative the snail, a slug hides nothing from the world. He goes through life as naked as — as a slug! They come in shades of pink, brown, beige, black, and gray, with or without spots.

Slugs can grow up to several inches in length, and their main features include the following: one long muscular *foot* that extends the length of the body; a flap of skin, called the *mantle* (where the shell would be were a slug a snail), under which the slug can withdraw its head; two sets of retractable tentacles on the head, the longer upper set holding simple eyes at the tips enabling the slug to "see" light and dark, and the shorter, lower pair holding scent receptors; and slime. Lots of slime.

A snail is a fancy slug, condo included. Common garden snails are much smaller than their sluggish cousins, usually reaching no more than 3 inches in length. They have the same body design as the slug: foot, mantle, tentacles, and even the slime. Most often they are a shade of dirty brown, with some spots or stripes. The most obvious difference is that snails have the protective shell.

Life Cycle

One of the things that makes slug and snail populations so large is their prolific reproductive habits. They are hermaphroditic, possessing both male and female sex organs, but need a partner to cross-fertilize. Although it can take all day for them to mate, at only a few months of age each can begin to lay hundreds of eggs a year, which hatch in only three weeks, ready to repeat the cycle.

The eggs are tough and elastic and not very vulnerable to small predators, but they will dry up if not kept moist. Look for them in damp, shady places or underground.

Extreme weather, either too hot or too cold, causes snails to stop laying eggs and go dormant, a condition they can tolerate for up to four years.

Range and Habitat

Found throughout most of the United States and southern Canada, slugs prefer a moist, moderate climate. They thrive in areas like the Pacific Northwest, California, and southeastern Alaska. Snails also depend upon a damp climate. However, they have one need that the slugs do not. Because of their shells, they must have calcium, so regions that are deficient in that element usually have fewer snails.

Habits

Slugs and snails require moisture and shade; they creep through shaded, low leaves of plants. They slowly inch along a self-made slime trail by means of muscular waves along the foot. Lacking shells, slugs are able to squeeze into small hiding places for shelter, while snails carry theirs with them. Food is shredded and ingested by the *radula*, a conveyer-belt–like organ covered with thousands of tiny teeth; they prefer to munch on decaying vegetable matter. Both slugs and snails are most active at night.

Garden Targets

Young, tender transplants, leafy vegetables, marigolds, delphinium — almost anything young and vulnerable is favored by slugs and snails.

Damage and Signs

The dried slime leaves a silvery trail of these pests' adventures. Most gardeners instantly recognize this evidence of slug or snail activity. The damage they inflict on plants leaves ragged, chewed foliage and can destroy entire plantings.

Perhaps this is their only redeeming quality: slugs are known to make even Great Dane–size piles of dog excrement vanish. When a few slugs congregate thereon, the pile mysteriously disappears over a period of a few days .

Deterrents

Since slugs and snails are fond of decaying vegetation, keep your garden rows or beds free of dead leaves and debris as much as possible, especially around target plants or seedlings.

Cultural Practices. While mulching is a valuable garden practice, it can create perfect hiding places for those seeking a cool, damp refuge. Hold off on mulching until plants are well established or until the temperature is over 70 degrees F., when slugs and snails are less active. Try mulches that compact, such as rice hulls or pine needles. (If you mulch with pine needles, you may need to counteract its acidity by adding lime to the soil.)

Some mulches can be used to form barriers that deter slugs and snails, as they don't like to crawl over rough or irritating surfaces. Some to try are eggshells, wood ashes, gravel, sand, oak leaves, cedar or oak bark, and tobacco stem meal. Sawdust around strawberries is especially beneficial, as the berries like the acidity and it keeps the fruit from touching the soil.

Also, beware of composting slug-infested plant material. You may wind up introducing slugs into your garden when you apply the compost.

In areas where winter crops are grown, plant seeds earlier, usually in August, so that plants are well developed by the time snails and slugs become more active in the fall.

Despite their seemingly universal appetites, slugs and snails won't pester some plants. These include: azalea, apricot, almond, basil, bean, cigarette plant, corn, chard, Jerusalem cherry, daffodil, fuchsia, freesia, grape, gopher plant, ginger, holly, hibiscus, Swedish ivy, Peruvian lily, parsley, pumpkin, plum, white winter radish, rhubarb, sage, sunflower, rhododendron, and California, Oriental, and Iceland poppies.

Repellents. Effective home remedies include interplanting repellent plants such as prostrate rosemary *(Rosmarinus officinalis)* or wormwood *(Artemisia absinthium)*. Wormwood is also effective when made into a tea and sprayed well around the base of likely targets. The U.S. Food and Drug Administration has declared worm-

wood "unsafe" when ingested, so care should be taken when handling.

Another very potent attack involves spreading powdered ginger around the plants, creating a barrier that slugs and snails will not cross. Crushed limestone spread near plants achieves the same results, as do 2- to 3-inch pieces of fresh-cut fennel scattered at the base of plants.

Handpicking. Another classic method of slug and snail control is a predawn flashlight raid — handpicking the offenders and dropping them into a pail of salted water to finish them off while they're still groggy. A spritz of white vinegar or a sprinkle of salt will also stop them dead in their track.

Leave old boards lying in the garden. Slugs and snails will congregate under the shaded shelter, and they can be easily collected.

Exclusion. Some advocate painting an inch-wide stripe of white paint (spray paint or whitewash) around plants to form a barrier. An alternative method is to use aluminum foil. Cut and fold the foil into strips 1½ inches wide and connect into pieces long enough to form a circle around the plant to be protected. Hold the foil in place with toothpicks, hairpins, or pieces of cut wire.

Construct a plywood barrier using 10-inch-wide boards, propped up on stakes to angle them away from plants. Or surround plantings with corrugated lawn edging that has had a 1-inch lip bent, using pliers, to face away from the plants.

Since copper carries a weak electrical current, slimy slugs and snails really get a charge out of it. A very thin (.002 inch thick) copper sheet, the type used in the electronics industry, can be cut into strips to line the border of each bed. Fruit trees can be protected with a 3-inch-wide strip of copper sheeting wrapped around the trunk about 1½ feet up from the ground.

Quarter-inch hardware cloth can be fashioned into either cages or fences that make excellent slug and snail barriers. By cutting through the mesh so that about ⅛ inch of sharp wire end

Plywood slug barriers can be propped up along rows of target plants.

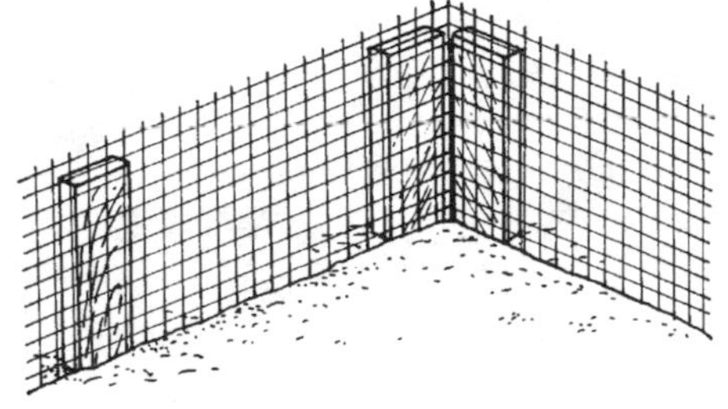

A bit of sharp wire is left on top of this slug fence, constructed of ¼" hardware cloth.

is left at the top of each piece you can put up a simple fence that no slug or snail can negotiate. In raised beds, staple the fence to the sides so that it protrudes 3 or 4 inches above the wood. Otherwise staple the cut wire to garden stakes, making sure the wire extends above the top of each stake, and drive them into the ground; the fence should stand about 4 inches aboveground. Fences can be made in segments so that they are easily pieced together, and later easily removed and stored.

Another way to take advantage of how much slugs and snails dislike rough surfaces is to use old window screens cut up to form collars to go around the base of each individual plant. Cut squares 6 to 10 inches wide and then cut a slit to the center of each square. Make a few snips in the center so that the mesh can be folded up out of the way, allowing you to place the collar around the stem.

Sprays and Dusts. Spray a 50/50 vinegar and water solution directly on plants or slugs. A stronger solution is no more effective and may burn plants.

Along with the spritz-of-death of vinegar are several other sprays to experiment with. A hot pepper spray is useful either directly on slugs or on or around their targets. It is also effective against many insect pests. To make, blend hot chile peppers with water and a few drops of liquid dish soap (to help the solution stick to foliage). Strain and spray. Test it on a few leaves first.

A direct hit with fresh lime juice kills, as does a concoction called "slug juice." This is made by putting the remains of a cup or two of dead slugs into a blender, pureeing them, and then straining the resulting mush.

Hair can also be used to kill snails. By snipping coarse hair, such as human or horse hair, into tiny pieces and scattering it in areas frequented by snails, you can eliminate many of them. Tiny hairs irritate the soft, moist skin of the snail and he dehydrates himself to death in his effort to expel the irritating hairs clinging to him.

Predators. Not surprisingly, mucous-covered slugs and snails are considered unappetizing by much of nature and therefore have few predators. Garter snakes, moles, shrews, ducks, and goslings will dine on them. But moles can cause more problems than the slugs and snails, and ducks and geese must be fenced away from tender plants. Toads and turtles will devour them, and the decollate snail (*Rumina decollata*), a ravenous carnivore, happily plays the cannibal. Since these

snails have *no* known predators, careful thought should be given to introducing them into your garden. (See Appendix 4 for suppliers of predators.)

Removal. One favorite slug solution is beer. In a more or less scientific study of nearly 4000 slugs and a dozen different beers, it was concluded that the fermentation of the lager yeasts, and not the alcoholic content, lured the slugs to the beer bait. The slugs preferred a near beer, Kingsbury Malt Beverage, over Michelob and Budweiser, the runners-up.

If you find the prospect of pouring premium beer for slugs unlikely, here are several variations of home brews that will substitute nicely:

Home Brew Slug Beers

- Mix cider vinegar with sugar
- Allow fruit peelings to ferment in a quart of water, along with ½ package of dry yeast and a ½ cup of beer
- Mix 1 pound of brown sugar with ½ package of dry yeast in a plastic gallon jug and fill with warm (80 degrees F.) water. Let this ferment for one or two days, uncovered.

To set the trap, find a shallow dish, deep enough to drown a slug. Pie tins and empty tuna fish or cat food cans work well. Pour in an inch or so of

Slugs in beer.

the brew of your choice and leave it in a shaded spot wherever you suspect slug activity. Press the dish down into the soil until the rim is even with ground level. The slugs crawl in, get sloshed, and drown. Empty out the dead slugs and refill the dishes every two or three days.

Both slugs and snails delight in citrus rinds. Make cups from oranges or grapefruit by cutting them in half and scooping out the insides. Place the hollow halves open side down in a likely spot in the garden in the evening and collect them, and the creatures hiding beneath, in the morning.

Commercial Products. Many commercial choices are available for slug and snail control. Deterrent fences fend them off with either an electric shock or a chemical irritation. There are also a lot of poisons on the market. Interestingly enough, however, these are often not fatal. This is because the active ingredient in most of these, metaldehyde, acts on slugs and snails the same way as salt does. It can cause them to secrete up to half of their body moisture, potentially lethal to be sure. But if the poison is ingested when it's rainy or humid, the

hallmarks of slug and snail season, both are perfectly capable of rehydrating themselves.

Nonpoisonous slug and snail deterrents on the market include Snail-Barr, a copper barrier you staple or clip into place, and Snailproof, a mulch made of sawdust and cedar shavings. (Both are listed in Appendix 4.)

Diatomaceous earth, available under several brand names and local nursery store labels, has also been used successfully against slugs and snails.

Turtles

(Reptiles, Family Testudinidae)

Turtles are very beneficial in the garden, being excellent slug and bug eaters, but they have been known to cause damage. Therefore, they will be included here, as well as in chapter 7, where details for creating an inviting habitat for them will be discussed.

Physical Description

Apparently content with their lot in life, these plodding reptiles have seen little need for change in millions of years. In fact, it would be difficult to distinguish the modern version of the turtle from one of its ancestors.

The turtle's most instantly recognizable feature is his seemingly impervious shell. It is both the stubby knight's castle and his armor. The top half of the shell is the *carapace* and the plate covering the belly, the *plastron*.

The shell of a mature adult box turtle is about 6 inches long; the carapace is spotted with yellow, orange, or olive markings. Another common garden visitor, the wood turtle *(Clemmys insculpta)*, has a grayish brown shell, and the carapace appears to be etched or carved. He averages 5 to 8 inches in length. Gardeners who dare the sandy soils of the Southwest may even encounter the brown, rounded shell of a tortoise (various *Gopherus* spp.), which reaches up to 16 inches in length.

Turtles have no teeth, but rather snap their groceries off with their beaklike mouths. They have good vision, but despite very well-developed ears they don't hear well. Instead, they

Range and Habitat

Turtles are common in the eastern United States, while tortoises are found in the desert Southwest as well as parts of the south central United States and Florida.

Turtles that venture away from water usually don't wander far from the pond or marsh. Wood turtles, as the name implies, spend much of their time in the woods.

rely on sensitivity to vibrations, such as those made by footsteps.

Life Cycle

The young turtles' fancy turns to love in the spring when they mate. Eggs are laid in the summer and buried to protect them from predators. The defenseless babies emerge in fall to a motherless world, and may spend their first winter hibernating on an empty stomach. Baby turtles can go weeks, even months, without food. Turtles are known for their longevity. Box turtles, for instance, may live for more than a century.

Habits

Turtles spend the winter dozing in mud at the bottom of ponds or ditches and the like, or in loose soil beneath the frost line. Since they, like all reptiles, are cold-blooded, their internal body temperature depends on the temperature of their immediate surroundings. Survival depends on finding suitable sleeping quarters. Tortoises, more often facing hot rather than cold extremes, feed during the cooler hours and seek a cool, shady napping place when the sun is out.

Garden Targets

A turtle's tastes are seasonal. Spring greens that tantalized the tongue early in the season appear to bore the palate by the time strawberries ripen. Accordingly, they will munch on tender leaves and blossoms, berries, strawberries, tomatoes, and cantaloupes, and devour mushrooms anytime.

Note: Turtles also savor slugs, snails, and insect larvae, making their presence in the garden welcome by many gardeners.

Damage and Signs

Targets will be damaged low to the ground; bites will be taken at random, and usually from the best fruits.

If the soil is loose and moist, tracks may be observed.

Deterrents

Exclusion. Even though some turtles, especially wood turtles, are notoriously good climbers, a trellis is usually one of the best ways of discouraging unwanted nibbling. Tomatoes and melons can be trained to grow upwards, with melon fruits being supported by a sling made of old pantyhose, netting, or similar material tied to the trellis. Keep the base of plants pruned up a few inches to make climbing less inviting.

Training vine crops to grow up a trellis is simple and inexpensive, and carries many added benefits. The design of the trellis depends on the plant, the materials you have on hand, and how much thought or effort you care to expend.

For tomatoes or melons, try driving 6-foot stakes into the ground at about a 30-degree angle, slanting towards the west. Connect the supports with several rows of heavy twine. As the vines grow, tie them to the twine.

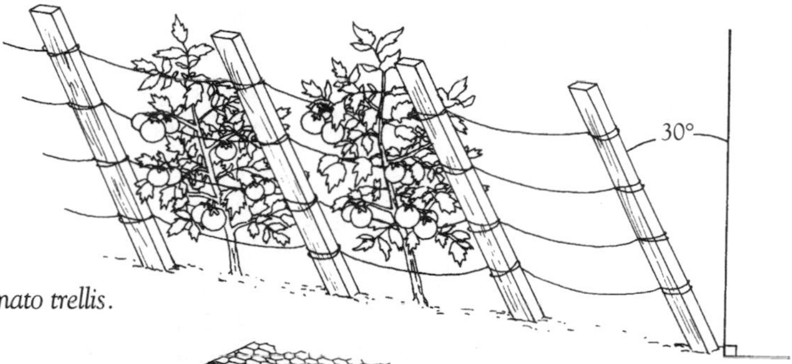

A slanting vertical tomato trellis.

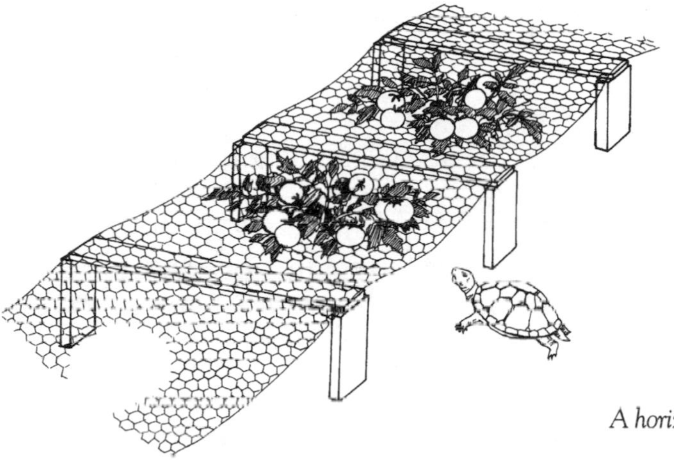

A horizontal turtle-proof trellis.

The fruits will hang down under the stakes, clean, healthy, and easy to reach. But not for turtles!

For low-growing varieties of tomatoes a horizontal trellis can be built off the ground using chicken wire and scrap lumber. Drive 15-inch 2x4 stakes into the ground about 3 feet apart both along and across the row, creating two lines of stakes, one on each side of the row. Link the stakes across the row with pieces of 1x2. Drape 3-foot-wide chicken wire over these supports and down the length of the row, and fasten both ends to stakes to hold the chicken wire in place. Cut a hole in the center of the wire between each set of stakes, then set a tomato plant beneath each hole.

When you have trained the growing plants up through the holes and onto the trellis, place straw or a similar mulch on top of the wire to protect the fruits. This mulch will also shade the soil underneath, keeping the roots cool and cutting down on watering and weeding needs.

Train melons up poles tied teepee style, up woven fencing wire, or up a redwood or lattice rose trellis. Support the weight of each melon with a sling tied to the trellis.

Trellising your vining crops offers many pluses aside from keeping

ground-level pests from devouring the fruits of your labors:

- Most vine-grown varieties produce more, over a longer time period, than bush varieties.
- Weeding and watering, as well as pest control, are easier, more efficient, and safer to the plants.
- The trellised plants create shade that can be used to cool other types of plants.
- Trellises allow you to use vertical space in the garden that otherwise is wasted.
- The produce is clean and easier to harvest.

Cages or fences made from ½- or ¼-inch hardware cloth or similar wire mesh protect strawberries and seedlings. Fit cages over individual plants or over entire sections of rows or beds.

Eighteen-inch-wide pieces of plywood stuck in the ground to form a fence and angled away from the plants have been successfully used to stop turtles as well as slugs.

For ripening melons try this trick: Push the open end of a large (2- to 5-pound) coffee can into the soil so that the bottom of the can sits about 6 to 8 inches above ground level. Do this with as many cans as you need so that each fruit can be placed on a can. This method has the added benefit of helping the melons ripen more quickly as the metal cans absorb and reflect heat.

Predators. Bears, raccoons, skunks, coyotes, dogs, cats, large lizards, alligators, crocodiles, and shore birds include turtles, eggs, and babies in their diets.

Traps. If turtles are causing more trouble in the garden than they are worth, they can easily be caught in a live trap, either a homemade box type or a commercially produced variety. Some turtle species are endangered, however, and should not be kept as pets. Check with local wildlife officials to be sure the turtle in question is not a protected species. Mushrooms make the best bait, but any of what the turtles have come for in your garden will attract their attention. They are not leery of foreign objects, so no special preparations are necessary. (See Appendixes 2 and 3 for more about traps.)

Chapter 6

What Bugs You?

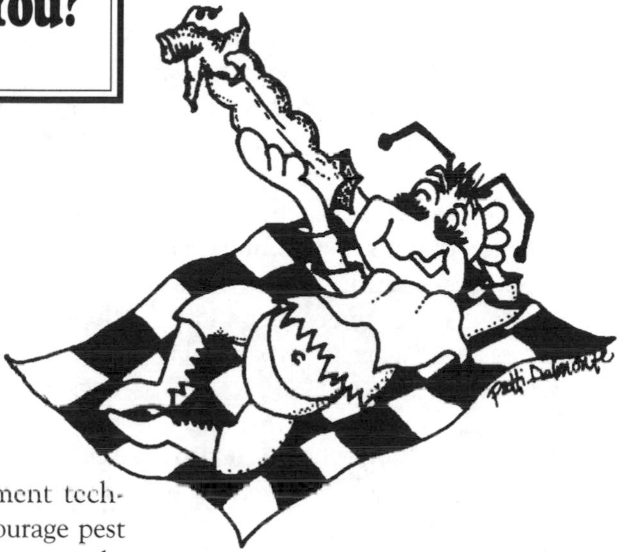

Just as general management techniques can lure or discourage pest birds or animals, so can they contribute to insect management. The goal of these techniques is not to wipe out every bug in the garden, but to establish and maintain a controlled balance. A few pests must survive to maintain populations of the beneficial insects who prey on them. Also, you must consider where your personal margins of acceptable insect presence or actual damage lie — you can lose a few plants to insects and still have a good garden. By using a combination of natural defenses, the organic gardener relies not on the spray bottle of insecticide, but on careful observation, planning, and a good deal of trial and error.

Clean gardening practices are essential, as many insect species breed or overwinter in piles of garbage, weeds, and clippings. These supply the little beasties with food and shelter and are considered an open invitation to a great variety of bugs. Likewise, allowing diseased or dead vegetation to collect near growing plants promotes plant diseases.

Many practices will deter a wide range of bugs, and certain methods zero in on specific invaders.

Plant Health

Simply put, healthy plants in healthy soil do not attract insects or disease organisms.

Ever notice that bugs seem to besiege plants that were already in a weakened state? It's true. But why and how do they know?

Insects relate to one another and the rest of the world through a complex network of senses and signals. Many have sophisticated sensory centers in their antennae that pick up everything from scent to vibrations, including infrared vibrations given off by other insects and the plants themselves. Senses of taste, smell, touch, "hearing" in the form of receiving and interpreting vibrations, sight, and even electromagnetic sensitivity are adapted in varying ways to give each individual species an edge in its particular garden niche.

Tests consistently confirm that healthy plants tend to stay healthy while sickly ones are in for a struggle. A plant that has been weakened by disease, transplant shock, improper hardening off, poor nutrition, or other insects is an easy target. The plant's color changes, and some bugs pick up on that. It may smell or taste different to the insects' superior sensitivity in these areas (a compound known as stress ethylene is often released by plants under stress). Too, sick plants are physically less sturdy, stems lose the stiffness associated with adequate water retention, cuticle (outer surface) composition changes, and wilting softens the plant tissues, making them easier for bugs to chew or suck. Any holes chewed into plant tissues cause microscopic amounts of volatile essential oils of that plant to be given off into the atmosphere, and insects can be attracted by only a few molecules of their favorite fare.

One tactic toward raising "tougher" plants is to water them less. When plants are subject to slight water shortages they react by developing a tougher outer layer to protect the plant from loss of moisture. Therefore, while plenty of water produces plants that brag about being tender and juicy, slightly underwatered plants may have tougher, less bug-appealing stems, leaves, and other parts. While it's unlikely that the human consumer of these garden goodies will detect any differences in produce quality, to the bugs such differences may be substantial enough to send them buzzing off.

Soil Health

The nutrients plants use come from two sources within the soil: organic matter, or humus (the product of the natural breakdown of animal and vegetable remains), and minerals.

Organic Matter

Besides supplying the soil with nutrients needed by plants, humus improves garden soil merely by its physical presence. In heavy clay the organic matter creates tiny air pockets, loosening the soil and making it more workable. In sandy ground the organic particles bind together, creating a more stable soil while improving its capacity to hold water.

How do you get more organic matter into your soil? One of the most efficient answers is **composting**. There are many methods and recipes for cre-

ating compost, but the idea is simple. Layer vegetable (weeds, leaves, clippings, trimmings, thinnings) and animal wastes (excluding meat or fat), along with a few shovelfuls of garden soil and a good sprinkling of water, in a bin or pile no less than 3 feet wide in all directions. It takes a minimum of these measurements to generate enough heat to turn those ingredients into compost.

Provide oxygen for the millions of tiny microorganisms that are breaking down all that organic matter for you. The easiest way is to grab a pitchfork and turn the pile over from time to time. Make sure to toss what was the outside of the former pile into the center of the new pile so that it also gets acted on by these tiny workers. In a few weeks to a few months, depending on temperature, humidity, pile components/proportions, and design, you will have dark, crumbly, sweet-smelling compost! Keep your pile covered during rainy or snowy weather so all that valuable nutrition won't get washed away.

Till compost into the garden soil before planting time or mix it with soil and spade it into individual planting areas during seeding or transplanting.

Another good way to incorporate organic matter into the soil is to raise **cover crops**. While usually grown to cover the soil and protect it from erosion, they have a valuable second use: to improve the soil. Used this way, they are often called green manure. There is a variety from which to choose. Legumes, such as clovers, hairy vetch, and soybeans, provide the added bonus of fixing nitrogen from the air into the soil where plants can use it. Others include winter rye, wheat, spring oats, and mustard. Seed your garden, or a portion of it, with one of these, let it grow, then till under at least six weeks before the next crop planting. Some cover crops have a heavy top growth that should be chopped up before turning them into the soil. This makes the tilling job easier and insures quicker decomposition of the organic matter. A few passes with a rotary lawn mower does the job nicely. A small area can be turned under with a spade and a measure of sweat.

Soil Elements

The major elements required by plants — nitrogen, phosphorous, and potassium, or potash — can be added through use of such amendments as colloidal (soft) phosphate, bone or blood meal, and greensand.

Nitrogen is essential for the development of lush, green leaves. It promotes rapid growth and improves the color, quality, and density of foliage. The protein content of food crops depend on this important element. Its overuse may cause overgreening and lack of flowering or fruit development.

Phosphate, as a source of phosphorus, stimulates early root growth and formation, gives rapid and vigorous growth to plants, and speeds maturity. It is responsible for flowering and winter hardiness of perennials,

and aids in seed germination.

Potassium adds to the vigor and disease resistance of plants, serves to stiffen stalks and stems, aids in protein synthesis, and is essential to the production of starches, sugars, and oils, as well as their movement through the plant. It is important in the development of quality fruit and in the formation of color in fruit and leaves.

Plant food labels refer to these critical elements by their chemical symbols, N (nitrogen), P (phosphorous), and K (potassium), and list them in that order with numerical values, such as 10-10-10, signifying the percentage of each in that fertilizer.

Trace elements are also necessary for development of healthy plants. Cobalt, boron, zinc, copper, magnesium, calcium, iron, manganese, molybdenum, sulfur, and others can be incorporated through the use of greensand, compost, or green manure.

Careful observation of plants can tell us a lot about the state of garden soil. For example, signs of many deficiencies show up quite obviously in tomato plants. Those lacking in nitrogen develop *chlorosis*, or yellowing, in the leaves. This condition is common with a number of deficiencies, but occurs mostly in the older leaves near the base of the plant when a nitrogen shortage is responsible. Leaves first turn yellow, then "fire" (develop a burnt look). Plant growth may be stunted.

An iron deficiency causes the leaves to turn yellow or pale green while the veins within them remain green.

Not enough sulfur causes yellowing in the youngest leaves.

Lack of potassium makes plants more prone to disease. Leaves develop yellow streaks, with older ones curling and forming spots.

A lack of phosphorous inhibits proper development of the tomatoes and causes stunted plants to produce very dark green to blue leaves with purple to red veins.

A classic indication of calcium deficiency is blossom-end rot in tomatoes. Other signs may occur in young leaves as they may appear hooked or wrinkled and remain folded at the tops or die.

Broccoli or cauliflower with stems that turn brown and mushy inside result when the soil is low in boron.

pH

The pH level of soil plays a role in the ability of plants to use the nutrients that are present. The pH level can be checked with a soil test, available through nursery outlets or your local county extension agent. Most crops do best if the pH falls within the 6.2 to 6.8 range. Too high or too low a pH level interferes with a plant's ability to use available nutrients. If too high — above 7 — the soil is alkaline, and the addition of acidic manure (horse, chicken) or a sulfur-based product will bring it down into that ideal range. If the pH level falls below 7 it is considered acid. A slight amount of acidity is desired, but if it

drops too low, it can be raised with the addition of ground limestone.

Try to keep a healthy balance of mineral components in your soil. Excesses can cause as many problems as deficiencies, such as allowing soluble nutrients to be leached out of the garden soil and into the groundwater. By using natural additives, which are more easily utilized by microorganisms and plants, you lessen the chances of upsetting the balance of the soil's composition. Have your soil tested to see what, if any, additives your soil needs.

Soil Texture

Soil texture is important to growing healthy plants. A dark, rich, friable loam is every gardener's dream dirt. Texture, of course, depends on soil composition. The extremes of sand and clay both have their drawbacks to gardeners.

You can get a good idea of your soil's texture with a simple home test. Fill a jar with one-third soil from the garden and two-thirds water. Shake well and then place it on a windowsill and ignore it for a few days. Then check the layers in the jar.

Ideally garden soil should contain about 45 percent sand, which settles out first to form a bottom layer; 35 percent silt, which, being lighter than sand, settles to a layer on top of that; and 20 percent clay, which settles into a top layer. Organic matter will float to the top — the more the better. Soil with 70 percent or more sand at the bottom is sandy, while that with much over 30 percent clay on the top layer is clay.

Soil Solarization

If there were a sure way to destroy virtually every kind of harmful insect egg and larvae in your garden soil, would you be interested? How about if the process were easy, cheap, and carried a host of other benefits along with it? **Solarization** is a simple, five-step process that kills insects, plant diseases, nematodes, harmful fungi, and weed seeds. At the same time helpful microorganisms within the soil apparently benefit, possibly from the lack of competition, and thrive. Soil that has been solarized allows plants to draw on the nutrients, especially nitrogen, calcium, and magnesium, more readily. Seeds germinate more quickly. Plants grow faster and stronger, often maturing earlier with substantially higher yields than in unsolarized soil.

What exactly is this miracle cure and how does it work? Solarization works in the same way as a greenhouse, where a transparent covering, in this case 3 to 6 mil plastic sheeting, traps the sun's heat. After several days of sunshine, soil temperatures rise to as high as 140 degrees F. at the soil surface and well over 100 degrees F. as far down as 18 inches. It takes four to six weeks of sunny weather to pasteurize the soil. For most of the country that means planning to spread

plastic somewhere between the end of June and the first of September.

Any size plot, down to a 3-foot-wide bed, will retain enough heat to do the job, although the larger the area the more heat is generated and maintained, *and* the longer lasting the effects. It's easier to lay plastic down in a narrow strip than a wide patch, so that is a major consideration. And therein lies the solitary expense in using the sun's energy to improve your soil: a strip or roll of clear *(not black)* plastic large enough to cover your area and overlap on all sides by at least a foot. That, and perhaps the cost of bribing a helper or two!

Five Steps to Purifying Your Soil through Solarization

1. Prepare the soil. Pull any weeds or old crops. Turn in any soil amendments and then rake the surface smooth. It's important to remove any stones or clumps that might raise the plastic and create airpockets that could cause uneven heating.

2. Water thoroughly. Leave a sprinkler on for several hours or overnight to soak the soil. This creates 100 percent humidity under the plastic, which acts with the heat to kill all those unwanted critters.

3. Dig a trench all around the bed or plot 6 to 8 inches deep.

4. Lay a clear plastic sheet, 3 to 6 mil thick, over the area, overlapping the trench on all sides. Fill the trench back in, weighing down the plastic while pulling it as tight as possible. (This is where you need helpers.)

5. Sit back, relax, and wait. Although cloudy weather will slow things down by cooling the soil under the tarp, a few weeks of sunshine will improve your soil dramatically, easily, and inexpensively.

If you live in an area with cool or cloudy summers, or if you just don't want to *wait* all season, you can speed

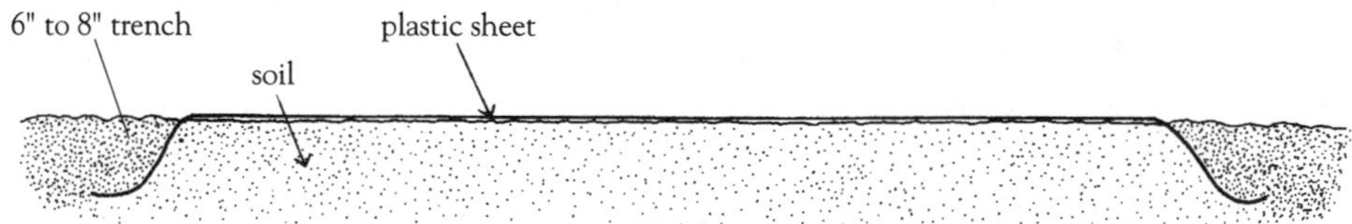

"Solarizing" soil to rid it of insect eggs and larvae.

up the process by adding a second sheet of plastic. Using the hoops commonly used to elevate row covers or bird netting, raise the second sheet of plastic over the ground-level sheet. The airspace in between acts as a temperature buffer zone during cloudy weather, and the combination of the two sheets of heat-absorbing plastic serves to raise the soil temperature as much as 6 degrees F. Using this method, you can expect to see the same soil-conditioning results in thirty days that would ordinarily take at least ninety days with a single layer of plastic.

Crop Rotation

Crop rotation is a sound practice that farmers and gardeners have used for centuries. By never growing the same crop or family of crops in the same place two years in a row, many soil-borne diseases and insects can be controlled. Rotating, or moving crops to different locations at each planting, works by interrupting the life cycles of harmful organisms. Insects that lay eggs, pupate, or otherwise overwinter in the soil wake in the spring ready to devour those first tender shoots (or roots). They expect to find the same feast before them that they saw the previous season. By planting a crop from an entirely different family, you can cut them off from their food source. For instance, root maggots waiting for tasty broccoli roots can starve in a healthy pea patch.

Certain pests are more resilient than others. This is one reason it is often necessary to plan on *not* using a patch of garden for the same crop for three to five years. This is especially true for brassicas, or cole crops, such as broccoli, cauliflower, brussels sprouts, cabbage, and kale.

Some crops such as corn, celery, and tomatoes are considered to be "heavy feeders" because they demand more nutrients than other crops. Your soil, and thus future plantings, will benefit greatly by alternating such crops with peas, beans, or another legume, or cover crops to replenish nitrogen and other nutrients.

Timed Planting

Every year at about the same time the same old bugs make their spring debuts. Their first appearance depends on the temperature, humidity, and food supplies as well as the time of year. But barring extremes their emergence can be predicted. By carefully checking for insects in your garden on a daily basis and keeping notes on what you find (type of insects, stage of development, and numbers present) and where (geographic location within the garden, type of plants, including differences in varieties, and whether the bugs appeared on the tops, bottoms, flowers, leaves, or fruits of plants), in a few seasons you can consider yourself a (regional) expert!

Your county extension agency or nursery can tell you what to expect,

and you can build on that from your own observations. The benefits of knowing when certain insects will stage their yearly coming-out parties are substantial. If you know, for instance, that the striped cucumber beetle will be out and hungry in early May, you can delay setting out your transplants a few weeks. By this time the beasties will have scoured your plot, found it sadly lacking in sustenance, and either moved on or perished.

If you plan to release predators to gobble up the gobblers, it makes a world of difference if they find their intendeds readily. Otherwise they may wander off in search of their supper. Release them when their prey is plentiful. By knowing precisely when pests will be bursting on the scene, you can plan your planting, transplanting, and release of beneficials much more effectively.

Companion Planting

For generations gardeners have noticed how some plants seem to do better in the presence of others. Part of this happy coexistence is attributed to the ability of certain plants to repel, ward off, or confuse insect attacks. Staggered plantings of different crops — a patchwork garden — will interrupt the spread of insects. It's easiest for them to go down a neat row of vegetables, one plant after the other.

Rather than barring insects, some plants, by attracting them, serve as a *trap crop*. The bugs actually prefer them to your main garden crop. Trap crops can be removed and destroyed when infested to eliminate the pests, or may be left in place to keep them otherwise occupied. Some trap crops, for instance dill for tomato hornworms, attract the pests and thus make them more vulnerable to other means of control, such as handpicking.

Resistant Varieties

What makes some plants more resistant to bugs than others? Nature builds defenses into wild plants, and as humans have altered and invented plants to suit their own tastes, some of those natural defenses have become lost in the process. Cuticle composition, sticky hairs, tighter cornhusks, even naturally occurring bug toxins within the plant cells are being rediscovered by plant breeders and crossed into garden vegetable strains. Check with your state university for any resistant varieties they may be testing, and with your nursery for commercially available resistant varieties.

Plant Coverings

There is a variety of horticulture fabrics on the market capable of excluding insects if used properly. They provide a physical barrier between the crops and the critters, discouraging bugs, bunnies, and birds. There are also fringe benefits to covering certain plants, such as season-extending heat

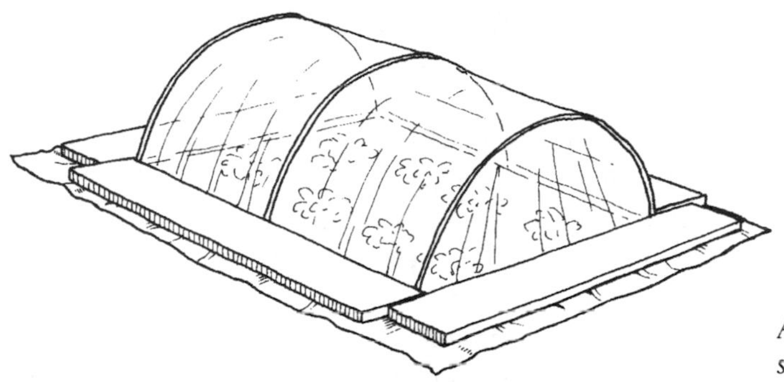

A "floating" row cover, suspended by hoops.

retention, wind and hail protection, and the exclusion of airborne weed seeds.

Some coverings, such as Reemay, are made of spun-bonded polypropylene. They are porous, allowing air and water to pass through freely, and translucent, letting 70 to 80 percent of available sunlight through to growing plants. Though extremely lightweight (barely ½ ounce per square yard), these fabrics have spun-bonded fibers that make them very strong and tear-resistant. They can be used for several seasons if treated with care. Avoid walking on the coverings, lift and place them out of the way when cultivating, and store them when not in use.

Other polypropylene fabrics such as Agronet and VisPore are constructed differently. Agronet is a nearly transparent mesh that is made like an ultrafine screen. It allows up to 95 percent of the sun's rays to penetrate it. VisPore is clear and less porous, only 5 to 7 percent, but allows plenty of air and water and nearly all light to pass through it.

All of these plant coverings trap heat. This makes them wonderful season extenders, both by aiding early planting and by protecting crops in the fall. But in spring and summer they can raise temperatures underneath by 15 to 35 degrees F., too much for many plants. Of these three, Agronet retains the least amount of heat while VisPore retains the most.

Lay these fabrics over the crop as soon as it goes in the ground. Weigh the edges and ends down securely with soil or boards so that nothing can creep underneath and to prevent the wind from blowing the fabric off plants. Leave extra headroom for the plants as they grow. The cover can rest on the plants with no ill effects or can be draped over hoops or supported by other structures, even by intercropping with taller, faster-growing plants.

Gardeners report success against flea beetles using the fabric as a 3-foot-tall fence around plants. Make individual cages to cover peppers, tomatoes, eggplant, or other large plants. Build a frame to size with scrap 1x2 or

other available material and staple the fabric securely to all sides and over the top but not at the bottom. Center the cage over the transplant and secure it to the ground. Cages built with "legs" that extend below the covering can be pushed down into the soil until the fabric meets the ground. Mound soil around the base of each cage to seal the plants in and the bugs out.

Cages made with fine window screening or cheesecloth will protect cool-weather, shade-loving plants such as broccoli and other cole crops, lettuce, and spinach. Design cages to fit over a single plant, row, bed, or section of a bed. Rather than raising the temperature, such coverings will help to minimize the sun's effects while keeping plants free of bugs and their damage.

Regardless of the type of covering used, keep a close watch over covered crops. Be sure you haven't caged in more than just plants — one trapped mouse can munch a lot of strawberries! Also, bear in mind that many pests overwinter in the soil and may emerge after the plants have been covered. The covers will keep out most airborne weed seeds, but cultivation will most likely still be necessary. And don't forget that while fabric or screening keeps out harmful bugs, it also prevents bees and other beneficial insects from doing their jobs. At some point, whether to prevent overheating, to weed, or to permit pollination, almost all covers will have to come off.

Ultrasonic Devices

A new weapon in the bug wars is the ultrasonic noise box. Using radio-type sound waves of the same frequency received and believed by bugs, the box's emissions chase bugs away from plants electronically. The "sounds" emitted from these devices are not audible to people or most pets, but are supposedly unbearable to a range of garden pests. (Unfortunately, some even advertise that they will drive off bats, one of the best bug eaters around.)

This field is wide open for development. Understanding how insects communicate and navigate through their "radar" literally allows gardeners to tell the bugs "where to go."

Sprays and Dusts

It may be okay to spray or just dust if you must. But some insecticidal preparations are more acceptable, in an organic sense, than others. Sometimes a powerful stream from a garden hose is enough to dislodge unwanted visitors from plants, without side effects. The dazed bugs can then be collected and disposed of.

Chemical pesticides cause enormous health and environmental problems and like (other forms of) war, seldom solve the problem. One of the major advantages of organic pesticides is that they break down quickly, posing no threat of chemical buildup in soil or plants, or groundwater contamination. This speedy decomposi-

tion may also be considered one of their main disadvantages, however, as it often makes several applications necessary, especially after rainfall.

Soap Sprays. Soap sprays are among the safest of preparations and are very effective against a variety of soft-bodied insects. Aphids, mealybugs, spider mites, spittlebugs, stinkbugs, crickets, and grasshoppers can all be washed up by a soap spray. Mix 3 tablespoons of mild soap such as Fels Naptha, Ivory Snow (laundry soap), or Safer's Insecticidal soap to a gallon of water and apply to foliage with a hand sprayer.

Most bugs will die within an hour, done in by the fatty acid salts of the soap. To kill requires a direct hit, as the solution degrades quickly, so spraying must be repeated often. Whether insects are killed by desiccation, suffocation, or some other means is unclear, but happily whatever the mechanism, many beneficial insects are apparently immune.

Some plants are more susceptible to damage from soap sprays than others, particularly Chinese cabbage, cucumbers, melons, and other large leafed plants. A residue from repeated sprayings can cause leaves to brown on the edges and curl. Rinsing the plants with water a few hours after spraying may prevent this. If a growing tip is damaged, plant maturity can by delayed. Any soap spray may somewhat reduce crop yields.

One important note: Stronger concentrations of soap are *no more effective* at killing bugs, but *cause significant plant damage*.

Dormant Oil. Dormant oil spray is used primarily on fruit and nut trees. It must be applied early, when no leaves or buds are present (during dormancy) but after temperatures are above freezing (when insect eggs begin to hatch). Late winter is usually best. Its use should be considered as a last resort, *only* against a known insect problem, as it harms beneficials as well as such pests as aphids, mites, and thrips. Improper application may damage trees.

Select a product that is 97 percent petroleum oil with 3 percent inert ingredients. Avoid those that include arsenate of lead, lime sulfur, or Bordeaux mix. A lightweight (#10) motor oil can be used. Mix ⅔ cup per gallon of water and spray to coat each tree thoroughly, paying particular attention to joints. The solution cuts off air to the tree, and this suffocates insect eggs and emerging larvae. Dormant trees obtain most of their oxygen through their roots, so they are not affected unless the oil is applied after buds have appeared. This can also cause leaves to burn, or leaves or fruit to drop.

Bug Juice. This is a remarkably effective method of insect control. Here it takes bugs to break bugs. After determining which pest is doing the damage, collect about ½ cup and (yep!) put them in a blender with about 2 cups of water. Liquefy, strain (through cheesecloth), pour about ¼

cup into a 1-gallon hand sprayer, dilute by filling with water, and spray away. Cover the entire plant, hitting both sides of leaves. Some successes have been reported by treating the soil (drenching) as new seedlings emerge to prevent bugs from getting started. This stuff can be diluted many times for repeat uses. (You don't want to have to do this again, do you?) Freeze any extra promptly to prevent bacterial contamination. (Please mark the container clearly!)

How does it work? Possibly through the release of alarm or escape pheromones given off by the insects as they are collected or going through the blender that warns others away. Perhaps a few sick bugs are ground up in the process and spread their "bug." Or maybe the smell attracts the bugs' predators to the area. All these as well as other factors may be at work.

Bug juice has been reported to work against a variety of pests, including aphids, pill bugs, Mexican bean beetles, cutworms, stinkbugs, and armyworms — even slugs! *Warning: Do not try this against fleas, mosquitoes, or others that feed on blood and transmit diseases.*

Plant Juice. Plant juice is a simplification of the bug juice method. It's especially good for tiny insects such as aphids, which are too much trouble to handpick. Load the blender with infested leaves and proceed as before.

Another variation is to make an extract from leaves of nonpoisonous plants that are not bothered by bugs. Try pine, poplar, or various herbs. Spraying such concoctions on afflicted crops repels such pests as scale, beetles, codling moths, mealybugs, and boll weevils.

Garlic and hot pepper sprays as well as several herbal brews are effective against many insects, as the bugs are very sensitive to differences in the smell or taste of their preferred foods. Naturally occurring sulfur compounds in garlic repel a great many pests, from insects to large animals. Butterflies even have taste receptors in their feet, which tell them upon alighting whether dinner is underfoot.

Teas. Often, home remedies call for a "tea" made from this herb or that plant, leaf, or flower. Technically, this means an *infusion*, which is prepared much the same way as a cup of tea. Place the required amount (when specified) of fresh or dried material in a glass or porcelain container and pour in boiling water. Let it steep a few minutes to draw out the volatile oils (the active ingredients in the tea), then strain. Unless specified in the directions, do not boil or simmer, as this may alter or destroy the delicate balance of the oils. For some plants, it is enough to soak the leaves in tepid or even cool water.

Homemade remedies often call for adding a teaspoon or so of liquid soap, such as dishwashing liquid. This helps to make the spray stick to the leaves of plants, and can be added without compromising most recipes to improve their effectiveness.

Bacillus thuringiensis (Bt). Bt is a naturally occurring bacterium that infects and destroys a multitude of insect pests, most notably leaf-chewing caterpillars such as cabbage worms, loopers, and hornworms. It kills through a toxic protein crystal that adheres to the insect's gut and perforates it, allowing the critter's vital fluids to seep out. It must be eaten to work, so application must be timed for when pests are feeding. Plants must be sprayed thoroughly, including all parts and the undersides of leaves. Stickers and wetting agents increase effectiveness.

To get the most from Bt, spray while the caterpillars are small, preferably under ½ inch long. The smaller bugs are more susceptible than large ones.

Researchers continue to be surprised by Bt. Hundreds of varieties exist in nature, each carrying a different type of poison crystal, effective against a different pest. The proteins of each strain are deadly only to certain types of insects while having little or no effect on others. It is possible that eventually there will be designer strains isolated to zero in on almost any specific bug. To date mosquitoes, beetles, and nematode roundworms have joined the ranks of the conquered.

Since Bt residues break down almost immediately (fastest when exposed to sunlight), it poses no health risk and may be applied right up to harvest time. Bt is available under several brand names through nursery outlets, in either a spray or a wettable powder.

Botanical Insecticides. Rotenone, pyrethrum, ryania, nicotine, sabadilla, and neem are natural plant derivatives that are nearly harmless to people and animals. They decompose much more quickly than their chemical cousins, so they present little environmental threat. However, they are still potent bug killers that often don't discriminate among their victims.

Buy the purest form of botanical insecticides. This is not made easy by manufacturers who often combine products or include additives. One additive, a synergist called piperonyl butoxide (PBO), should be avoided.

Rotenone is a tropical plant extract, made from the roots of Asian *Derris* plants and South American cubé plants. It is commercially available as a powder or wettable dust. Lethal to a vast array of insects including bees and other beneficials, it should be applied in the evening when bees are least active to minimize casualties. A powerful stomach poison to insects, it is extremely toxic to pigs and fish (it's also toxic to humans in sufficient amounts), and should never be used near waterways. Allow three to seven days before harvesting treated crops, as it takes that long for residues to disappear, despite the one-day claim of many products labels.

Nicotine is an alkaloid commonly derived from tobacco but present in other plants. It performs best against

soft-bodied insects. A strong contact poison, nicotine is (surprise) very toxic to humans. Residues break down quickly, allowing nicotine solutions to be applied to plants within forty-eight hours of harvest.

After using, wash your hands with milk to neutralize tobacco mosaic virus, which can be spread by homemade solutions. This even eliminates the risk of smokers spreading the disease!

Pyrethrum, another powerful insecticide, is made from the blossoms of the pyrethrum flower, *Chrysanthemum cinerariaefolium*. It is sold as a concentrate or in combination with other botanicals. It controls dozens of pests while not affecting birds, animals, or humans (except in cases of allergic reaction), but is just as lethal to fish as rotenone.

Passing quickly through the cuticle (outer covering) of insects, pyrethrum acts on the nervous system, delivering a quick knockdown of its victims as it stuns them senseless. Confused bugs stumble out into the open where they can be finished off, either by the pyrethrum or a backup method.

Apply in the late afternoon or evening as sunlight accelerates the degrading process. Don't combine with a soap spray or lime program, as they are mutually incompatible.

Ryania comes from the roots and stem of the South American shrub *Ryania speciosa*. It is most often sold in compounds with rotenone or pyrethrum, which are toxic to bees and fish. Both a contact and stomach poison, ryania in its pure state makes bugs so violently ill that they forever avoid any plants treated with it after a brief initial encounter. It is most effective against the codling moth, corn earworm, and other caterpillar pests.

Sabadilla has been used for bug control since the sixteenth century. Its toxic alkaloids are derived from the seeds of a South American lily, *Schoenocaulon officianale*, and is made into a dust or wettable powder. Many hard-to-kill bugs succumb to its effects as a contact or stomach poison. Harlequin bugs, stink bugs, lygus bugs, striped cucumber beetles, cabbage worms, and leafhoppers are among the defeated. Wear a face mask when applying, as it can be irritating to mucous membranes.

Neem oil is made from the seeds of the native Indian neem tree, *Azadirachta indica*. It acts upon many insects as an appetite suppressant and on some as a growth or development inhibitor. Aphids, cucumber beetles, mealybugs, mites, and more shun plants treated with this extraction.

Many other flowers and herbs have insect-repellent qualities and are valuable either as companion plants or in home bug remedies. Marigolds (not the scentless varieties), nasturtiums, tansy (not ragwort), rue, feverfew, chamomile, lavender, southernwood and other artemisias, and many kinds of mints, especially pennyroyal, have long been relied upon for their abilities to repel bugs. Most cooking

herbs also keep bugs at bay and at the very least are pleasant to work around. It seems the more wonderfully aromatic the herb, the more unappealing they are to insects.

Diatomaceous earth is the skeletal remains of tiny prehistoric sea creatures called diatoms. The shells of these single-celled fossils are broken down during processing into needlelike silica particles that penetrate the bodies of insects on contact. Since a bug's outsides are all that holds its insides in place, they gradually ooze out and the bug dies of dehydration. Dusting after a light rain or mixing the powder into a spray will help insure that it stays where you put it. Note: Although considered safe to people and animals, it does irritate some people's lungs. It is also harmful to beneficials, including earthworms. Be sure to buy the diatomaceous earth produced specifically for garden use, and not the product used for cleaning swimming pools.

Legally speaking, any material used to control a pest, even a home remedy, is considered a pesticide. State and federal laws regulate the use of *all* pesticides and require registration of the product as well as establishment of residue tolerances if they are used on foods. In California, for instance, this would apply even to such materials as ground-up garlic, liquid soap, or anything else used to control pests.

Although this may sound like overregulation, laws like these are established to protect those who eat the

Guidelines for Spraying

To make the use of any pesticides as safe and effective as possible, always follow these basic guidelines:

1. Read and follow directions. Ask your nursery or county Extension Service for advice if you are ever unsure about handling pesticides. Some products call for wearing gloves or goggles — do so.

2. Store pesticides in their original containers locked away from children and pets.

3. Mix only what you can use at one time.

4. Mix wettable powders in a separate container, not the sprayer. Filter the mixture through cheesecloth, *then* transfer it to the sprayer. This avoids the frustration and delays of clogging the applicator.

5. Don't spray in windy weather. You want your pesticides to land where you aim them.

6. Clean up carefully when finished. Thoroughly rinse out applicators, wash hands, and throw the garden clothes into the wash.

7. Never reuse containers. Dispose of leftovers responsibly, as indicated on the product package.

produce and those who mix and apply the materials. Obviously most home remedies are harmless, but certain naturally occurring plant products can be very poisonous. Also, certain home-remedy ingredients, such as soaps or oils, were not manufactured to be applied to food products. We can't always be sure what is in them or what all the effects of their residue might be. The purpose of the registration process is to require testing of the ingredients to determine if they have any adverse health or environmental effects.

Keep in mind that even though many home remedies have worked for generations, they may not always be recognized as legitimate practices due to a lack of scientific study. This also means that there could be undocumented side effects.

Know thy Enemy

Understanding that a little knowledge can be a dangerous thing, the conscientious organic gardener tries to educate himself or herself on the ecology of the garden and the nature of any specific pest problems.

Identification of insect problems is a two-step process. As mentioned at the beginning of this chapter, the mere presence of insects may not necessarily justify bringing out the heavy artillery. Just because you have *insects* doesn't automatically mean you have an *insect problem*. Often it is better to accept a level of infestation or damage than to launch a control program. Certainly a small amount of cosmetic damage is preferable to the brother, expense, and ecological disruption of chemical intervention.

Assuming damage is significant enough to warrant some measure of control, the next step is to determine which little beast is responsible. Bugs have several built-in evasion tactics that make this especially challenging.

To begin with, the sheer number of species and the adaptations of each serve to fill every imaginable nook and cranny of nature, and some you never even want to imagine! In the garden, bugs are in the air, on the ground, under the ground, and in the foliage, fruits, and flowers. Some burrow into roots, some bore into stems, some tunnel in between the surfaces of leaves. Besides all these bugs, things like soil deficiencies, plant diseases, and pure gardener error (like planting shade-loving crops in full sun) can make it difficult to figure out what exactly is making a plant sick.

As if the vast diversity of bugs weren't confusing enough, insects came up with the remarkable concept of metamorphosis. Unlike a baby gopher, who looks like any other gopher, only smaller, a baby bug often bears no resemblance whatsoever to its parents. And just to keep things interesting, there are two types of metamorphoses. Some insects undergo complete metamorphosis, involving a dramatic emergence from a pupal stage; some go through an incomplete

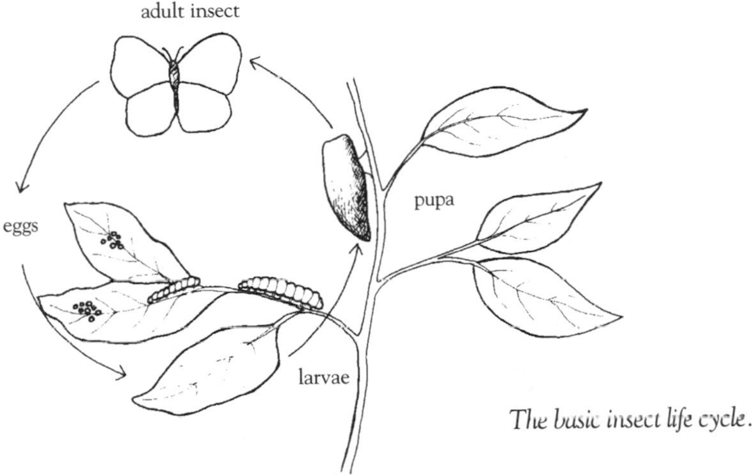

The basic insect life cycle.

metamorphosis; and some seem to fall in between.

Insects that undergo incomplete metamorphosis begin life as eggs. The eggs hatch into larvae, called nymphs, which grow and proceed through stages, referred to in bug lingo as *instars*. As the larvae grow, the hard outer covering, the exoskeleton, gets tighter and tighter until finally it is shed and the nymph grows into its next form. Some nymphs do resemble the adult form of their species; others look totally different.

Other insects go through a total change. They also begin as eggs, hatching into larvae. The larvae grow, and may or may not pass through various instars, but at a certain point, ordained by nature, they make a dramatic change. They pupate. Some spin cocoons, some retreat to underground cells, and while to an outside observer they appear to be dormant, they go through such drastic physical changes that they lose forever their previous forms to emerge as adults.

Typically, adult forms of insects have six legs and three main body segments, which may not be obvious in each species. The head, with or without antennae, is followed by the thorax (middle segment), with the abdomen bringing up the rear.

So, the challenge of identifying a bug problem is not only to find out *if* the bugs are a problem, or *which* bug is a problem, but *what form* of the bug is a problem. Sometimes only larvae do damage, sometimes only the adults, and sometimes all stages cause trouble. In any case, adults are unwanted because they perpetuate the species.

Realizing that the task is not a simple one, the following sections highlight common pests and offer some successful defenses. Realistically, though, the only limit to practical pest control lies in the determination and ingenuity of the one being pestered!

Aphids

(Order Homoptera)

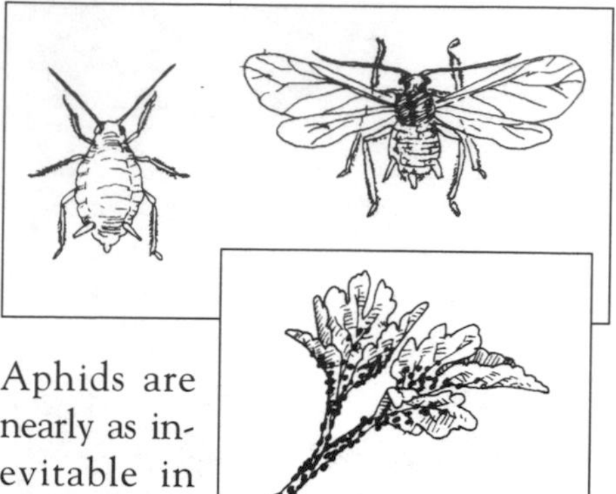

Aphids are nearly as inevitable in the garden as seeds! There are dozens of species, often named for their favorite food, such as the bean aphid, woolly apple aphid (no, he doesn't eat fuzzy apples), and root aphids.

Physical Description

Despite the diversity of aphid species they all have common features. Aphids are tiny individuals, most under 1/10 inch long. Their soft bodies are pear shaped, with two long, whiplike antennae at the tip of the head, and a pair of tubes, called *cornicles*, jutting from the other end of the body. The cornicles fire a defensive spray when the aphid is threatened.

Mouthparts are specialized structures designed to pierce plant tissues and suck out the sap.

Aphids come in a variety of colors ranging from the translucent green of cabbage aphids to the pearly black of bean aphids, with pink, red, purple, and blue varieties included in the spectrum. The wooly apple aphid resembles a mealybug with his tufts of cottony fluff. Many species are winged, but even within these only intermittent generations develop wings.

Life Cycle

Aphid reproduction is geared to produce the most bodies in the least amount of time. Most species have many generations each season. Generally the first generation that emerges in the spring consists exclusively of ravenous females. They feed en masse and almost immediately give birth to more ravenous females, all without the benefit of male companionship. This all-girl system of reproduction without fertilization is called *parthenogenesis*. As conditions become too crowded a winged generation is produced, which flies off to other plants to begin the process all over again. Eventually, overcrowding due to rampant reproduction and lowering fall temperatures trigger a generation of true males and females. These mate in the fall, producing the all-female eggs, which overwinter the population into the following spring. Individual aphids survive only a single season.

Habits

Due to their rapid and constant reproduction, aphid populations can build up tremendously. Since they tend to congregate, they are often found in clumps on stems or under leaves. Aphids are drawn to the color yellow, possibly as a means of zeroing in on weak plants or the pale green,

Range and Habitat

Found throughout North America, aphids inhabit orchards, fields, gardens, and meadows.

tender growing tips of plants.

Through feeding they transmit diseases among their host plants. They also secrete honeydew, a sticky, sweet goo that promotes damaging mold growth on leaves and attracts ants. The ant-aphid relationship is similar to that of the farmer and his cows. In exchange for honeydew, Farmer Ant protects his herd of aphids from predators and even moves it to greener pastures when food supplies are depleted.

Garden Targets

Considering the many species of aphids, the targets in the home garden may be narrowed down to almost everything! Most vegetables and ornamentals are susceptible. Cabbage aphids infest brassicas to the point where entire plants are not worth harvesting. It's nearly impossible to dislodge the masses once they have accumulated inside the heads of brussels sprouts, broccoli, or cauliflower. Pea aphids mob peas and beans, while bean aphids swamp not only peas and beans but spinach, chard, beets, and rhubarb as well. Apple, pear, and other orchard trees can be damaged — even stunted — by wooly apple and green peach aphids. Root aphids are taken by ants to feed on the roots of beans, carrots, corn, lettuce, and parsley, to name but a few.

Damage and Signs

Aphids feed in such numbers that leaves often turn yellow as the entire plant begins to weaken. Leaves of potato plants turn brown and curl. Tomatoes suffer from blossom-end rot, dead spots on leaves, leaf roll, and stunted plants. Fruit trees with swollen twigs and branches, covered with a white fluff, have been taken over by the woolly apple aphid.

Deterrents

Cultural Practices. Garden management practices of removing plant remains from previous crops, especially cole crops, and tilling soil afterward to displace and kill eggs are mandatory steps against aphids. Repeated tillage helps to discourage ants that nest underground. Rotating crops will help. Aphids are especially fond of plants that have been overnourished with nitrogen, so don't overfeed.

Plantings of sunflowers and milkweeds make good trap crops.

The reflection from aluminum foil mulch disorients flying aphids, keeping them from lighting on plants surrounded by it. The shiny surface also reflects light and heat back into the plants. Lay out strips of foil around the base of vulnerable plants and hold them in place with rocks or bricks. Keep a close watch to be sure that the

increased temperature does not harm the plants. If plants wilt from heat radiated by the foil, remove it.

Repellents. Alliums such as garlic and chives, as well as anise, coriander, nasturtiums, and petunias can be interplanted as repellent plants.

Exclusion. Row covers effectively protect vegetables and can be left on cole crops until harvest, temperatures permitting.

Traps. Using their attraction to yellow against aphids, sticky traps can be made of bright yellow tiles, boards, or banners coated with motor oil, petroleum jelly, or commercial stick-em such as Tanglefoot. Place these near target plants. Bright yellow plastic plates filled with a little soapy water will drown any aphids that fly into them. These work best positioned at the base of target plants.

Bio-control. Gardeners have long thought of ladybugs as the aphid predator of choice, and granted they will consume a comforting share of the sticky little bugs. But they can be fickle gals who don't think twice about crossing property lines. Lacewings devour aphids to the tune of about 100 each per day. Spiders, assassin bugs, big-eyed bugs, and soldier bugs also dine on aphids and may be easier to keep at home.

Parasites such as the chalcid wasps and others can help reduce aphid populations once they become established. Look for "aphid mummies," the hollow remains of aphids who have already been parasitized. Do not disturb. Friendly bugs have left their legacy within and when the eggs hatch, more parasites will emerge to claim more aphids. The orange wormlike larvae of the gall, or aphid midge, will also do in gobs of aphids. They are invaluable greenhouse allies that, unlike many other beneficials, will keep busy year round. There are even aphid diseases, most prevalent in damp weather, and a lethal fungus that may come to the aid of aphid-plagued gardeners.

Sprays and Dusts. Soap sprays are highly effective against aphids on garden vegetables. One study found a 97 percent reduction in aphid numbers just one day after application, and aphid predators and other beneficials were unaffected.

Dormant oil spray for fruit trees and roses will prevent larvae from emerging from eggs laid on bark or stems. Both of these methods *can* harm beneficial insects as well as aphids.

Many homemade sprays have been successful against aphids. Water sprayed with force directly at infestations can wash them away. Tea made from 1 part mint to 4 parts water, steeped and filtered, will deter them. Tea made from tobacco stems or soaked cigarette butts is effective, but toxic to people and animals. Don't plan to use it on roses, however, as it turns the blooms black. Also, tomatoes, peppers, and potatoes are susceptible to tobacco mosaic virus, which tobacco preparations can spread. Boiling rhubarb leaves distills

oxalic acid, poisonous to man and beast as well as aphids if consumed. Use 2 pounds of leaves per quart of water and after boiling add 1 teaspoon of liquid soap. Use elder leaves instead of rhubarb to spray rose bushes. Teas made from garlic or green onions work. Strong limewater is an old-time cure. Three parts 70 percent rubbing (isopropyl) alcohol to 4 parts water with a tablespoon of liquid soap added makes a very effective desiccant. Finally, plant juice made from infested leaves will wipe aphids out.

Both rotenone and diatomaceous earth will kill aphids, but beneficial insects will suffer as well.

Beetles

Flea Beetles

Although there are about twenty varieties of flea beetles, only a handful bother garden crops: striped *(Phyllotetra striolata)*, cabbage *(P. albonica)*, cucumber *(Epitrix cucumens)*, eggplant *(E. fuscula)*, spinach *(Visonycha xanthomeloena)*, horseradish *(P. armoraciae)*, grape *(Altica chalybea)*, and sweet potato *(Chaetocnema confini)* flea beetles are all members of the same troublesome tribe. They are beetles, not fleas, but are probably so named because of their tremendous, flea-like jumping ability.

Range and Habitat

Flea beetles are found throughout North America. Habitat is nonspecific.

Physical Description

Flea beetles are tiny (most under 1/10 inch long), hard-bodied insects. Colors range from high-gloss black to iridescent blue, green, or bronze. Some have yellowish legs, antennae, or wing markings (not that you'll ever get close enough to see them!).

They have exaggerated hind legs, like those of their namesake, allowing for powerful jump starts.

Life Cycle

Adults overwinter in garden debris or nearby weeds. Warm spring weather rouses them from their sleep just in time for breakfast. After feeding for several weeks, each female lays roughly 100 eggs in the top 1/8 to 1/4 inch of soil, usually near the future host. After a week or two these hatch into larvae that munch roots for another two weeks before pupating and emerging as hungry adults in another twelve days or so. At this point, new and overwintered beetles descend on crops together, which is why the early- to midsummer season sees the worst damage. A third generation may be produced, depending on the climate. Throughout the summer the oldest die off, leaving the new generations to sleep through the winter and carry on again in the spring. Winter conditions will cause numbers to vary from one year to the next. Flea beetles do not survive more than one summer.

Habits

Boing! Ping! Spring! These little guys are jumpy! Any approaching threat sends them off leaping tall eggplants in a single bound.

Flea beetles are chewers who do so in earnest during hot, dry spells, often attacking their hosts in large numbers. Apparently believing it's the early flea beetle that gets the greens, they start in on weeds before the garden is in, and later pounce voraciously on tender seedlings.

Flea beetles find their hosts through sensitive scent detectors along their antennae. Once holes have been chewed through leaves, the volatile oils released draw even more little munchers to the scene, like sharks in bloody water. All this chomping from place to place helps to spread plant diseases.

Garden Targets

As names of different types imply, most flea beetles are specialized in their feeding habits. That is, certain kinds of flea beetles eat only certain kinds of plants. Throughout the United States the most common targets are young tomatoes, eggplant, potatoes and related plants, cole crops, spinach, beets, radishes, and turnips.

Damage and Signs

The hallmark of flea beetle damage is plants that look as though they have been riddled with tiny buckshot. Most plants can survive a surprising amount of this early damage, one glaring exception being eggplant, which often does not recover.

Deterrents

Cultural Practices. Knowing the flea beetles' preference for hot, dry conditions, you can slow down their feasting by keeping plants moist. Regular misting, not soaking, will dampen their appetites. Combined with rapid, healthy growth as afforded by good soil and growing conditions, this may suffice to get seedlings through the worst of the feeding frenzy.

Cultivate early and often to expose eggs; a depth of ½ inch will do.

Interplanting crops helps to diminish flea beetle activity by giving out mixed signals as to a host plant's availability. Since most are host specific and locate their food by odor, the easiest way to *attract* flea beetles is to plant one big smelly patch of their favorite meal.

Try to plant resistant varieties. De Cicco, Atlantic, and Italian Green Sprouting broccoli, Snowball and Early Snowball cauliflower, Mammoth Red Rock and Early Jersey Wakefield cabbage, and Sequoia potatoes are less vulnerable than many other varieties of these crops. Plant marigolds to repel flea beetles.

Prevention is better than cure. Keep garden debris (their winter home) cleaned up.

Exclusion. Crop covers will keep young, tender targets free of damage.

Traps. A shallow beer trap, similar to that used for slugs, has worked for some people.

Sprays and Dusts. Teas made from repellent plants such as wormwood, mint, or catnip can help to botch up the flea beetles' odor radar, as can sprays from garlic, onion, or hot peppers.

A sprinkling of wood ashes or ground limestone discourages flea beetles, who dislike the dustiness. Resort to rotenone for serious infestations.

Colorado Potato Beetle

(Leptinotarsa decemlineata)

For many gardeners the Colorado potato beetle is one of the most reliable crops in the garden. This potato bug is so common it's not surprising that it is also very resistant to controls, including most pesticides.

Physical Description

Adult beetles are about ⅓ inch long, with a hard, very rounded outer shell. The wing covers alternate creamy yellow with ten black stripes. The head and thorax are decorated with irregular black marks.

The fat, reddish larvae sport two rows of black dots along either side, as well as a black head and legs. They plump up to about ½ inch long before going into the pupal stage.

Range and Habitat

The Colorado potato beetle ranges throughout North America, except in the South and Pacific Northwest. It had its origin in mountain meadows but now will settle in just about anywhere.

Life Cycle

Overwintering as adults, several inches underground, potato beetles awaken when spring soil temperatures are in the mid-fifties, and are ready to eat and lay eggs. Eggs hatch in about a week and then go through four instars before returning to the ground to pupate. All this takes three to four weeks, after which the females stop eating long enough to mate and lay more eggs. Up to four generations are produced each season. The average life span is five to six weeks.

Habits

As chewing insects, all stages of larvae and adults eat and eat and eat, pausing only long enough to mate and lay more eggs. Such a life!

Garden Targets

Members of the Solanaceae family — potatoes, tomatoes, eggplant, and peppers — are particularly vulnerable. Cabbage and petunias are also susceptible.

Damage and Signs

These pests can strip plants of foliage. They do the most damage in small plots, killing plants and at the very least reducing harvests. Characteristic black excrement can be found on damaged leaves and stems.

Deterrents

Cultural Practices. Rotate solanaceous crops with other types of plants, and try resistant varieties, such as Sequoia potatoes. Potatoes can be grown aboveground, making it nearly impossible for grubs, or larvae, to move up into the plants from the soil. Keep a foot-deep layer of mulch over the developing tubers to protect them from sunlight (it turns them bitter and green) and to further stymie the grub migration.

Repellent plants like snap beans, marigold, garlic, onions, flax, catnip, coriander, nasturtiums, tansy, dead nettle, and especially horseradish can be interplanted to keep the beetles away.

Because they're not very enthusiastic climbers, fat grubs can be halted by a thick mulch.

Exclusion. Crop covers tucked over vulnerable plants will protect them from incoming beetles but can't help to keep ground-level grubs from their regularly scheduled trek from the soil up into plants.

Bio-control. A strain of Bt, *Bacillus thuringiensis san diego*, sold as M-One, is reported to be about 90 percent effective when applied early (against newly hatched larvae).

Predators include toads, paper wasps, and ground beetles. Normally considered stink bug predators, *Perillus bioculatus* and *Podisus maculiventris* also enjoy a fat potato beetle.

The parasite wasp *Edovum puttleri* and a fungus (*Beauveria bassiana*) can keep them in check. Tachinid flies also parasitize these beetles, but not until so late in the season that the damage has already been done.

Sprays and Dusts. One great remedy against potato beetles is to feed them to death. Sprinkle plants with water, then dust well with wheat bran. The bran, once moistened, swells to a point where the beetles' cuticle gives under the pressure. Greedy beetles down the bran as they devour plant leaves, expand, explode, and expire! Teas or sprays made from basil or boiled cedar boughs have been reported successful as repellents. Spraying a solution of 2 tablespoons epsom salts dissolved in a gallon of water also turns them away.

"Beetlejuice," the beetle version of bug juice, destroys the small percentage of beetles it doesn't deter. Triple Plus (rotenone, pyrethrum, and ryania) annihilates them.

Cucumber Beetles

(Order Coleoptera)

Here is a pair of outlaw cousins, the striped cucumber beetle *(Acalymma vittata)*, the common garden criminal, and the spotted cucumber beetle *(Diabrotica undecimpunctata howardi)*, alias the notorious corn rootworm. The only difference between them is their chosen repast.

Physical Description

The adult striped cucumber beetles grow to ¼ inch long, while their white wormy larvae grow to about ⅓ inch. An adult beetle is bright yellow, with three broad, black stripes running down the length of the wing covers and a black head. His accomplice, the spotted cucumber beetle, fits a similar description except his greenish yellow wing covers are disguised with eleven large, black spots (twelve in western species). Destructive larvae grow to ½ inch in length and are beige with a brown head and brown spot at the rear.

Life Cycle

Adults of both species overwinter in spent vines or other garden refuse, hitting the garden just before cucumber seedlings emerge. They feed mercilessly, mate, and lay their orange or yellow eggs at the base of cucumber or other host plants. After hatching, the larvae dig down into the soil to munch on roots and ground-level stems. After a few weeks, the larvae pupate and adults emerge to produce from one to three more generations, depending on climate. The cucumber beetle survives only for a few weeks.

Range and Habitat

Both the striped and the spotted cucumber beetles are found in the eastern United States and in parts of southern Canada. Similar species of beetles occupy the west. "Stripes" is most frequently seen in home gardens west of the Rocky Mountains, while "Spot" frequents large cornfields from Mexico to Colorado, and going northeast into Canada.

Habits

These greedy eaters will tunnel underground to go after germinating seeds before the sprouts can push through the soil. So gluttonous they can strip entire plants practically overnight, they do their worst damage early on, devouring seedlings before they can get a roothold. Although adults will take on almost any part of the plant, they can most often be found on the underside of leaves.

Garden Targets

Starting with cucumbers and other cucurbits (related plants such as melon, squash, and pumpkin), "Stripes" will

proceed to vandalize beans, peas, corn, beets, eggplant, tomatoes, potatoes, and more, including flowers such as daisies, cosmos, dahlias, roses, zinnias, and sweet peas. "Spot" goes for corn, cucurbits, tomatoes, eggplant, potatoes, and even some tree fruit.

Damage and Signs

Holes chewed through foliage, flowers, even fruit may indicate cucumber beetles. They can decimate plants. Their crimes also include transmitting deadly bacterial wilt and cucumber mosaic virus.

Deterrents

Cultural Practices. "Spot" is most easily kept from corn by crop rotation.

Traditionally, heavy mulching has been used to discourage the upward mobility of "Stripes." Larvae find it tough to negotiate through it on their journey from ground level into plants. Late planting, in zones that will allow for it, helps to avoid the heaviest damage inflicted by the first wave of emerging adults. Interplanting is helpful, especially with repellents like catnip, tansy, marigolds, or radishes in and around hills. These beetles are also reported to dislike goldenrod.

Exclusion. Crop covers placed over transplants will keep adult beetles from getting to them. Be aware, however, that these will trap larvae emerging from the soil.

Traps. A trap can be made from a stiff paper milk carton using a piece of bitter melon as bait.

Sprays and Dusts. A spray made of equal parts wood ashes and dehydrated lime, mixed with water, is said to banish the beetles. Make sure to apply to all sides of foliage. Juice from geranium stalks and leaves repels "Stripes." Whiz up a batch in the blender, dilute, and strain into a sprayable consistency. While you have the blender out, a batch of cucumber beetlejuice makes a lethal preparation.

Rotenone, pyrethrum, and neem are all effective.

Japanese Beetles

(Popillia japonica)

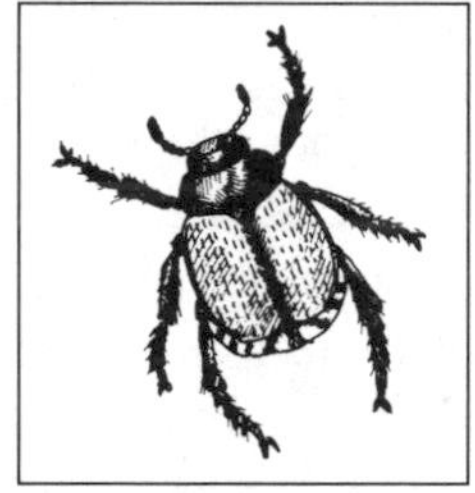

Think of Japanese imports and most likely the first things that come to mind are cars or electronics. However, long before these came our way, around 1916, we received the first of what has turned out to be a glut on the beetle market.

Physical Description

The adult Japanese beetle is metallic green with copper-colored wing covers. Peeking out from under the wings are small tufts of short, white, bristly hairs, and downy gray hairs cover the belly. Japanese beetles are about ½ inch long and ¼ inch wide, males being somewhat smaller than females.

The maturing larva is a dingy white grub with a brown head. It grows to 1 inch long and has ten abdominal segments. The underside of the last segment has two rows of spines that form a V, an identifying mark found only in Japanese beetle larvae.

Range and Habitat

The Japanese beetle's territory is the eastern United States and is expanding westward. Originally found in open woods and meadows, the Japanese beetle can now be found in any park, lawn, or garden.

Life Cycle

Though it takes nearly two years to complete their life cycle, only thirty to forty-five days of it are spent as an adult. Both adults and larvae overwinter in the soil. Grubs spend about ten months underground, usually maturing in the spring. They undergo about ten days in a dormant stage just before pupating in their subterranean chamber. Eight to twenty days later, the adult beetle evolves as a soft, vulnerable creature. It stays in the protective cell a few days while the exoskeleton stiffens, before crawling to the surface.

After mating, females return underground a few inches and lay their eggs, which hatch in about two weeks.

Habits

So sociable, masses of Japanese beetles will feed on one host plant, leaving the next one untouched. They also consider mating a group activity. A moving mass of up to thirty males may engulf a single female, all with the same idea at the same time. No wonder she sometimes hides out underground for a few days after laying eggs!

Preferring to dine in direct sunshine, they feed heaviest in temperatures between 83 and 95 degrees F. Temperatures of 70 degrees F. and above keep them active and flying about, while low humidity (below 60 percent) reduces flight activity and promotes feeding. Cool weather, wind, or clouds slow both activities, and rainy days bring them to a halt.

Garden Targets

Upon arrival in the United States, the hungry beetles were greeted with a smorgasbord of new foods. Versatile little guys, they found no fewer than 275 to their liking. Among these are various fruit and nut trees, especially those bearing ripe or overripe fruit, ornamentals, raspberries, rhubarb, corn (silks), and, for the grubby kids, lawn after yummy lawn. Grassy areas such as lawns and golf courses, especially those that are frequently mown, provide their favorite fare of tender grass roots.

Damage and Signs

Leaves of victims are skeletonized, with only the lacy pattern of veins remaining. Flowers are consumed and

fruits are devoured down to the pits.

Lawns may sustain extensive damage due to feeding larvae. Large patches of brown, dead grass appearing in late summer or early fall may be the work of these grubs.

Deterrents

Cultural Practices. Keep trees free from overripe fruit and put off planting corn until after the beetles have staged their main feast. Maintain a high pH level in lawn soils wherever grubs are a problem, as this discourages them.

Grow borage as a trap crop; white geranium, garlic, and rue are repellent plants. The beetles avoid forsythia, honeysuckle, and privet; lay out boughs or use these in sprays. Larkspur not only attracts the beetles, it is fatal to them.

Handpicking. Handpicking can greatly reduce the number of beetles. Try placing a tarp under infested foliage and shaking the beetles onto it. If done early in the morning while it is still cool and damp, the groggy beetles can't fly off. Dunk your catch in a little kerosene and dispose of them.

Exclusion. Here again covers offer absolute protection from flying adults. Since some adults as well as larvae overwinter in the soil, crop covers may trap them in with plants.

Bio-control. Milky spore disease *(Bacillus popilliae)* is another Japanese beetle control that is catching on quickly. It is a naturally occurring infection, so named because it turns the

Build Your Own Japanese Beetle Trap

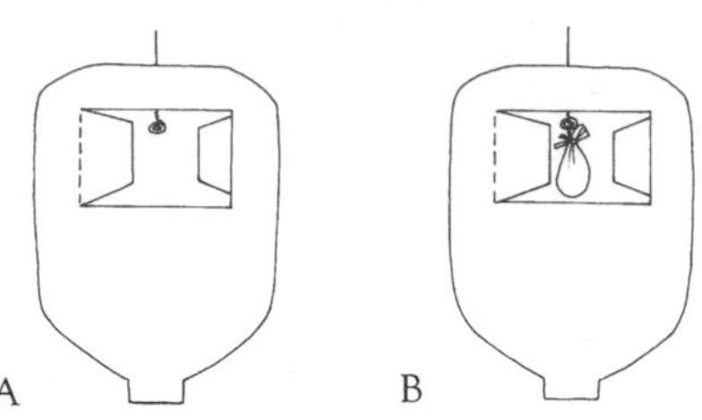

A. *Cut a door out of the lower half of a plastic milk jug, leaving a hinge on each side. Punch a hole through the center of the bottom of the jug and push through a 12" piece of hanger wire. Wrap the end of the wire through and around a washer to secure it inside the jug.*

B. *Make a bait bag by cutting several layers of cheesecloth into a 6" square. Place 1 or 2 teaspoons of bait in the middle and draw all the corners together. Tie closed with a twist-tie. Use the twist-tie to fasten the bait bag to the hanger wire inside the jug.*

C. *Tie a garbage bag tightly around the neck of the bottle, making sure the bag is open and flared around the outside of the bottleneck. (If the bottle came with a screw top, cut out the top of the cap and feed the bag through it.) Screw in place. Punch several holes in the bottom of the bag for drainage. Hang the trap in a sunny area at least 200 feet **away** from the plants you want to protect. Leave the bagged beetles in the sun to finish off any survivors. Bury the dead beetles.*

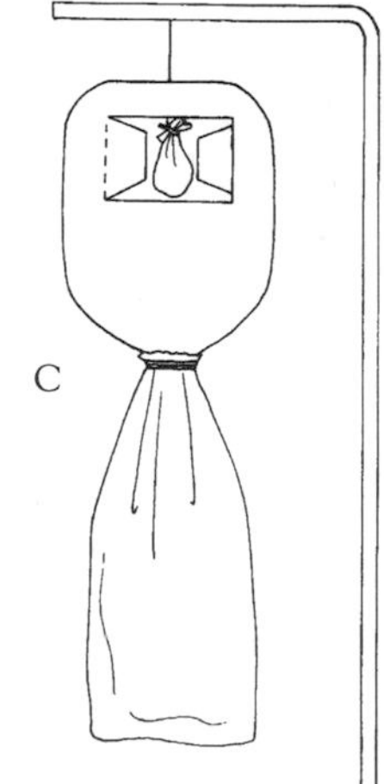

larvae's blood from clear to milky white. Lethal to grubs but harmless to plants and animals, it is sold in the form of a dust, and may be applied to lawns or other grassy areas anytime except when the ground is frozen. Don't apply with an insecticide, as this wipes out the host for the disease and it will be useless.

It may takes years for this infection to become established, and unless near neighbors are cooperating with your efforts, it may never get a fair chance. Ask your county extension agent for help in coordinating a community effort.

Many birds eat the beetles, and there are several parasites. A parasitic nematode, *Heterohabditis heliothidis*, tested 90 percent effective against the grubs while still in its experimental stages. Begin application of this agent in mid-May. Two wasps, the fall tiphia *(Tiphia popilliavora)* and the spring tiphia *(T. vernalis)* also attack the larvae. Two tachinid flies, *Hyperectein aldrichi* and *Prosena siberita*, parasitize the adult beetles.

Traps. One of the most popular methods of dealing with the adult beetles is to put out traps. These can be homemade or commercial and baited with either food or sex attractants (pheromones). Suggested lures include geraniol (rose scent), anethole (a flavoring made from anise or fennel oil), eugenol (from clove oil), and commercially produced lures, as well as pheromones Japonilure and Integralure. Be forewarned that these lures work! Combining food and sex lures multiplies the effectiveness.

Sprays and Dusts. Teas made from branches of plants that beetles naturally avoid may detour them around garden plants. Japanese beetle-flavored bug juice will also repel them. Rotenone is effective.

Mexican Bean Beetles

(Epilachna varivestis)

The black sheep of the ladybug family, the Mexican bean beetle's resemblance to its helpful cousin is only wing-cover deep.

Physical Description

Young adult beetles are yellow, maturing to the characteristic ladybug copper color. Wing covers are sprinkled with sixteen black spots, but there are no white markings between the head and body — a sure sign that this beetle is no "lady." They are rounded, about ¼ inch long and nearly as wide. Larvae are light yellow, covered with bristles, and about ⅓ inch long.

Life Cycle

Adults spend the winter in the garden or in nearby fields or woods. Rising with the first bean seedlings, they feed on leaves for several days. Females lay eggs in large clusters on the undersides of leaves. Each can lay

more than 450 eggs. When larvae hatch, they eat, grow, and wriggle out of their old skins until it's time to retire to the sheltered underside of a leaf and pupate. Adults emerge about one month from the time the eggs were laid. Depending on the region, there will be from one to three generations per year.

Range and Habitat

Different species of bean beetles occur throughout the United States; the Mexican bean beetle is found in the eastern United States as well as parts of Texas, Arizona, Colorado, and Utah. Habitat is nonspecific.

Habits

Both adults and larvae prefer to feed from the bottom side of leaves, but will occasionally nibble on stems or beans.

Garden Targets

Beans; also cabbage, kale, collard, and mustard greens.

Damage and Signs

Feeding habits of all stages skeletonize the leaves, leaving only the lace-like skeleton of veins intact.

Deterrents

Mexican bean beetles are sensitive to high temperatures and drought; some summers nature will contribute to their control.

Cultural Practices. If possible, plant early. Clear away plant remains as soon as the harvest is finished. Keep the garden free of debris that could provide winter quarters.

Interplant beans with potatoes (each plant benefits), nasturtiums, garlic, or savory. Rosemary and petunias are somewhat repellent. Try resistant varieties of beans such as Wade, Logan, and Black Valentine lima beans. Other resistant varieties include Copenhagen Market 86 and Early Jersey Wakefield cabbage; Dwarf Siberian kale; Georgia Longstanding, Green Glaze, and Vates collards; and Green Wave mustard.

Handpicking. Search and destroy by daily handpicking and you will reduce much of the current season's problems as well as some of the potential for future generations. Turn over leaves to look for clusters of the rounded yellow eggs. Toss the collected beetles in a can of water with a little kerosene, or reserve them for Mexican beetlejuice. Olé!

Exclusion. Row covers work well on bush beans. Other plants can also be well protected, but pole beans are awkward to cover.

Bio-control. Predators include assassin bugs and soldier bugs. A wasp, *Pediobius foveolatus*, is a commercially available parasite. Some ladybugs seek out the eggs and larvae.

Sprays and Dusts. A spray made from boiling cedar chips reportedly deters these beetles. Another sugges-

tion is a spray made from corn oil and mashed turnips. Resort to rotenone or pyrethrum only when necessary.

Borers

Squash Vine Borers

(Melittia satyriniformis)

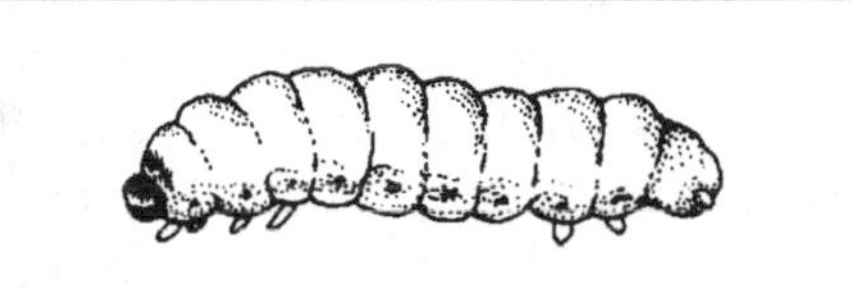

Symptoms of bored plants don't appear until it may be too late to save the victim of this insidious plant predator.

Physical Description

The adult is an elusive, quick, red and black moth, with clear red wings. Up to 1½ inches long it may, at a glance, look like an oversized hornet. Larvae are ugly, wrinkled, white caterpillars with brown heads, growing to about an inch in length. Eggs are flat brown circles, about ⅒ inch across, attached to stems at the base of the host.

Life Cycle

Squash vine borers overwinter underground as larvae or pupae. Adults emerge in late spring and lay eggs just as cucurbits begin to flower. The borers hatch in one or two weeks and feed for four to six weeks more before returning to the ground to pupate. Usually one generation per year is produced in the North and two in the South.

Range and Habitat

Found in the United States and southern Canada east of the Rocky Mountains, the squash vine borer's habitat includes any cultivated open area.

Habits

The larvae bore into the base of stems shortly after hatching, crawl within, and feed on the soft insides. They leave the plant only at maturity to go underground and pupate. Adults visit plants only momentarily while depositing eggs and are rarely even seen. Females locate the egg site on the stem by touch and will settle for any place within a few inches of where the stem touches the ground.

Garden Targets

Targets include summer and winter squash, pumpkin, melons, and cucumbers.

Damage and Signs

When all seems well until vines suddenly wilt, suspect the squash vine borer. Deposits of crumbly greenish yellow residue called *frass* collect at the base of stems or near holes in vines.

Deterrents

Cultural Practices. Early plantings may resist attack, and late plantings may be timed to miss the main July onslaught. Mounding soil up over the plants to the flowers or over any leaf joints encourages rooting and decreases vulnerable surface area. Keep old vines cleaned away, and scrape and squish any eggs you find.

Radishes interplanted in hills of the garden targets help repel vine borers as do wood ashes, camphor, and black pepper sprinkled around potential egg-laying sites. Butternut varieties of squash are the most resistant.

Handpicking. The historical treatment for borers involves major surgery from which plants seldom fully recover. Split the vines with a razor blade at the borer's entrance hole and gouge out (a small crochet hook works great) or stab the culprit to death. Several larvae per stem often must be removed or killed to prevent further damage. Heap moist soil over all plant wounds to aid healing and rooting.

Exclusion. Crop covers, foil collars molded around the base and lower stems of plants, or nylon panty hose wrapped around the stem from the ground up all serve to exclude the egg-laying moths. No eggs, no caterpillars.

Bio-control. Injections of Bt or beneficial nematodes *(Neoplectana carpocapsae* or *Heterorhabditos heliothidis)* into the stems, using a 3cc syringe (from the drugstore, doctor, or vet's office) placed about an inch and a half above the soil line, can control borers remarkably. Administer just after the first flowering to hit the invading larvae and prevent them from ever entering and damaging the plants. If the caterpillars are already inside the vines, inject at 4-inch intervals along the stem and repeat every few weeks.

Tiny trichogramma wasps parasitize the borers.

Sprays and Dusts. Rotenone or pyrethrum powder will control them if applied regularly as soon as the vines start to run.

Mound soil over squash plants to the first leaf joints or flowers to reduce the surface area vulnerable to borers.

Bugs

Harlequin Bugs

(Murgantia histrionica)

Pretty to look at, but not nice to be near, harlequin bugs can devastate entire crops in a season.

Physical Description

A designer original! Vivid orange-red and black patterns decorate the flat shield-shaped adults, which grow to about ⅜ inch long. Barrel-shaped eggs are laid in precise double rows on the flip side of leaves. White and black bands around them make them easy to identify. Nymphs are red and black. Harlequin bugs at all stages have an unpleasant odor.

Life Cycle

Adults overwinter in piles of garden debris, laying their distinctive eggs early in the spring. Nymphs hatch to feed. In about two weeks, after several molts, they mature into adults. Three or four generations in a season are common, except in the Deep South, where they may reproduce continuously.

Habits

Adults and nymphs feed by piercing plant tissue and sucking out fluid.

Range and Habitat

The harlequin bug can be found in fields, orchards, gardens, and meadows in southern regions of the United States.

Garden Targets

Harlequin bugs feast on cabbage and related crops, such as broccoli, cauliflower, brussels sprouts, turnips, radishes, kohlrabi, as well as horseradish and mustard.

Damage and Signs

Harlequin bug feeding causes bleached spots on leaves and may lead to wilting, brown, and dying plants.

Deterrents

Cultural Practices. Thorough garden cleanup is essential. Trap crops of turnips or mustard may lure them from other plants. Pull up these crops when they are infested and dunk them into a bucket of water and kerosene. Resistant varieties include Grande, Atlantic, and Coastal broccoli; Copenhagen Market 86, Headstart, Savoy Perfection Drumhead, Stein's Flat Dutch, and Early Jersey Wakefield cabbage; Early Snowball X and Snowball Y cauliflower; Vates, Morris Improved Heading, and Green Glaze collards; Vale kale; and Red Devil, White Icicle, Globemaster, Cherry Belle, Champion, and Red Prince radish.

Exclusion. Crop covers will keep adults off plants.

Sprays and Dusts. Soap sprays offer good control. If faced with a heavy infestation, sabadilla or pyrethrum are recommended.

Range and Habitat

Squash bugs inhabit fields and gardens throughout North America.

Squash Bugs

(Anasa tristis)

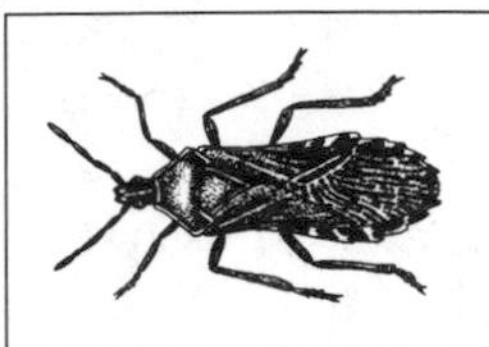

What a stinker! Not only does this pest ravage and ruin garden crops, but the malodorous wretch exudes an unpleasant odor (like that of bitter almonds) upon impact. That is, it stinks when you squish it — hence one appropriate nickname, "stinkbug."

Physical Description

Mature adults are dark brown, 5/8 inch long, with flat backs, long legs and antennae, and piercing mouthparts. Young nymphs are a pale pearly green with a reddish head and legs. Eggs are shiny gold when laid, changing to red-brown. Arranged in patterns around the center leaf vein, each is about 1/16 inch long.

Life Cycle

In winter hibernating adults hide out in old vines, under boards, or in piles of trash. Mating and egg- laying commence in the spring. Nymphs hatch in from five to fourteen days. There is usually one generation per year.

Habits

Hatching from clusters of eggs, the young tend to stay in groups. Both adults and nymphs feed by piercing plant tissue and sucking out the sap, while injecting digestive juices toxic to the host.

They seek dark, damp hiding places.

Garden Targets

Squash, pumpkins, melons, and cucumber are the squash bug's preys.

Damage and Signs

Young plants are easily killed by squash bugs. Older plants suffer wilting leaves that eventually blacken and die. Yields may be drastically reduced or eliminated.

Deterrents

Cultural Practices. Garden cleanup of previous vine crop residues, piles of trash, and boards removes overwintering sites. Rotate vine crops as far away from previous plantings as possible. Start plants indoors so that they are large and healthy when transplanted.

Radishes, tansy, marigolds, and nasturtiums interplanted with squash help repel the bugs. Interplanting with

peas has also deterred squash bugs.

Trellising (growing plants upward on supports) gets foliage off the ground, reducing the moist, covered areas that the bugs seek (see chapter 5, Turtles, for ideas). Avoid loose mulches, like hay, and opt instead for paper, plastic, compost, or sawdust.

Look for resistant varieties like Table Queen, Royal Acorn, Early Golden Bush Scallop, Early Summer Crookneck, Early Prolific Straightneck, and Improved Green Hubbard squash.

Handpicking. Crush eggs and toss any adults you can catch into a can of water with kerosene.

Exclusion. Crop covers or screening left on until flowering helps young plants get established before having to fend off any attacks.

Bio-control. Predators include wolf spiders and a red and black tachinid fly, *Trichopoda pennipes*.

Traps. Leave a board out as a trap near the squash plants for the bugs to congregate under. A quick stomp will flatten any takers. Toss any dichards into a can of water with a little kerosene.

Sprays and Dusts. Soap sprays work well if started at the first sign of adults and kept up throughout the season. A liberal misting of imitation vanilla apparently fouls up their squash sensors. Try sprinkling plants with water that has soaked with a handful of wood ashes and a handful of lime for at least twenty-four hours. Sabadilla dust works, too.

Caterpillars

Cabbage Loopers and Imported Cabbageworms

(Trichoplusia ni and Pieris rapae)

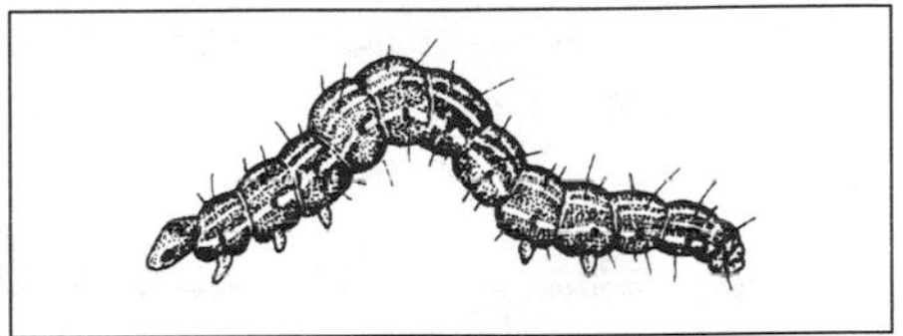

These two caterpillars are very similar in habits and appearance as well as in the damage they do. They may be confused with diamondback moths, garden webworms, or alfalfa loopers.

Physical Description

The cabbage looper is green with white stripes down the back and sides. He is most easily recognized by his "humpback." With no legs between his front and hind ends, he moves one end at a time, "looping" or "inching" along. The nickname inchworm comes from his way of going rather than his length, which is more likely to be about an inch and a half.

Adults are bark brown moths, with a silver marking at the center of each wing.

Imported cabbageworms are a paler green with a yellow stripe along the back. They are about 1¼ inches long and covered with velvety hairs. Adult moths have white wings, 1½ to 2 inches across, decorated with black wing tips, yellowish undersides, and black spots (two for females, one for males).

Range and Habitat

Cabbage loopers and cabbageworms can be found throughout the United States and parts of southern Canada. Habitat is nonspecific. Loopers may appear in any garden where brassicas are grown.

Life Cycle

Both cabbage loopers and imported cabbageworms spend the winter as pupae; loopers hang from a leaf, and worms tuck themselves snugly underground in tough, comfy chrysalises. In some northern regions adult looper moths fly south for the winter. Adults return in the spring and lay their eggs on host plant leaves. Within a week these hatch into tiny caterpillars that eat their way to full size in about two weeks. After about two more weeks of pupation, they reappear as egg-laying adults. Several overlapping generations are produced throughout the year.

Habits

Larvae are chewers, preferring leaves to other plant parts.

Garden Targets

Both worms and loopers are primarily cabbage or cole crop (broccoli, cauliflower, kale, kohlrabi, radish, turnip) pests. They will also eat lettuce and some flowers. Loopers expand their diets to include peas, beans, tomatoes, spinach, celery, parsley, potatoes, and carnations.

Damage and Signs

These caterpillars chew large, irregular holes in leaves. As they mature they may bore into the center of heads to feed. Cabbageworms leave green fecal pellets to punctuate their damage.

Deterrents

Cultural Practices. Early damage can cost plant vigor and affect yields. If these pests are a chronic problem, consider planting earlier to give crops a head start. Winter pupation sites for loopers can be eliminated by keeping weeds away from the garden area.

Varieties like Mammoth Red Rock, Savoy Chieftain, and Savoy Perfection Drumhead cabbage are more resistant to damage because of the tight formation of the heads.

Plants repellent to cabbageworms can be interplanted or used as a border for garden targets. Try onion, garlic, tomato, tansy, celery, hyssop, mint, sage, rosemary, or thyme.

Handpicking. Regular handpicking and destruction of the eggs (greenish white spheres on the tops of leaves for loopers and yellow "bullets" for worms) will prevent damage from the caterpillars. Check both sides of leaves, and do away with any stages of the pests you find.

Exclusion. Crop covers help to extend the growing season as well as to prevent the adults from depositing

their eggs. Often they may be left on fall cole crops until harvest. Since the cabbageworms pupate underground, crop rotation is necessary to avoid trapping them under the covers as they emerge.

Bio-control. Bt is even more potent than chemicals against these caterpillars. Be sure to hit them while they are still small, preferably under ½ inch long.

For a homemade pathological control for loopers, make "sick juice." This takes advantage of a naturally occurring disease, nuclear polyhedrosis virus (NPV). Infected caterpillars turn chalky white and lethargic, and usually die in three or four days. They often just sit on leaves motionless. Gather a few loopers (four will successfully treat a quarter-acre garden) and proceed as for bug juice. The difference here is that rather than repelling potential offenders, you are killing present pests with past pests.

Predators and parasites include yellow jackets, trichogramma wasps, and braconid wasps, but most birds will turn up their beaks at them.

Sprays and Dusts. Repellent sprays work better against cabbageworms than cabbage loopers. Try a mixture of some or all of the following: chopped onion, horseradish root or leaves, garlic, mint, hot peppers, black peppercorns, or powdered limestone. Many gardeners have had success shaking pulverized flour and salt, rye flour, or even plain table salt onto wet cabbage heads.

The Last Resort. If all else fails, and you end up with wormy produce, soak it in a tub of either warm salt water or a solution of vinegar and water for about fifteen minutes before preparing it to eat, can, or freeze. The caterpillars shrivel up and float to the top. Some are sinkers, but either way, they die and fall out of the vegetables.

Corn Earworms
(a.k.a. Tomato Fruitworm or Cotton Bollworm)
(Heliothis zea)

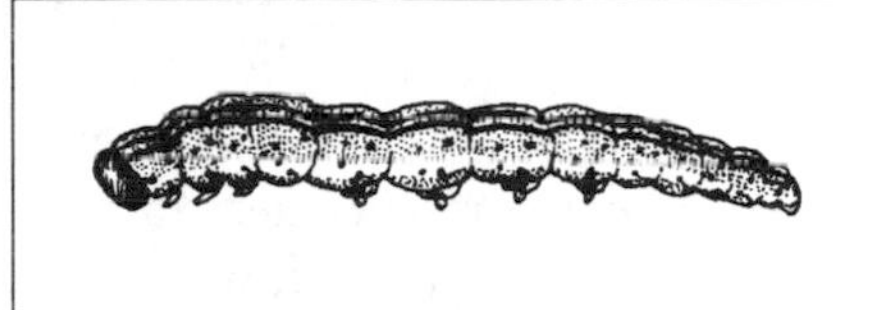

Unfortunately, the aliases don't reveal a split personality. On the contrary, all three sides to this character are pretty much the same — trouble! (To make matters worse, another insect villain, the European corn borer, uses a similar modus operandi to terrorize northern gardeners.)

Physical Description

The "earworm" is actually an unattractive caterpillar. It grows to about 2 inches long and comes in shades of green, pale yellow, or brown, with light or dark sidewalls. Adults are dull beige or gray moths, decorated with a few black spots and bearing 1½-inch wingspans.

Range and Habitat

Earworms are found throughout North America. Habitat is nonspecific; they may appear wherever host plants are found.

Life Cycle

In regions where the ground does not freeze, an earworm spends the winter as a pupa, a few inches down in the soil. In other areas, adults migrate to more temperate climes. Emerging in the early spring, they lay single, dingy white eggs on host plant leaves. These hatch into the irksome earworms. As many as seven generations each year can be expected, with population peaks coming about two weeks after a full moon.

Habits

Adults are night flyers, attracted to lights, and more amorous during a new moon. This accounts for the cyclic fluctuations in their numbers according to lunar phases.

Garden Targets

Favorite targets include corn, tomatoes, cotton, peppers, eggplant, okra, potatoes, squash, beans, and peas.

Damage and Signs

In corn, earworms begin munching the tender shoots as soon as they break ground, especially on late plantings. They are most infamous for their work on the corn ears. Chewing the silky tassels interferes with the plants' pollination and kernel development. Later, earworms worm their way through the husks into the ears, where they ruin kernels and leave gobs of fecal material. The results are ears that are deformed and open to mold and diseases.

They chew a hole in tomatoes through the stem end of the green fruit, sometimes feasting on one, sometimes moving through many.

On other crops they eat chunks out of tender new leaves and buds. Peppers will show brown, pinhead-sized holes where the worms move into and out of the fruit.

Deterrents

Cultural Practices. Fall and spring tilling helps by exposing the pupae to wind, weather, and predators. Early plantings of corn may avoid damage, and cold, damp weather discourages earworms almost as much as it does the corn. (Note: The European corn borer *prefers* the earlier plants.)

Corn varieties with tight husks are physically more resistant to earworm damage. Try Country Gentleman or Silver Cross Bantam. Clipping a clothespin on the tip of each ear can help to keep husks tight.

Plant cosmos as a repellent, or smartweed or sunflowers as trap crops. Grassy strips between corn rows help to attract predators.

Handpicking. Earworms can be

handpicked from corn (after silks have browned) by carefully pulling back the husk and picking them out with a crochet hook. Infested tomatoes or other crops should be culled and discarded or burned. Trim damaged ends of ears of corn and enjoy the rest.

Bio-control. Bt sprayed on at the first sightings of caterpillars will do them in. Once they have penetrated the ears (or fruit), they are harder to control.

Tachinid flies, wasps, brachonid wasps, and ichneumon flies are important egg and larvae parasites. Elcar, a commercially available virus, and nuclear polyhedrosis virus are lethal control agents. NPV can be spread by finding a few infected earworms and turning them into sick juice. (See explanation under Cabbage Loopers.)

Moles and soldier beetle larvae attack on the ground. Lacewings, fire ants, damsel bugs, bats, redwing blackbirds, woodpeckers, English sparrows, and even grackles assault from the air. Birds can do more damage to the corn than the earworms, as they enthusiastically dig for the hidden caterpillars.

Even earworms eat earworms.

Traps. Blacklight traps will destroy the moths, and any elevated outdoor nightlight draws a crowd for bats to feast on.

Sprays and Dusts. Garlic and onion teas have been used successfully against young earworms. Some gardeners sprinkle ground lime on corn ears as soon as silks show to deter the pests.

A mineral oil treatment has long been recommended as a useful remedy. By squeezing an eyedropperful of mineral oil into the tip of each ear (half is enough for smaller ears), any resident earworms are suffocated. Some gardeners give this an extra punch by mixing with pyrethrum or pureeing with African marigolds or geranium leaves.

While plain mineral oil will not affect the taste of corn, it may cause spoilage of the ears, especially in hot, dry weather. Also, don't apply until pollination is complete and silks have turned brown and withered, as the oil can hinder or even prevent this essential process. (Corn is pollinated by the breeze, not insects.)

Rotenone will control earworms.

Cutworms

(Order Lepidoptera)

"Cutworm" is a catchall name for the destructive larvae of hundreds of different species of moths. They may be subdivided according to their means of attack — as climbers, tunnelers, subterraneans, and armyworms, who attack on all fronts.

Physical Description

Soft, ugly, fat, bristly caterpillars, ranging in color from gray, brown, or

black to greenish white and red; their average size is 1½ inches. Often their common names come from distinguishing marks or colors, such as stripes or patches in a variety of hues including yellow, bronze, red, and black. The black cutworm *Agrotis ipsilon*, which is dirty gray to black with a lighter strip down its back, and the variegated cutworm *Peridroma saucia*, marked by yellow side panels and blotches along its back, are among the most common examples found in home gardens.

Adults are generally small, plain-looking brown moths, about ¾ inch across.

A cutworm can be positively identified with a touch test. If it coils up into a ball, it's a cutworm.

Life Cycle

Larvae overwinter burrowed into the soil. Crawling out of their winter quarters, they get right to work chewing through tender seedlings, while adults lay their round, white eggs in weeds or grass. After a few weeks, small larvae hatch, eat, grow, and eventually return to a few inches underground to pupate. From one to four generations are produced every year (the first being the most damaging), ending with the larvae hatched from the last eggs laid in the fall. Wet fall weather interferes with egg-laying and may result in fewer cutworms the following spring. It is these last hatchlings that return to the soil to hibernate until spring.

Range and Habitat

Cutworms are found throughout North America. Garden plots that were in grass or weeds the previous season are especially attractive to them. Unless tilled and left open all winter, or solarized, such areas provide ideal conditions for the emerging larvae.

Habits

Cutworms flourish in warm, moist spring weather, happily chewing through stems or leaves or underground parts of plants, depending on the species. Most surface feeders do their dirty work at night, curling up under cover of soil or nice, cozy mulch (they *love* mulch) during the day to rest up for the next all-nighter. The moths are also active at night, and are irresistibly drawn to light.

Garden Targets

Favorites are tender seedlings or transplants. Older plants may sustain less obvious damage. Cutworms aren't particular, but will start with brassicas, beans, corn, and tomatoes, and move on to everything else.

Damage and Signs

Though some species climb into plants to feed, the classic sign of busy cutworms is seedlings gnawed at the base until they fall over. A telltale tunnel, about ¼ to ½ inch wide, may be found near the base of the victim.

The damage is done during the night, so if tender plants look fine in the evening but are felled (or even missing) in the morning, suspect cutworms.

Deterrents

Cultural Practices. By tilling soil as early as it can be worked in the spring and not planting for two weeks, weed seedlings that the first wave of larvae depend on are destroyed. Reports of near total population control have been attributed to removing their earliest food source. Soil displacement also exposes larvae to predators.

Keeping a garden area free of weeds and grass removes egg-laying sites.

Interplant onion, garlic, or tansy to repel cutworms. Or plant sunflowers as a trap crop.

Handpicking. Handpicking is easiest and most productive following a rain or thorough watering, and done after dark. Spot cutworms with a flashlight and pluck them in the act. Scratching gently around the base of seedlings, especially in the early morning, will also expose their hiding places. Use a clump of clover, mullein, milkweed, or sprouts, half buried, as bait to draw a crowd that can be easily collected or stomped. No need to locate the bait away from other plants, as the caterpillar won't travel away from its main food source.

Exclusion. The most effective line of defense against cutworms is to put a collar between them and the objects of their digestion. These should be about 3 inches tall and can be made from toilet paper rolls, pieces of paper towel or wrapping paper rolls, tar paper, linoleum, foil, bottomless paper cups, or any material stiff and flexible enough to fashion around the stems and push about an inch into the soil. Some materials such as most paper or peat pots with the bottoms removed will degrade, while others can be collected and reused. If wind or other pests are problems, find something sturdy, such as foam pipe insulation, that can serve double duty as a plant support. By the time most seedlings outgrow their collars they are strong enough to tolerate some cutworm damage.

Other barriers that have reported some success are rings of wood ashes, eggshell, or chicken manure, or a mulch of oak leaves.

Bio-control. Predators that relish the fat, juicy caterpillars include robins, meadowlarks, blackbirds, bluejays, moles, shrews, toads, ground beetles, and firefly larvae. Chickens or hogs re-

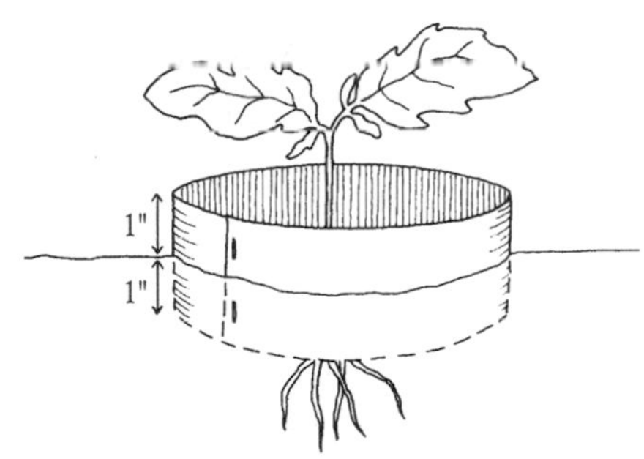

For maximum effect, sink a cardboard collar 1 inch underground to exclude cutworms.

leased on a freshly tilled plot will pig out!

Commercially available parasites include trichogramma wasps and the caterpillar nematode, *Neoaplectana carpocapsae*.

Bt can also be used.

Traps. Cutworms will devour cornmeal, which may do them in on its own, since they can't digest it. Or cut it with powdered Bt for a fatal feast. They also go for molasses. An old-time trap is to mix molasses, hardwood sawdust, and wheat bran and spread it around susceptible plants. Lured to the molasses, cutworms wallow around in the stuff, which stiffens as it dries into an immobilizing cast that leaves them vulnerable to the elements and predators, including vengeful gardeners.

Adult moths can't resist their fatal attraction to light. Bug zappers will fry a fair share. Or just run a light up a pole or tree to give your friendly neighborhood bats an easy midnight snack.

Tomato Hornworms

(Manduca quinquemaculata)

Surprisingly, this large and decorative caterpillar, because of its color, can be a tough one to spot on foliage. A close cousin, the tobacco hornworm, is nearly identical in appearance and practice.

Physical Description

A large and distinctively marked caterpillar, the hornworm is easily identified. The larvae grow to a length of 4 inches. They are stem green with seven or eight diagonal white stripes down the sides, each shadowed by a row of black dots and punctuated by a "false eye" spot. The telltale tail is black on the tomato hornworm and red on the tobacco hornworm.

Adults are huge grayish brown moths, known as sphinx, hawk, or hummingbird moths. They have wings up to 5 inches across, covered with wavy lined patterns. Orange spots mark the body.

Pupae hibernate in hard cases in the shape of a 2-inch-long spindle with a curved handle.

Life Cycle

They winter in a hard-shelled pupal case a few inches underground. Adults emerge in late spring and lay their greenish yellow orbs on the underside of host leaves. These hatch within days, and within a month the larvae eat their way to their full, ghastly size. While only one generation invades the North, Southern gardeners can look forward to two more.

Habits

Expert at camouflage, larvae chew leaves in broad daylight, while the monster moths take flight at dusk.

Range and Habitat

Found throughout North America, hornworms prefer open, cultivated areas.

Moths may be mistaken for hummingbirds as they hover before flowers, feeding on nectar.

Garden Targets

Hornworms dine on tomatoes, peppers, potatoes, eggplant, dill, or tobacco, in the case of tobacco hornworms.

Damage and Signs

Sometimes nibbling at fruits, the hornworms consume a tremendous amount of leaves. Little souvenirs, very similar to rabbit pellets, are left behind.

Deterrents

Cultural Practices. Fall tilling helps to destroy underground pupae. Rotating crops and providing crop covers will keep hornworms off the plants. Borage, opal basil, and marigolds serve as repellent plants. Dill makes an excellent trap crop, as the lumbering giants are easily spied clinging to the delicate stems.

Handpicking. Handpicking is the most recommended method of control. Although hornworms are huge, there usually aren't all that many to contend with. Spraying plants with a blast of cold water sends them into a thrash dance, making them easier to spot.

Bio-control. Spray susceptible plants with Bt and you can forget about hornworms.

Braconid wasps lay eggs on the caterpillar's body. If you happen to find a parasitized hornworm, you'll know it. The body is covered with tiny cocoons of these wasps. Do not disturb this hornworm, as he is about to expire anyway, and he is carrying the next generation of a very beneficial insect. Trichogramma wasps parasitize the eggs.

Earwigs

(Order Dermaptera)

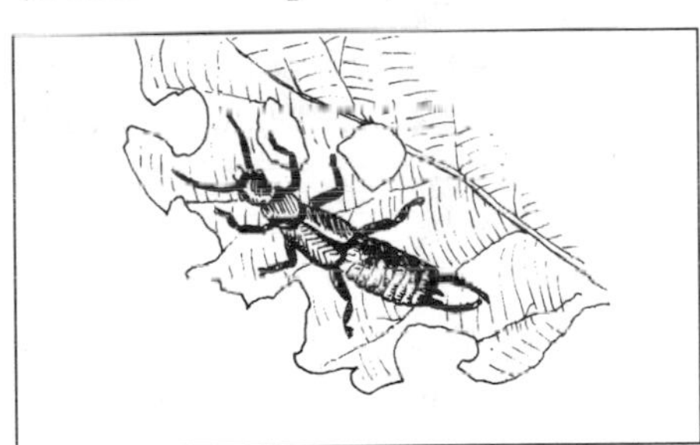

Contrary to ludicrous legend, earwigs do not crawl into your ears while you sleep. In fact, their scary appearance is the only threatening thing about them.

Physical Description

About ½ to ¾ inch long, red-brown with small, nearly useless wings, earwigs are instantly recognizable by their nasty-looking pincers at the hind

end. White, globular eggs are laid in the soil.

Life Cycle

Eggs laid in the fall will hatch in the spring. Several stages of nymphs follow, finally resulting in the recognizable adults. One or two generations are produced each year.

Habits

Earwigs like to sneak around in cool, dark hiding places by day. They come out to feed at night, sometimes in overwhelming numbers. They can't hurt you — they use those dangerous-looking pincers to stave off rear attacks from ants.

Garden Targets

They eat the foliage and flowers of many plants — bean and beet seedlings, sweet corn, lettuce, celery, potatoes, strawberries, dahlias, zinnias, and hollyhock. However, decaying matter, and even other garden pests, make up the mainstay of their diet.

Damage and Signs

Holes in foliage or flowers and young plants or shoots nibbled down mark their presence. To be sure earwigs are at fault, you must grab a flashlight and catch them in the act.

Deterrents

Unless you actually see them doing damage, controls are not generally recommended. But if they are indeed your culprits, follow the remedies below.

Bio-control. Earwig predators include a tachinid fly, *Bigonicheta spinipennis*.

Traps. If necessary, earwigs can be trapped in hollow tubes left out in the garden overnight. Bamboo, sections of pipe, or garden hose will work. Pick up the traps each morning and dump the contents into soapy water or water and kerosene. A beer trap will lure and do in vast numbers. Place fresh beer in old cat food or tuna fish tins around susceptible plants or sink them flush with ground level. Empty and replace every few days.

Another trap uses bacon grease smeared in a ring around the inside of a can or jar about 2 inches from the top. Fill the container with water and a dash of soap to just below the grease line. Bury the works so that the opening is flush with the ground. Attracted to the grease, earwigs crawl in and, plop!, you know.

Sprays and Dusts. Corn can be protected by dusting silks with boric acid.

Range and Habitat

Various species can be found throughout North America. Earwigs like dark hiding places, underneath objects.

Fire Ants

(Solenopsis invicta [red]* and *S. richteri [black])

The name *S. invicta* fittingly translates to "invincible." While these red devils are meaner than their cousins, *S. richteri*, the black ants can tolerate cold. The shattering news is that the "mean" red ant and the "tough" black ant are joining forces to create a "meaner, tougher" hybrid.

Black ants were introduced into the United States around 1918 and the red in the 1940s. The problem with newcomers such as these imported fire ants is that they upset the balance of things. Having no natural enemies, they can take over, even to the point of altering their environment to suit their tastes. Other species, poorly equipped to compete with the prolific and aggressive imports, are wiped out.

Horror stories abound of unsuspecting innocents suffering terrible, painful attacks — baby birds killed in their nests, baby animals attacked before they are old enough to stand, and even children who stumble unknowingly upon their nests.

Their nasty habits and persistence have earned the fire ants the status of "weed species." Usually, when confronted with masses of undesirables, humans summon up their superior intellect, technology, and firepower and proceed to eliminate the beasties. But not these guys.

Even aerial bombers showering the land with toxic chemicals (dieldren and heptachlor in the 1950s and chlordane and mirex into the 1970s) were no match for the sheer biological willpower of the ants. Rather than eliminate the fire ants, all that those tactics accomplished was to strengthen their dominant position by destroying any competition. A few fire ants *always* survived to propagate the next, stronger, more resistant generation. In fact, since government eradication programs began in 1957, the fire ants have spread from an area of 28,341,000 acres to well over 400 million acres. Combine their manmade resistance with man's ever helpful distribution through contaminated nursery stock and sod, and it seems as though the fire ants could scarcely get along without us! For though we loathe the ground they

Range and Habitat

Found in southeastern regions of the United States, fire ants gravitate toward ecologically disturbed areas such as roadsides, lawns, landscapes, garden beds, windfalls, and flood areas. Raised garden beds are particularly appealing to them. They prefer open, sunny places and avoid shady or wooded places and areas where soils are too sandy to compact for tunnel digging.

walk under, fire ants may justifiably consider us unwitting humans as their best friends in all the world.

Physical Description

Individuals look much like any other picnic pest, ⅛- to ¼-inch-long reddish or black ants. Identification depends more on finding the hard-domed mounds, or (yikes!) observing their nasty tempers in action.

Life Cycle

Life begins as one of thousands of eggs laid by the queen within the mound. The female workers tend to the eggs and maturing larvae, moving them up or down the mound to keep them in the ideal temperature range of 85 to 90 degrees F. Those destined to be workers live only about six months, as do males, but queens typically live two to three or more years.

Several times a year, on a warm day most likely following a rain, the fire ants swarm in what is romantically dubbed their nuptial flights. Fertile queens and males meet in mid-air, 300 to 800 feet up, and the males perform their sole function in life, followed by a quick plummet to their demise. The queens, carrying the seeds of an entire colony, then fly off to find a suitable nesting site. On landing, they pop off their wings and dig in — that is, if they survive the many perils encountered on the ground.

From predators to drought to starvation, and attacks by workers from other colonies, the odds are 90 to 99 percent *against* any one queen ever reproducing. If she does, only about ten to twenty eggs are laid and cared for until they mature into workers, in about a month. These then take over everything but egg-laying, which then becomes the queen's sole purpose. Within a year she will produce about 11,000 workers, and by the time the colony matures in 2½ to 3 years there may be more than a quarter of a million residents.

Now for the bad news. Forty mounds per acre used to be considered a severe infestation, but today there may be as many as 800. In fact, there is evidence that these colonies communicate and cooperate as "super colonies."

Habits

As if single-queen colonies were not ominous enough, the ants have teamed up to produce multiple-queen cooperatives. Commonly dozens, even hundreds, of queens may inhabit the same mound, with as many as 3000 being documented.

Extremely sensitive to ground vibrations, hordes of angry fire ants swarm from the mound attacking anything in sight whenever it is disturbed. They grab their victim with powerful jaws and sting repeatedly, injecting a painful alkaloid venom.

They are omnivorous (eat anything), voraciously attacking both plants and animals. Their society is exquisitely organized: the youngest workers tend the nursery, older ones pull K.P., and the most mature forge

out at night for food. Special workers tend to the queen's every need. Males spend their entire existence doing nothing but waiting for their "big day."

During floods, masses of ants climb aboard anything that floats and set sail for a new home. Much of their dispersal can be accredited to their seaworthiness.

Garden Targets

Gardeners, okra, potatoes, strawberries, citrus, and seed corn are favorites of fire ants. Their appetites are unlimited. They also attack boll weevils, aphids, earwigs, corn earworms and other caterpillars, and even ticks and fleas. They find compost piles and raised beds attractive and frequently excavate nests inside.

Damage and Signs

Identifying mounds, especially those less than a year old, can be tricky. Often only a slight bump may be visible, and sometimes not even that. Mature mounds are stone-hard domes, up to 1½ feet high and 2 feet in diameter. They often extend as far as 3 feet deep.

Damage includes devoured plants, difficult to impossible harvest conditions, and painful stings to humans, which result in pustules prone to infection and scarring, and not infrequently hypersensitive or allergic reactions, even death. Every year upwards of 80,000 people receive medical attention for fire ant stings, and that accounts for only a fraction of those actually stung. A mixture of half chlorine bleach and half water, or a paste of meat tenderizer and water, if applied within fifteen minutes of a sting, helps to minimize the pain and swelling. See a doctor if anything other than localized pain develops or if pain is severe.

The cement-hard mounds damage farm equipment and ruin real estate. Severe infestations may drive off (or kill off) every other living creature around the mounds.

Deterrents

Some practices may persuade the ants to set up housekeeping away from your preferred areas. Most controls only send the ants packing, rather than doing them in.

Cultural Practices. Avoid planting in raised bed; in this case the problems can outweigh the benefits. Create shade by trellising vine crops. Drench garden soil with manure tea to discourage foragers from frequenting the area. Fill walkways with sand or pea gravel to prevent mound building or tunneling.

Composting in a commercial, enclosed bin raised off the ground minimizes the chances of ants moving in.

Exclusion. Sticky barriers around raised beds or potted plants stop ants, but must be kept free of "bridges," such as twigs, debris, or ant bodies. Placing flowerpots or greenhouse table legs in containers filled with a sticky substance such as used motor oil creates a moat that prevents ants in your plants.

Bio-control. Predators that will go after fire ants include ground beetles, earwigs, mites, and spiders. Combining the parasitic nematode *Neoplectana carpocapsae* with a bait makes it more likely to pass through protective screening processes in the workers' digestive system that are designed to eliminate hazardous substances. If undetected by the workers it will be introduced to the queen, thus offering a promising means of control. Bats may take down individuals distracted by the throes of their nuptial flights. Armadillos occasionally pillage the mounds, but offer no real control.

New ways to control fire ants are being studied. The ants are evolving before our eyes by hybridizing and developing resistance to chemicals. They keep getting better and better at surviving. That coupled with their means of distribution, from winged queens on the breeze to entire colonies hitchhiking in nursery stock, makes control frighteningly difficult.

Fighting Fire with Water. Eliminating a mound depends on eliminating the queen(s). This is tough to do since her "court" of special workers tests her food, preventing most poisons from reaching her, and whisks her to safety deep within the mound whenever it is disturbed. Success requires attacks on warm sunny days when the queen(s) are most likely to be near the surface of the mound. Work quickly.

One old cure advised plunking a shovelful of ants from one mound into a neighboring one and letting them fight it out. Evidence now suggests that this may only contribute to cooperation between the mounds to establish a multiple-queen mound.

Tried and true is the practice of pouring three or four gallons of boiling hot water into the mound. Have a helper (maybe someone you don't like all that well?) poke a stick into the nest while you saturate it with the hot water. This often requires several treatments, but many people report success in that the mound is no longer active. Could be the ants are only retreating to cooler quarters.

A drench of 3 to 4 tablespoons of liquid soap per gallon of water, for a total of 3 to 4 gallons, is also effective when applied in the same manner as boiling water. Any ants contacted are killed instantly. When all is still, dig into the mound and drench some more. Check the mound periodically for survivors and repeat as necessary.

Pyrethrum is fatal to the ants. When injected into the mound (a job for a professional), it will get the queens.

The best bet is to use slow-acting poisons that are not detectable to the ants until it's too late. They are quick to recognize dying ants and move to avoid danger. The tradeoff on the time it takes to produce results is that entire colonies can be *destroyed*.

Two highly recommended products are Logic (active ingredient fenoxycarb) and a poison bait, Amdro (active ingredient amidinohydrazone). Logic interferes with the queen's ability to lay eggs. Those that are laid develop into useless males or sterile queens, no workers. Eventually no one is left to tend the mound and it dies off. Amdro is an insidious ant poison, as is boric acid. These are applied by sprinkling a few tablespoons around (not on) the mound at times when the foragers are most active, in the morning on warm spring or fall days, and in the late afternoon in the summer.

Flies

Carrot Rust Flies

(Psila rosae)

This sneaky pest does its damage underground, undetected until harvest time.

Physical Description

The adult is a ⅕-inch-long fly with a shiny greenish black body. It has a straw-colored head and legs, and huge red eyes. Larvae are yellowish white maggots that grow up to ⅓ inch long.

Life Cycle

Winter may be passed underground, either as pupae or hibernating maggots. These develop into flies that lay their eggs in the tops or crowns of host plants. Within days these hatch into the voracious larvae, which feed for about a month before pupating. Two or three generations emerge each year, and the last one causes the most damage.

Range and Habitat

Carrot rust flies are most prevalent in the Pacific Northwest, and are also found in Utah, Wyoming, Colorado, and Nebraska. Sadly, these flies seem to favor soils rich in organic matter. They also prefer plots surrounded by brush or woods, or those next to buildings.

Habits

As is frequently the case, it's the kids who cause the trouble. Hatching from their crown-point eggs, they tunnel ever downward through the stem and feast on the smaller fibrous roots, as well as main taproots.

Garden Targets

Carrots, parsnips, celery, celeriac, parsley, fennel, and dill are eagerly consumed by carrot rust flies.

Damage and Signs

Unfortunately, the visible tops of victim plants usually appear fine, while the underground portion silently suffers. Tunnels carved throughout carrots are marked with rust-colored fecal matter. The roots may be stunted or yellowed and are very susceptible to rot. The damage generally gets worse the longer the carrots are left in the ground.

Deterrents

Cultural Practices. Don't store carrots in the ground. It's far too convenient for these pests. Late plantings or early fall harvesting may sidestep damage. Keep weeds, especially stinging nettle, away from the garden to avoid supplying alternate hosts. Rotate carrot and other target patches.

Repellents. Onions and other alliums, pennyroyal, rosemary, sage, coriander, black salsify, and wormwood planted nearby repel the flies. They won't lay their eggs in carrots that have been dusted with pulverized wormwood or rock phosphate. The maggot larvae avoid carrots planted with a pinch of used tea leaf in the hole.

Exclusion. Crop covers are effective in preventing damage from carrot rust flies. Put in place at planting time and left there until harvest, they will virtually eliminate damage.

Cut It Out. When all else fails, cut away and discard affected plant parts when harvesting. The remainder is still edible.

Grasshoppers/Locusts

(Family Acrididae)

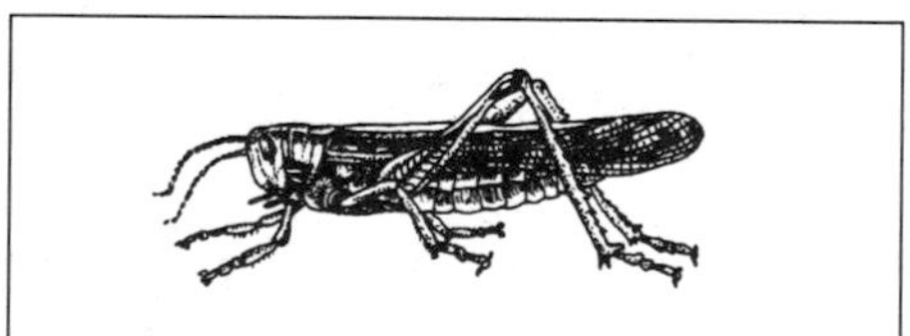

Best known as the plague of dust bowl farmers, grasshoppers are not a major pest to most gardeners. Given the right circumstances, however, their sheer numbers can rattle the reserve of even the best-prepared growers.

Physical Description

Full-grown grasshoppers of some species can top 4 inches in length, but those most likely to find their way into the home garden are barely knee-high to those grasshoppers, usually under 2 inches long. They may be green or various shades of brown. Large jaws and oversized hind legs have won them their two claims to fame — unrelenting chewing and spring-loaded jumping.

Life Cycle

Overwintering about 3 inches down in the soil, masses of grasshopper eggs begin to hatch with the first warm spring days. The newly hatched nymphs begin feeding and within forty to sixty days blossom into reproductive adulthood. Females can lay up to 400 eggs each and continue feeding until finished off by cold weather. Most species produce one generation each year.

Habits

Famous for swarming in hordes during drought, the masses that appear are triggered by the optimum hatching conditions and the inability of predators to keep up with their sudden numbers. When disturbed, they combine the forces of their powerful hind legs and wings for a quick getaway. They are active during the day.

Range and Habitat

Different species can be found throughout North America. Grasshoppers thrive in areas with long, hot summers and are legendary for their outbreaks in the Midwest. They are most common in dry areas — those averaging from 10 to 30 inches of rainfall a year. Before they make it to garden sites, they infest overgrown grassy or weedy areas such as roadsides, ditches, or fencerows. Solid, unworked ground is preferred for egg-laying.

Garden Targets

Grasshoppers prefer grasses, clovers, and some weeds to garden vegetables, but when faced with famine will gratefully digest whatever you have to offer.

Damage and Signs

Leaves and stems can be stripped if sufficient numbers are present.

Deterrents

Grasshoppers in the egg and nymph stages are highly susceptible to weather fluctuations. An early warm spell followed by cold can coax the eggs into hatching prematurely and then retard or kill the immature nymphs. Wet and cold weather hampers hatching and nymph development and fosters disease.

Cultural Practices. Fall tilling exposes eggs to weather and predators, and the turned earth discourages further egg-laying. Freeing the garden and surrounding areas of weeds and grasses further reduces available egg-laying sites.

Exclusion. Crop covers will protect plants from grasshoppers.

Bio-control. All stages of grasshoppers are vulnerable to predators and parasites. Many birds, and animals from cats to skunks to coyotes, will pounce on them. Snakes, toads, spiders, mantises, and rodents will eat 'hoppers; some will even excavate for the underground egg clusters. Red mites and nematodes parasitize the eggs, while ground beetles, blister beetles, and bee flies lay their own eggs with those of the grasshoppers as a handy food source for their hatching larvae. *Nosema locustae*, a commercially available parasitic protozoa, will kill up to 50 percent of the available grasshopper population within four weeks of application. Currently, viral control agents, such as Entomopox, are being tested. This one offers a 50 percent kill rate within as few as ten days.

Traps. Clover and ryegrass make appealing trap crops, which may be combined with a contraption called a "hopperdozer" to catch multitudes of 'hoppers. Make your own by attaching wooden strips for runners to the bottom of a large pan and adding a backboard of aluminum sheeting to one end of the pan. Fill the pan with water and a little kerosene and drag it across the infested areas. Disturbed grasshoppers spring up and either land

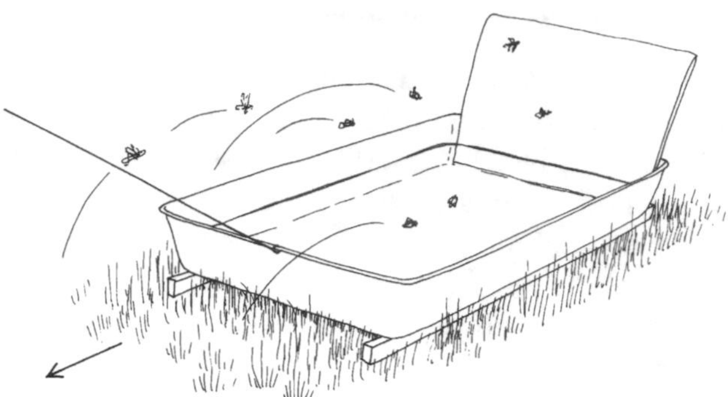

The hopperdozer is dragged through grasshopper-infested gardens.

in the pan or ricochet into it from the backboard. Repeat often and destroy your catch.

Another trap involves setting several large jars of water and molasses around the garden. Drawn to the sweet stuff, 'hoppers that enter don't exit.

Sprays and Dusts. Add grasshoppers to the list of those repelled by hot pepper sprays.

Leafhoppers

(Family Cicadellidae)

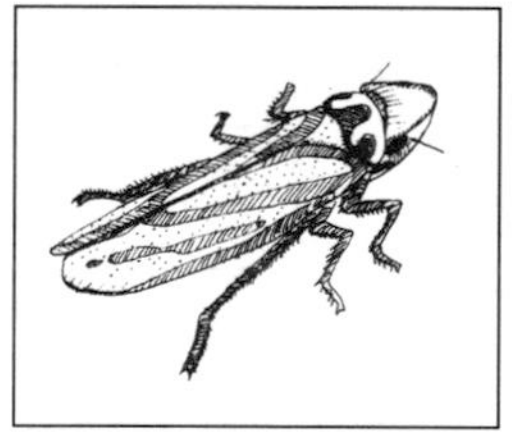

Frequently the most serious damage from these fancy-looking bugs is caused by the two diseases they spread, curly top and aster yellows.

There are many varieties of leafhoppers, the more common garden pests being the aster (six-spotted) leafhopper, the beet leafhopper (*Circulifer tenellus*), the potato leafhopper (*Empoasca fabae*), and the red-banded leafhopper (*Graphocephala coccinea*).

Physical Description

Shaped like a tiny wedge, most species don't exceed ⅕ inch long. Aster leafhoppers sport six black spots over greenish yellow, beet leafhoppers lack the spots, potato leafhoppers are light green with white spots, and the fhashy red-banded leafhopper displays bright red, green, and blue markings. Nymphs are usually a smaller, paler version of the adults.

Life Cycle

Hibernating adults spend winter among weeds or in garden debris. They often lay eggs within the veins or stems of host plants. Most species produce several generations per year, each living only a few weeks.

Habits

Leafhoppers feed by puncturing plant tissues and sucking out vital juices, usually from the underside of

Range and Habitat

Various species of leafhoppers are found throughout North America. Most prefer dry, sunny, open areas.

leaves. In the process they transmit plant diseases.

Population booms can occur quickly as adults migrate in from the South, traveling on the prevailing winds. They fly off suddenly when disturbed, while nymphs scuttle away in a sideways "crabwalk."

Garden Targets

Beans, beets, potatoes, tomatoes, eggplant, vine crops, rhubarb, celery, and other vegetables; some flowers, including asters and dahlias; and many weeds are all favorites.

Damage and Signs

Many plants withstand a great deal of leafhopper feeding without showing any significant signs of injury. However, saliva injected while feeding is toxic to plants and with heavy infestations can cause stunting and discolored leaves. Hopperburn or tipburn caused by potato leafhoppers affects potatoes, beans, eggplant, and rhubarb. Edges of leaves curl up, turn yellow or brown, and die, reducing the plant's ability to photosynthesize. Serious infestations can reduce yields.

Some of the worst plant damage caused by leafhoppers is secondhand, caused by the diseases these bugs spread, aster yellows and curly top. Both can cause serious crop losses, manifesting differently in different plants. Aster yellows, *Chlorogenus callistephi*, affects many hosts, including carrots, celery, cucurbits, endive, New Zealand spinach, potatoes, onions, strawberries, and tomatoes, as well as many annual and perennial ornamentals and weeds. Affected plants commonly crack and yellow, with the veins turning clear and plants developing uncharacteristic or distorted stems, leaves, and roots. Carrots grow short, thick, hairy, and discolored. Lettuce pales. Tomato and potato leaves roll, while stunted celery stalks twist.

Curly top, *Ruga varrucosans*, also called Western yellow blight, is limited to the western United States, unlike aster yellows, which is prevalent throughout the United States and southern Canada. Among the many plants affected are beans, beets, carrots, celery, crucifers, cucurbits, New Zealand spinach, Swiss chard, and many ornamental plants. Symptoms depend on the plants affected, but thick, curling leaves and characteristic plant yellowing in tomatoes give this ailment its common names. Beet veins turn clear, then leaves curl up, yellow, wilt, and die. Abnormal root growth is common. Growing tips on cucurbits darken and turn up, while older leaves yellow. Other plants also show discoloration and curling of leaves.

Deterrents

Cultural Practices. When practical, plant in sheltered areas away from weeds. Shading and crowding plants close together reduce light and increase moisture, conditions leafhoppers avoid. Leafhoppers dislike perennial grasses, so these can be maintained near susceptible crops. Petunias and geraniums also repel them. Providing windbreaks (try interplanting with corn or sunflowers) makes it harder for the windblown hoppers to light on protected plants. Remove affected plants and keep the garden area free of weeds and debris. Experiment with resistant varieties such as Delus potatoes and Roza, Columbian, Rowpac, and Saladmaster tomatoes.

Exclusion. Crop covers are as close to a sure thing as you can get in dealing with these pests. Apply at planting or transplant time and leave on until plants flower. You may wish to re-cover plants after they are pollinated in times of heavy infestations. Remove any hoppers before putting the covers back.

Bio-control. Predators include some wasps and flies as well as big-eyed bugs and lacewing larvae.

Traps. Black light traps will draw and destroy adults.

Sprays and Dusts. Some types of leafhoppers can be repelled or killed with soap sprays. Diatomaceous earth helps cut down numbers, and either rotenone, pyrethrum, or a combination product will control them.

Leaf Miners

(Liriomyza spp.)

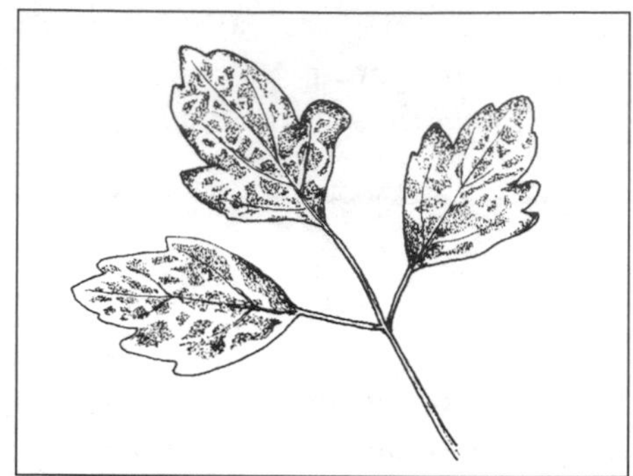

Several species exist to pester the home gardener. Probably the most familiar is the spinach leaf miner, *Pegomya hyoscyami*.

Physical Description

Adults are small flies, about half as big as a housefly. They are hairy and black with yellow markings. The troublesome miner larvae are miniature plump green maggots.

Life Cycle

Overwintering underground as pupae, flies begin to hatch in the spring. They lay more tiny, white, oval eggs in clusters on the underside of leaves. Hatching within days into larval "miners," they feed for two or three weeks before dropping to the ground to pupate. Several generations are produced during the growing season.

Habits

The miners burrow between the surfaces of leaves almost immediately upon hatching and proceed to "mine"

Range and Habitat

Leaf miners infest target crops throughout North America.

the middle layer. This makes them unaffected by insecticides.

Garden Targets

Spinach leaf miners go for spinach like Popeye, but will also ruin chard, beets, and lamb's-quarters. Other miner species violate blueberries, blackberries, potatoes, peppers, and cabbage, as well as some flowers, including columbine, roses, nasturtiums, and chrysanthemums.

Damage and Signs

The miners eat out tunnels inside the leaves. The tunnels show as random squiggly lines or blotches and may result in yellowing foliage.

Deterrents

Cultural Practices. The most effective defense against leaf miners is to cover susceptible crops. Rotate crops to avoid the leaf miners emerging from the soil. Early plantings may avoid damage. Fall tilling will destroy pupae. Crush any eggs found on leaves. Cut and burn any infested leaves.

Sprays and Dusts. Soap and hot pepper sprays are effective against some varieties. Soak chopped rhubarb leaves in water with a touch of liquid soap for a few days, then strain. This makes an effective spray. Sabadilla dust will kill miners, but nothing affects them once they dig in. Sprays must be applied before or while the eggs begin to hatch to kill the larvae as they emerge. Timing is critical.

Mites

Spider Mites

(Class Arachnida)

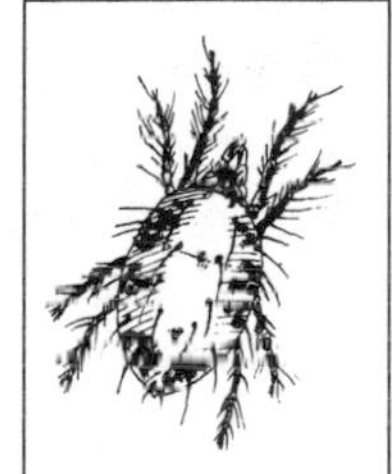

These tiniest of garden wildlife are not insects, but are miniature cousins to spiders and scorpions. Red spider mites and two-spotted spider mites are the most likely garden pests.

Physical Description

Mites are barely noticeable specks, about the size of a grain of salt. Their color apparently varies according to their diet, from red to yellow to green. Through a magnifying glass eight pairs of legs are seen, but not wings or antennae.

Life Cycle

Adults hibernate through the winter under garden trash. They arise to lay eggs in the spring and warmer months. These hatch in about three days, and the young mites reach maturity within a week. With a life of only days, scores of generations come and go each season.

Range and Habitat

Found throughout North America, spider mites thrive in hot, dry areas.

Habits

Like their cousins, spider mites spin fine, silky webs. These are not fancy to look at and are strictly for defense. Though the flimsy webs cause no physical damage to plants, they can spoil the appearance of flowers.

Spider mites feed by piercing leaf tissue and sucking up the plant fluids.

Garden Targets

Strawberries, melons, beans, corn, tomatoes, eggplant, flowers, and other garden plants suit spider mites.

Damage and Signs

Leaves turn yellow, first along the veins, then throughout. Foliage wilts and the plant's health declines. To identify mites as the cause of these problems requires some detective work with a magnifying glass. Angelhair-like webs found clinging to leaves and stems mean that mites are around somewhere.

Deterrents

Cultural Practices. Mites are not in the least repelled by marigolds. They love them! *Never* plant marigolds if you have mite trouble. Keep weeds down in the garden area, especially lamb's-quarters, another mite favorite. Onions, garlic, and chives repel them. A blast of cold water from the hose may dislodge them. They dislike both wet and cold conditions, and heavy, moisture-retaining mulches may help by making the area less comfortable for them.

Bio-control. Ladybugs and lacewings both enjoy mite appetizers. One of the most promising means of mite control is a commercially available cannibal, *Amblyseius californicus*, itself a predatory mite.

Sprays and Dusts. It may seem ironic that the more pesticides used on a given plot, the worse the mite problem becomes. This is just another inescapable example of Mother Nature's pesky logic. Such spraying kills off their natural enemies, and with such quick life cycles, the mite populations soon skyrocket.

Soap sprays are effective against them, while not eliminating their natural predators. Many gardeners swear by a buttermilk spray. Mix ½ cup buttermilk with 4 cups wheat flour to 5 gallons of water. Garlic or onion sprays repel them. Alcohol spray, made from 4 parts water, 3 parts rubbing alcohol, and a squirt of dish soap, makes a lethal spray that kills by desiccation. A tea of rhubarb leaves will kill mites. Be sure to coat both sides of leaves when using any sprays.

Nematodes

(Meloidogyne spp.*)*

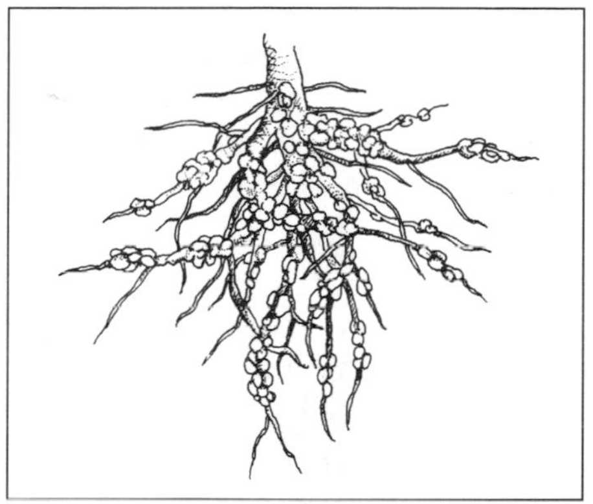

What unseen plague renders soil totally unfit for crops, paves the way for plant diseases, and is so resistant to control that it can survive nearly two years underwater? Did you say nematodes, eelworms, mini-roundworms from the depths? Believe it or not, there are actually some varieties of nematodes that are beneficial in the garden (see chapter 7), but the bad guys discussed here are one of gardening's most frustrating adversaries.

Physical Description

Without a microscope, or at least a magnifying lens, you'll probably never see a nematode, no matter how many of them you have. They are tiny threads of life, as small as ¹⁄₁₂₅ inch long, tapered at both ends. Root-knot nematodes are the most common garden pests, although lesion, lance, and stubby root nematodes are found in some areas. Names suggest the damage they do. In many species, males are considered unnecessary (sorry again guys!). Occasional egg masses can be seen in the soil as small, pearly lumps.

Life Cycle

Adults lay eggs in soil or plant roots. Larvae hatch, feed, and grow into more egg-laying adults. Dormant larvae or eggs overwinter in soil or plant roots.

Habits

Nematodes ruin crops, reproduce, and never leave the underworld.

Garden Targets

More than 2000 plants including strawberries, potatoes, beans, cabbage, lettuce, peas, turnips, carrots, tomatoes, cucumbers, squash, and other garden vegetables are susceptible.

Damage and Signs

Plants are deformed, sometimes chloriotic (yellowed) or dying. Root-knot nematodes cause knobby, grotesque-looking roots resulting in stunted, yellowed, and wilted plants with distorted roots and poor yields.

Range and Habitat

Various species found throughout the United States. Nematodes are most abundant in coarse soils. They are widespread, thanks to contamination by farm machinery moving from place to place and infested drainage water.

Other varieties also affect plant development, health, and yields.

If plants are failing inexplicably, a soil test may expose the culprit. During the growing season take several soil samples from different places around the affected plants' roots, from the surface down to about 6 inches deep. Mix and put about a cupful in a plastic bag to keep it from drying out. Your local nursery or county extension agency can direct you to a testing facility.

A home soil test requires collecting enough samples to fill six planter pots. Keep half in a plastic bag and freeze the other half — and thereby any invading nematodes — for at least three days. Divide the soil. The freezer-treated soil goes into three pots and the plastic bag soil into another three pots. Plant radish seeds in all six and judge their progress. If the freezer-treated dirt samples do noticeably better than the untreated samples, suspect nematodes.

Deterrents

Cultural Practices. Never plant in infested soil if at all possible. Sterilize soil and garden tools (soak tools in bleach water and let dry in sunshine), and work in as much organic matter as possible to help build up parasitic fungi and other predators. Incorporate compost, then grow and till under cover crops. Rotate crops with, or interplant with, those that are immune or resistant, such as marigolds, brassicas, alliums, mustard, cress, rutabaga, and ground cherry for root-knot nematodes; watermelon or hot peppers for sting nematodes; or beets, rutabaga, yams, or radish for meadow nematodes. Cyst nematodes flounder in pH extremes. Two years of immune or resistant crops, or fallow ground, should starve them out.

Repellents. Plants toxic to nematodes include asparagus, hairy indigo, velvet beans, crotalaria, salvia, and calendula. Tilled-under timothy, fescue, or ryegrass release nematode toxins as they decompose. French or African marigolds also release nematode poisons through their roots, but evidence suggests that these are most effective the season after the flowers are grown.

Bio-control. Predators in the soil include other nematodes, as well as fungi and other dirt-dwelling microbes.

Sprays and Dusts. Corn oil mixed with water suffocates nematodes when sprinkled near plant roots, used as a soil drench, or used as a root dip for transplants. A fertilizer of 70 percent fish emulsion and 30 percent yucca extract (Pent-A-Vate) seems to produce plants unappealing to nematode palates.

Clandosan, a soil amendment containing urea and a natural complex of proteins and chitin (a tough, protein-based component that gives the shells of crabs and other arthropods their strength), works by stimulating microorganisms found in the soil. These fungi and other tiny predators destroy the hapless worms.

Root Maggots

(Order Diptera, larval form)

Unfortunately, there is no shortage of subterranean demons at work ruining the very foundation of many garden plants. Root maggots destroy entire plants, or just as infuriating, the cultivated roots. Cabbage maggots *(Hylemya brassicae)* and onion maggots *(Hylemya antiqua)* are but two of several species.

Physical Description

Adults of most species appear similar to houseflies. The onion maggot fly has an odd humpback. The larvae are generally fat, whitish grubs, growing to ⅓ inch long and tapering to a pointy head. Up to 200 tiny white eggs may be laid in the crown or at the base of each host.

Life Cycle

Pupae spend the winter from 1 to 6 inches down in the soil. Flies emerge in spring and begin laying eggs within days. These hatch in three to ten days into the ruinous maggots, which feed for a few weeks before pupating. Two or three generations per year are common; the first causes the most damage in the garden.

Habits

Eggs are laid at the base of hosts. Upon hatching, the larvae begin a downward trend, eating their way through the root systems.

Range and Habitat

Root maggots prosper in moist, cool soil. Various species exist throughout the United States and southern Canada.

Garden Targets

Species abound to mutilate onions, cabbage, broccoli, cauliflower, brussels sprouts, turnips, radishes, and rutabagas.

Damage and Signs

In cabbage and related crops, all may appear well until seedlings suddenly yellow, wilt, and die. This is especially obvious during hot or dry spells. Yank up the victim and you'll find the grubby maggots clinging to the mangled roots. Interfering with germination, seed corn maggots affect many vegetables, including all vine crops.

Root crops may wilt somewhat, but the worst damage is also underground. Scars and tunnels, often further desecrated by rot and disease, mar the root and make it inedible.

Deterrents

Cultural Practices. Start seedlings under protection, in a cold frame or other cover. Cabbage and related plants survive better if given an early start. Onions are susceptible any time, but often sustain the worst damage

early. By interplanting onions throughout the garden, the maggots' lunch route is greatly complicated compared to a nice row or patch in which they can readily proceed from one onion to the next. White onions are the most susceptible, red the least, and yellow are somewhat resistant.

Radishes make good trap crops. Pull and destroy them once infested. Likewise, cull any infested plants and remove crop residues promptly. To protect "eating radishes," try interplanting with extra-hot radish varieties like Black Spanish.

Exclusion. The *most* effective means of controlling maggot damage is excluding the egg-laying flies. Crop covers perform this task admirably with astounding results compared to uncovered plants in the same plot. An old home remedy of placing 4-inch-wide tarpaper collars around each seedling at transplant time also works. The flies don't care for the tarpaper smell and look for other places to deposit their eggs. Cut a small hole in the center of the paper, just large enough to fit the seedling stem through. Slit the collar to fit it around the transplant, and slide into place. These measures also mandate crop rotation, as the pests originate in the soil.

Bio-control. The beneficial nematode *Neoaplectana carpocapsae* destroys cabbage maggots and can remain active in the soil for up to two years.

Sprays and Dusts. Sprinkling wood ashes, rock phosphate, or diatomaceous earth around the base of plants discourages the maggots. Oldtimers insist that improper lime content of the soil invites infestations and recommend a limewater drench. Soak 2 pounds of lime in 5 gallons of water for at least twenty-four hours, making sure the lime has settled to the bottom of the bucket. Pour off the clear water and use it to soak the soil at the base of target plants. A mulch of oak leaves is said to serve the same purpose.

A tarpaper plant collar should fit snugly around the stem.

Thrips

(Family Thripidae)

Never a single thrip, even if they did come that way, the word *thrips* is both plural and singular. These pests are often most obvious by their presence rather than by actual damage. Of the many varieties home gardeners face, onion thrips, flower thrips, and gladiolus thrips are among the most common.

Physical Description

Without a magnifying glass thrips are identifiable as throngs of tiny crawling spots before your eyes. Magnified, they are elongated, slim insects with double wings decorated with fancy fringe. No more than 1⁄16 inch long, they range in color from yellowish to near black. Larvae are smaller than adults, wingless, and pale yellow to white.

Range and Habitat

Seeking the security of close quarters, thrips seek places where plant leaves fit snugly together, such as the overlapping petals at the base of blossoms or inside cabbage heads. Various species exist throughout the United States and southern Canada.

Life Cycle

Of the 600 species of thrips found in North America, some lay eggs and some reproduce without male fertilization (parthenogenetic reproduction). Those that lay eggs may pierce stem tissue or hide them in crevices or folds. Eggs hatch into nymphs that look like miniature wingless adults. These develop into mature adults by passing through a cocooned pupal stage. Several generations, living but a few weeks, occur per year.

Habits

Thrips are gregarious, living and feeding in large groups. They are quick and constantly on the go. They feed by scraping plant tissues and slurping up the seeping fluids.

Garden Targets

Hosts include onions, beans, peas, carrots, tomatoes, potatoes, cucumbers, squash, and other garden vegetables and many flowers, especially gladioli and roses.

Damage and Signs

Affected leaves develop silvery spots or streaks from the drained surface cells. These are often punctuated with tiny dark spots of excrement. Serious damage can lead to wilting or rot, and very young plants may die.

Flower buds either turn brown or unfold into deformed, browned blossoms. Onions may become stunted as leaves die back. The necks swell and bulbs fail to fill out. Cabbage leaves are pitted and may develop dark patches.

Deterrents

Cultural Practices. Remove weeds and grass around the garden to eliminate alternate hosts. Immediately destroy any infested blossoms.

Foil collars and mulch, extending past the plant by at least a foot on all sides, are reported to work for low-growing plants. For those over 2 feet tall try foil-covered panels, suspended by stakes between plants or from branches, to foil the thrips traveling from one plant to the next.

Spanish-variety onions are more resistant than others. Also, Blueboy, King Cole, Early Jersey Wakefield, and Danish Ballhead cabbage offer some resistance. Gladiolus thrips can be eliminated by treating corms to a hot bath (110 to 125 degrees F.) for twenty to thirty minutes before storing for the fall. Corms should be dug and cured in the fall a few weeks before treating, then stored and replanted in early spring.

Sprays and Dusts. Try a blast of cold water to remove thrips from plants. Soap sprays are often very effective. Rotenone, pyrethrum, or diatomaceous earth dusted at the site of damage or around the crowns of onions will help, but shelter-seeking thrips are tough to discourage.

Wasps

Yellow Jackets

***(Vespula* spp.)**

The mere sight or buzz of these or other wasps is enough to send many a gardener running for the house.

Physical Description

Adults are from ½ to 1 inch long with bright yellow and black, or white and black patterned bands decorating the abdomen. Wings are transparent and folded back when not in flight. The "stinger" is actually a modified *ovipositer* (egg-laying apparatus) of the sterile female worker. It is sheathed within the abdomen until the worst possible moment.

Queens are twice as big as workers and males (drones) are also huskier than the working-class females. Eggs and larvae remain concealed in paper-like cells in the nest until they emerge as adults.

Range and Habitat

Found throughout North America, yellow jackets nest inground, often preferring open grassy areas or the edge of woods.

Life Cycle

Yellow jackets, as other wasps, have annual nests. The only member to overwinter is the new queen, which emerges just before winter. She mates and then looks for a sheltered spot to spend the cold months of hibernation. In the spring, queens emerge to feed and establish a new colony. Once inside, they rarely if ever leave.

The queen builds a few paper cells (the first and last menial task of her life), deposits eggs, and cares for the larvae for eighteen to twenty days, at which point they pupate and she rests. When these first adults emerge, they take over the housework and baby-sitting, freeing the queen to concen-

trate solely on her job as the royal egg-layer.

The colony grows (some species, such as *Paravespula germanica*, into the many thousands), peaking in population in late summer, and then begins to decline. Males and fertile females emerge from the paper cells instead of workers. Larvae are abandoned or even eaten. After mating, the males die and the new queens fly off in search of a winter home.

Habits

The most famous and fearsome aspect of the yellow jacket is the furious attack it makes in defense of its nest. Unlike a honeybee, who can sting but

Avoiding Run-ins with Yellow Jackets

Yellow jackets will usually not attack unless provoked. (Heard that one before?) The problem is, we never seem to know what we're doing to provoke them. In an effort to avoid starting it when out and about in yellow jacket season, observe the following survival tips:

1. Be on the lookout for nests and stay away!
2. Don't wear scent lures, such as perfumes, suntan lotions, floral soap residues, and hair sprays.
3. Avoid light blue or yellow (or other bright colors, just in case) clothing. Stick to beekeeper white or dull beige.
4. Try to fit garden work or other chores into early morning or evening when yellow jackets are less active.
5. If cooking or eating outdoors, set out a piece of fresh liver, ham, or sweets *away* from your area. Yellow jackets look for protein (meat), sugar (sweets), or water. Let them find it elsewhere.
6. Keep all garbage cans securely covered with tight-fitting lids.
7. Be aware that during hot, dry weather they may congregate around water. Tighten any outside dripping faucets or hose connections.
8. Stay calm if yellow jackets are near (or on) you. Don't run or swing at them, as this makes them testy. They seem to be able to sense panic.

If stung, treat the sting with a paste of meat tenderizer and keep a cold compress over the sting. Antihistamines, aspirin, or acetometaphine may help symptoms. If possible, elevate the sting site and stay still for an hour or more. Some people develop allergic reactions, which require immediate medical attention.

once, this wasp does not loose its stinger once it penetrates a victim. It can, and does, sting repeatedly.

Nests are constructed underground or within cavities such as walls or hollow trees. Even when hidden out of sight, they are built the same way: cells of chewed wood pulp connected into combs and surrounded by an envelope of "paper," with just one opening.

If you approach too near, you may get a warning as a worker charges, headlong and fast. Quick motions such as panicked running and arm flailing, especially when accompanied by screams, only agitate them.

Yellow jackets become more active and many believe more aggressive on hot, sunny days, and toward the end of summer when they are hungry and facing the bitter end of their way of life.

Their one weak point is that they don't see well in the dark. Nearly all of them return to the nest for the night.

Garden Targets

Adults lap up pollen and nectar and prey on garden insects. They will chew up sweet ripe fruit such as strawberries, blueberries, tree fruit, melons, and other fruits and berries. Perhaps the most notable target is gardeners themselves. The presence of yellow jackets makes harvesting a tricky job.

Damage and Signs

Sure signs are holes in ripe fruit, and one heckuva pain in your arm, or leg, or whichever limb gets in the way.

Deterrents

Live and Let Live. Even if you choose to *try* to eradicate the wasps, it is still in your best interest to understand the basics of peaceful coexistence.

Traps. Build this effective trap: Tie a slice of melon, fresh fish, or meat to a stick and suspend it over a 5-gallon bucket (a blue one is most attractive to the wasps) partially filled with water and a squirt of dish soap. Workers flock to the bait, gorge themselves, and plunk!, hit the water too full to float. The soap prevents them from treading water by breaking the surface tension. Place this trap away from people and protect meat lures with netting or by constructing a protective cage, or erect a tripod to raise the bait out of reach of any competing dogs, cats, or other animals.

Queens emerging in early spring can be caught in a shallow pan half filled with sugar water and just a drop of liquid soap. Use a blue or yellow pan if possible. The sweet lure attracts the hungry queens into the water and the soap makes it almost impossible to escape. Every queen trapped eliminates an entire future nest.

Destroying Nests. Underground nests can be eradicated by pouring in gasoline or rotenone, then covering the entrance hole. Work after dark and move swiftly.

Mother Nature will do the dirty work if you ask sweetly. Pile a mound of sweet molasses horsefeed, suet, or other tasty treat near the entrance

hole. Hungry skunks, opossums, or other night marauders will excavate your problem for you.

Elimination of aerial nests calls for chemical or even professional help. *Don't try to knock it down.* They will object! Even if you succeed, they will only rebuild and be all the more fierce in their defense.

Weevils

(Order Coleoptera)

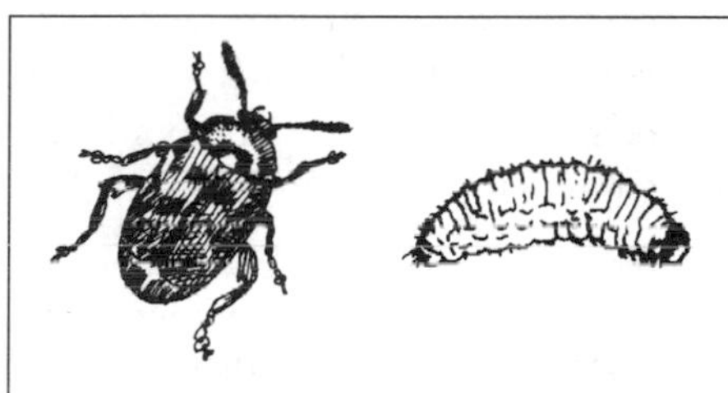

Though they are comical looking, an infestation of weevils, or curculios as some types are called, is no laughing matter. Many species exist to bedevil the home gardener, and most can be very frustrating to control organically. Bean weevils *(Acanthoscelides obtectus)*, cabbage curculio *(Ceutorchynchus rapae)*, carrot weevils *(Listronotus oregonensis)*, and vegetable weevils *(Listroderes costirostris obliquus)* are but a few of the many destructive pests at large.

Physical Description

Weevils are a form of beetle. Most are under ½ inch long and have hard wing covers. Garden varieties are usually dull colored, ranging from gray or brown to dark green. A distinctive snout, exaggerated and curved in the cabbage curculio, bears the mouthparts at the tip and a pair of antennae about halfway down.

Bean weevils are very tiny, ⅒ to ⅕ inch long, and come in shades of brown or dark camouflage green. The larvae are fat, whitish grubs. Cabbage curculios have the typical long, curved beak and are black with downy yellow hairs covering all ⅛ inch of their bodies. Carrot weevils reach a size of ⅕ inch, are dark brown to bronze colored, and have tough, hard wing covers. The larvae are dingy white with a brown head and no legs. They grow to about ⅓ inch in length. Vegetable weevils are dull grayish brown, marked with a V on the back. They grow to ½ inch long. The greenish creeping larvae resemble little slugs and will eat their way to ¼ inch long.

Eggs of most types of weevils are either gray or white and usually oval shaped. Often they are deposited in punctures or slits in plant tissue, making them difficult to find.

Life Cycle

Most weevils produce just one or two generations per year. Bean weevils may reproduce nonstop when present in stored beans. Outside, they overwinter as adults under garden debris. They emerge in late spring to lay eggs on beans. As these hatch the larvae crawl into the beans, where they feed until they pupate and finally emerge as adults.

Range and Habitat

Fields, gardens, woods — you name it and weevils can be found there. Various species are found throughout North America.

Cabbage curculio produce several generations each season. Adults winter in the soil, then emerge in the spring to deposit eggs inside the stalks and stems of the host plants.

Carrot weevils usually have two generations per year. Adults spend winter in garden debris or nearby in grassy or weedy areas. They lay their eggs in the crowns or carrots in the spring, and the grubs hatch to tunnel down into the roots of the host.

Vegetable weevils produce one batch per year. Adults emerge from their winter hiding places beneath garden trash or weed patches and lay their eggs on plant stems or in the crowns of host plants. The larvae begin feeding on foliage as soon as they hatch.

Habits

Bean weevils infest stored beans and may contaminate the next crop in so doing. They leave the seeds riddled with holes as the adults emerge from within the beans. Cabbage curculios enter stalks to feed and chomp on leaves as well. Carrot weevils burrow into the tops of host plants, leaving a wiggly tunnel behind them. They walk from their wintering places to their host plants, and therefore do not wander far from their place of origin. Vegetable weevils will chew their hosts down to the bare stems. The adults can be very damaging, but the larvae are by far the worst pests.

Garden Targets

Many weevils attack fruit trees, cotton, rhubarb, and various vegetables. The bean weevils infest both beans and peas. Cabbage curculios feed on broccoli, cauliflower, cabbage, and turnips, but will settle for other related crops if these are not available. Carrot weevils attack carrots, dill, celery, parsley, and parsnips. Vegetable weevils are pests of lettuce, spinach, carrots, beets, radishes, turnips, tomatoes, potatoes, onions, and cabbage.

Damage and Signs

Bean weevils leave hollowed-out bean shells, with holes in them where the adults make their exits. Cabbage curculios feed within the stalks, so little damage is seen. Carrot weevils damage the roots or hearts of crops with their tunneling. Often damage is not evident until harvest. Plants may wilt and die with serious infestations. Vegetable weevils may eat away at leaves until only bare stems remain.

Deterrents

Cultural Practices. Crop rotation is effective against carrot weevils because they don't travel far from their

place of origin. Cultivation may help eliminate hibernating adults.

To eliminate bean weevil infestations in harvested beans, dry the seeds thoroughly, then freeze for at least forty-eight hours. This prevents adults from laying eggs. Another tactic is to cure the harvested beans by heating them to 135 degrees F. for three or four hours, or by hanging bean plants up to dry, intact, for six weeks or so.

Bio-control. Parasitic nematodes will control any ground-level infestations of root weevils (soil-dwelling, root-eating weevils) or other weevils that come in contact with the ground.

Sprays and Dusts. Dusting with diatomaceous earth will deter vegetable weevils, or cabbage curculios before they enter stalks.

Whiteflies

(Trialeurodes vaporariorum)

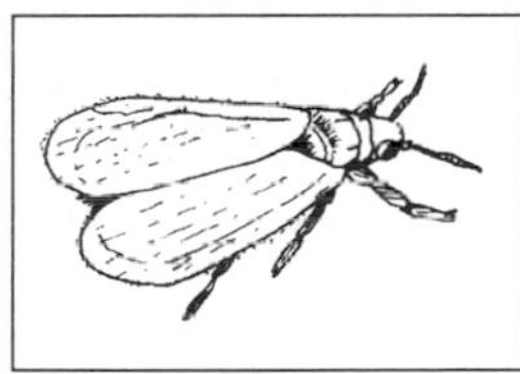

You may not even know they are there until you brush against a plant and suddenly a cloud of flying dandruff arises. Indoors or out, whiteflies can be a persistent presence, but unless populations are enormous, their damage usually is not.

Physical Description

Adults are very small, mothlike flies, from 1/20 to 1/10 inch long. Milk white, they are covered with a waxy powder. There are several stages of nymphs, the first and most active feeders appearing as greenish white, six-legged specks. Tiny eggs (1/100 inch) are yellowish when laid, fading to gray, and left attached to the underside of leaves.

Range and Habitat

These pests are most common in warm, sheltered areas, indoors or in greenhouses. Found worldwide, they will inhabit gardens in the southern United States year-round, or claim northern territories for the summer as they are introduced via infested nursery transplants.

Life Cycle

Winters are spent as nymphs. Adults feed and lay eggs on the bottom side of leaves; these hatch within a week. During the next two weeks several instars follow, each becoming less active, until finally they enter a pupalike state. Ten days later, adults emerge. Their life cycle takes about a month, with many generations occurring each year.

Habits

Nearly constant greenhouse occupants, whiteflies move in as the fall temperatures drop. They're also prevalent in outdoor gardens. Both nymphs and adults feed on tender growth, sucking out plant juices. They

congregate in thick crowds on the undersides of leaves and flutter like tiny snowflakes when disturbed. Whiteflies in all stages produce a sugary honeydew.

Garden Targets

Almost everything in the garden is subject to whitefly attack. Plants deficient in magnesium and phosphorous seem especially vulnerable.

Damage and Signs

Feeding weakens plants, which may turn yellow and dry, and may even die. Fungal growths often accompany the honeydew secretions and contribute to sickening the host.

Deterrents

Cultural Practices. Check nursery transplants thoroughly for pests. Nasturtiums, marigolds, and nicandra will help repel whiteflies, while catnip draws hordes of them and makes a fine perennial trap crop.

Bio-control. One parasite, *Encarsia formosa*, attacks the larval stages of whiteflies. It is native to the United States and Canada, and is available commercially. Lacewings and ladybugs also wolf them down.

Traps. Traps made from bright yellow boards (safety yellow) covered with a sticky coating (Tanglefoot, etc.) will attract and catch loads of whiteflies. Place the traps at plant level, either in the garden or greenhouse.

Sprays and Dusts. The many sprays to try range from a blast of plain water to the more extreme. Soap sprays will kill whiteflies. A mix of 4 parts water to 3 parts rubbing alcohol, plus a squirt of liquid soap, can be used to mist plants, indoors or out. This will desiccate these pests as well as many others. Wettable sulfur, at the rate of 1 tablespoon per gallon of water, with a few drops of liquid soap, is highly effective, but exposure to sulfur may carry health risks for humans.

Wireworms

(Family Elateridae)

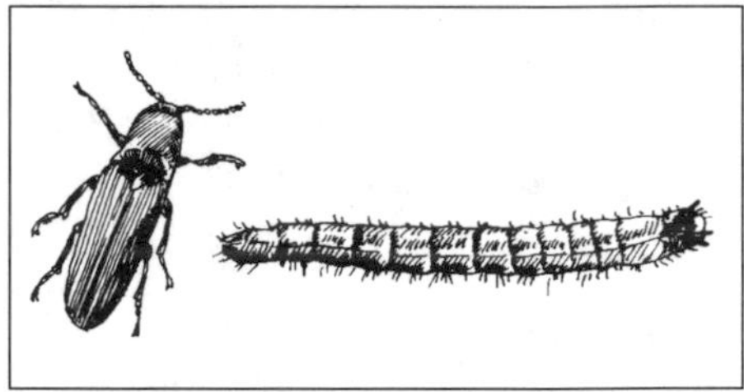

Perhaps one of the most underrated of garden pests, wireworms are often not fully blamed for the damage they do. Several species haunt the underground realm.

Physical Description

Adults, commonly called click beetles, are about ⅝ inch long, murky dark beetles with broad stripes on the wing covers. The larvae, wireworms, have hard, shell-like jointed skins that may be yellow to dark reddish brown. Some grow as long as 1½ inches. They are distinguishable by three sets of legs attached just behind the head.

Life Cycle

Adults, larvae, and eggs are present throughout the season. Larvae emerge from eggs laid under the soil surface and feed for two to six *years*, depending on the species, before pupating one autumn to transform into the adult click beetle the following spring.

Habits

An adult beetle can right itself if overturned by flinging itself with all its might into flips, until it happens to land right side up. The flip causes the beetle to strike the ground with a loud click. It usually takes many tries before that perfect belly-flop landing is achieved, hence the name click beetle; he might even be dubbed click click click beetle.

Wireworms chew on germinating seeds and underground plant parts throughout their larval period.

Garden Targets

Dinner may include seedlings of corn, beans, and peas; tubers of potatoes, sweet potatoes, carrots, rutabagas, radishes, and turnip; and the roots of cabbages, cucumbers, tomatoes, onions, watermelons, and others.

Damage and Signs

Attacks on germinating seeds destroy the young plants. Crops with root damage are less vigorous, less productive, and may wilt or ultimately die. Damage to root crops results in gnawed produce that is subject to disease.

Range and Habitat

Wireworms are often more of a problem in garden plots converted from sod within the previous two years and in soils with poor drainage.

Deterrents

Cultural Practices. Till the soil several times in the fall and if necessary leave the ground *totally* bare (this means weeds, too) for a season. Working in organic matter or even sand to improve drainage is helpful. Cover crops such as clover, alfalfa, or buckwheat are highly recommended.

Buckwheat and white mustard are unpleasant to wireworms, making them good repellent plants to mix with other crops.

Bio-control. The commercially available beneficial nematodes *Heterorhabditis heliothidis* and *Neoplectana carpocapsae* attack and destroy these as well as other soil-dwelling pests.

Traps. Traps made by burying a chunk of potato or a handful of sprouts a few inches under the soil and covering with an old board will draw a crowd of wireworms. Set several out, a few feet apart in the garden. Every few days dig them up and destroy the worms.

Chapter 7

Getting Help: Acquiring and Managing Beneficials

Look around any natural garden — that is, any ecosystem undisturbed by human intervention — and what do you see? Are all the plants devastated by insect infestations? Are gophers the only surviving life forms? With the exception of climatic extremes such as deserts and arctic glaciers, wouldn't you expect to see a variety of life, from plants to insects, birds and animals, coexisting?

The answers are, "no," "of course not," and "well, I certainly hope so!" Nature works in harmony with itself. The food chain follows a hierarchy: plants, plant eaters, and finally, plant-eater eaters. If one category is troubled the whole system is affected. Not enough plants and the plant eaters starve; not enough plant eaters and the plant-eater eaters go hungry; not enough plant-eater eaters and the populations of plant eaters expand until they eat up all the plants. A simple, yet easily disrupted balance.

So it is in your garden. By now you may have come to realize that you are not the only plant eater involved. There are plenty of others eager to get their share. So what is the solution? How does nature handle the problem? Of course. Plant-eater eaters!

Unless your garden has been saturated with poisonous chemicals, chances are good that at any given moment scores of plant-eater eaters, or predators, are at work. Cats are catching mice, birds are devouring fat caterpillars, ladybugs are gobbling up aphids, and lacewings are munching on a variety of bugs. One of the best

things you can do for your garden is to encourage this natural system of things. You can even help nature along by introducing predators into the garden.

Whether you are interested in sustaining existing predators or in introducing new species, three fundamental requirements common to all must be provided: shelter, food, and water. Without adequate supplies of any of these your predators will be forced to move away in search of them, perhaps to your neighbor's garden. This is especially critical when attempting to establish new species into your garden, as they will immediately fan out in search of these things.

As you may have guessed, it is your job to supply the shelter and water for your invited guests and on occasion, even supplement their diets. You must also tolerate a sustaining level of their main food supply — plant eaters — to keep those predator populations going. To eliminate all the troublesome critters in your garden would be to wipe out all the beneficial ones as well. The goal is to create a balance, with you designing and manipulating the food chain.

Some critters that are, for the most part, beneficial may also pose a threat to certain garden crops. Birds are an example. Often tender seedlings or berries will look just as appealing to them as those fat, juicy caterpillars. In cases such as this, don't abandon the idea of letting nature's system work for you. By adapting some of the management techniques described in this chapter, you can take advantage of predators without letting them take advantage of you.

For the Birds

Birdwatching and attracting birds to the home garden have long been intriguing pastimes throughout the world. From the comical antics of chickadees and nuthatches to the grandeur of a soaring eagle, there is something in the carefree wildness of birds that seldom escapes the notice of even the most jaded onlooker. They are, after all, free and unhindered by any artificial designs.

Aside from the pleasantries of admiring wild birds in their natural state, there is one decidedly practical motive for enticing them into the garden: they eat bugs. Some birds have diets that consist almost exclusively of insects, and others partake of weed seeds as well as bugs. Of course many have varied diets that include fruits, seeds, and greens as well as bugs. All it takes is a modest amount of observation time to discover which birds are your friends and which are not.

Friend or Foe?

Even if you don't have a lot of time to spend watching the birds around your garden, just a glance may identify the dietary needs of many birds. Essential in determining any bird's diet is the

equipment he has for obtaining and consuming food. Talons and a hooked beak, for shredding prey, dictate a diet of meat. Spindly legs and a short, thick conical beak relegate the owner to pecking at seeds. The beaks of most backyard birds reveal their food requirements even if you are unable to identify precisely what kinds of birds they are.

Beak Types Suggest Diet

By categorizing birds according to their beak type you can decide which you might want to encourage to stay on and which you would like to have move on. Four kinds of beaks most often pertain to the bug-eating birds that frequent home gardens:

1. Short, wide, gaping beaks are designed for opening and closing quickly. Birds with these are insect eaters that snap up their meals in flight. These include poor-wills, swifts, and nighthawks, as well as a dozen or so species of swallows, such as barn swallows and the ever-popular purple martins.

2. Thin, pointy beaks were made for eating bugs as well. However, the owners of these are more likely to catch their food at ground level, or snatch it from a hiding place. Some birds in this group include warblers, wrens, kinglets and the kingbirds, phoebies, and other flycatchers who also catch their prey in flight. The diets of these birds make them great garden allies.

3. A mid-size, sturdy beak is an all-purpose tool. Birds with this type of hardware eat a more varied diet, indulging in seeds, greens, and fruits as well as bugs. This can work as well for us as against us, as these are the birds most readily attracted to a feeder. Many birds fit into this category including robins, bluebirds, mockingbirds, cuckoos, towhees, chickadees, and elusive ground birds like the bob-

The short, wide beak of birds that feed in flight.

The mid-size, all-purpose beak of birds with varied diets.

The thin, pointy beak of many insect eaters.

The hooked beak of flesh-eating birds.

whites, as well as less welcome blackbirds, grackles, cowbirds, and crows.

4. Hooked beaks belong to the meat-eating birds of prey, the raptors. These include owls and hawks. Though you may not want the larger hunters near your garden, smaller hawks, especially kestrels, warrant a sincere welcome.

Owls are efficient predators. The larger owls are capable of taking on prey as large as woodchucks, small pets, and even geese. The bulk of most owl diets is made up of small rodents, particularly field mice (voles) and shrews, small birds from songbirds to pigeons, and many, many insects, including beetles, grasshoppers, and cutworms. They will eat almost anything active from dusk to dawn that they can manage to grab and carry away.

Home Turf

Your location determines which birds will visit your garden. Birds such as robins or swallows have adapted well to city life while others, such as bluebirds, are strictly country cousins. Geographic location and the type of terrain and native plantlife also prescribe the kinds of birds to be found. Many are native to grasslands, pine forests, or marshes and don't venture far from their preferred habitats. Some birds native to the South are unheard-of in the North, and vice versa. Get to know the birds present in your area and you can plan for those you would like to have help out with the garden chores.

Attracting Birds

A fascinating hobby in its own right, attracting birds to nest in your yard or garden will greatly increase the numbers and types of birds helping to rid the area of harmful bugs. The basic rules are simple: you provide water, a birdbath; supplement the food supply; and provide shelter, in the form of both nesting sites and cover for resting and roosting. In return you will have a garden filled with the heart-lifting melodies of bird song instead of the nearly audible noise of thousands of hungry, plant-munching bugs. Be aware, though, that even with the best of intentions and careful planning, enticing new birds to set up housekeeping in your garden may take a season or two. Mother Nature has endowed many of her favorites with a healthy lack of trust in humans and their surroundings.

Water

The first of the basic requirements for luring birds (or any other wildlife for that matter) to your garden is a water supply. Thirsty or dirty birds will make do with just about any collected puddle when need be, but to provide

a constant water supply is to ensure repeat business and tempt the users to nest nearby. Birdbaths as simple as a shallow pan filled with water or as fancy as a three-tiered fountain complete with a pump to circulate the water are available. Birds are attracted to the sound and sight of moving water. Leaving a garden faucet to drip or a full bucket with a hole dripping into a pan are simple ways of accomplishing this. Of course, some beautiful and elaborate drip fountains are sold to do the same job.

The most important responsibility, once a birdbath is installed, is to keep it filled. With regular use, a pan of water should be cleaned and refilled daily. Birds prefer to use pans placed at ground level to those on a pedestal or platform. A garbage can lid turned over works fine for this, but place a few bathtub stickers on the inside so that the birds don't slip. Ground-level baths should be located in an area free from bird predators such as cats. Keeping water sources away from potential kitty hiding places such as flower borders, iris or other perennial patches, and tall grass will reduce the risk of surprise attacks.

Another point to remember is not to overfill a birdbath. An average depth of 1½ to 2 inches is ideal, with no part being over 3 inches deep. The bath should have a gently sloping bottom with a surface textured to allow for confident footing.

Once you have enticed your friendly helpers to stay with you through the winter, it would be unfair and possibly fatal to deny them a reliable water supply as freezing weather sets in. This means either refilling the water at least once a day or investing in a heating element to prevent the water from freezing.

Feed

Most of the birds that rid your garden of bugs will also need some other source of food to round out their diets or to tide them over when pickin's are scarce. This is never more true than in wintertime. Once a feeding station is established, the well-being of the birds depends on its being thoughtfully maintained.

Feeders are just one alternate source of food to wild birds. Trees, shrubs, bushes, and vines provide berries, fruit, and seeds, more of the birds' natural diet. Many of these will hold their fruit well into the winter when they are needed most. Another benefit of using landscaping to supplement your helpers' meals is that shy birds prefer feeding from a natural source to the competition surrounding a bird feeder. The variety of food and the availability during any given season will, of course, depend on the types of plants in your landscape. Some trees and shrubs are more attractive and sustaining to birds than others.

Some popular landscape plants that appeal to the palate of a variety of birds include seed-offering trees such as alder, elm, birch, maple, pine, fir, and spruce. Mulberry, cherry

(black, choke, and wild), holly, dogwood, hawthorn, flowering crab apple, red cedar, and others produce fruits or berries. Many kinds of shrubs such as blueberry, Asiatic sweetleaf, blackhawk, coralberry, honeysuckle, barberry, juniper, elderberry, winterberry, highbush cranberry, and wild rose also provide fruits. Vines such as wild grape and Virginia creeper are good providers as well.

Diversity in what is offered at the feeder, just as in what may be had from the landscape, will help to lure a variety of birds, some with more of a bug-eating appetite than others.

As a rule, suet (beef fat) appeals to all bug eaters. Suet may be offered in a variety of ways. Place whole chunks in mesh bags, such as those onions and oranges are sold in, or in wire cages made from ½-inch hardware cloth. Either of these can be hung from limbs or attached to trees or feeders

Large pine cones can be filled with suet. Cut the suet into small pieces or force it through a meat grinder, then melt it in a double boiler with a little water. Allow it to cool until hard and then melt it a second time. This makes it easier to work with when filling the cone feeders. It is smoother and harder than raw or once-melted suet. Try pouring suet into molds or adding seeds, nuts, peanut butter, or cornmeal to create your own custom bird feeders to hang wherever they will be most appreciated.

Suet is especially important in the winter diet of birds when the high-energy insect portion of their diets may be temporarily eliminated, even though their bodies' need for it is greater than ever.

Other foods to offer birds at the feeder include sunflower or niger (also called thistle seed) seeds, nuts, peanuts, cracked corn, tablescraps, bread crumbs, and peanut butter. Commercially mixed birdseed often contains a large amount of milo, which is usually scratched aside and either eaten last or not at all. The mixture is also more expensive than mixing your own. When preparing your own bird mix you can gear it to those birds, specifically the bug eaters, that you wish to encourage. Ask your local garden supply outlet what they recommend for birds in your area.

Another essential element in bird diets is grit. Most wild birds must consume a modest amount of grit to grind their food into a size that can be digested. Most birds swallow their food whole, routing it directly to their crop, which stores food and "chews" it by pulsating muscle motion. The particles of grit swirl around inside this tough, muscled chamber, pulverizing the bugs, seeds, and other food. During much of the year, wild birds have no problem picking up grit, but in winter, grit, as well as food and water, may be in short supply. Sprinkling a little chicken grit around the bird feeder or supplying it in a shallow dish provides one more necessity for your feathered helpers. Grit can be as fine as sand or as coarse as tiny pebbles.

Feeders. A well-stocked feeder will invite many birds to the garden. Some are more welcome than others. To bar large birds such as starlings from hogging the food supply, hang the feeder from a branch so that it swings freely. Larger birds find this discomforting while smaller varieties don't seem to mind.

Glassed-in feeders with small entrance holes let smaller birds dine in peace. By offering an alternate meal to bossy ground feeders such as starlings and house sparrows, you may distract them from an elevated feeder. Sprinkle seed or bread crumbs on the ground, away from bird feeders. Another tactic is to remove perches from feeders, since generally only the larger and mostly unwanted birds use them.

Since many hawks prey on small birds, be sure your feeders don't turn into hawks' routine snack stop. Keep feeders in the open, but provide nearby cover so that eating birds don't turn into sitting ducks. Constructing bird feeders with cage-like covers built of large mesh wire will protect the visitors from a variety of would-be predators while allowing others free access.

Squirrels are notorious for their bird feeder raids. They can make a general nuisance of themselves by hoarding or spilling expensive seed or by damaging (or demolishing) the feeder. There are several easy methods to prevent them from getting at feeders.

One common anti-squirrel tactic is to suspend bird feeders from fishing line strung between two points (trees, poles, sides of buildings) that are at least 16 feet apart and 8 feet above the ground. Hang the feeder in the center and thread baffles or tumblers on either side. Empty thread spools, film cartridges, or sections of PVC pipe make good tumblers. Recycle those two-liter pop bottles into baffles by either cutting out the bottom or

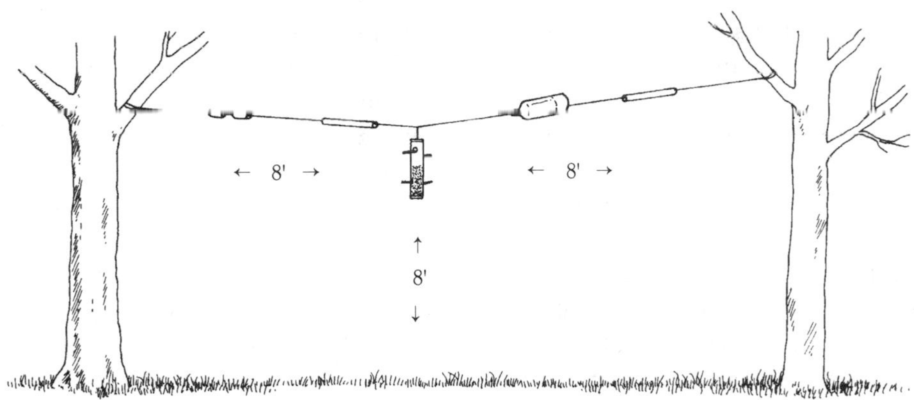

A truly squirrel-proof feeder is suspended at least 8 feet high from 2 points at least 16 feet apart.

threading the line through a prepunched hole. As the acrobatic squirrels attempt a crossing, the spinning tumblers will greatly reduce their chances of succeeding. Be sure that there are no jumping-off points from which the squirrels might launch an aerial attack. They can jump astounding distances, so allow at least 8 feet in any direction, including from the ground.

Other squirrel-foiling devices are designed to keep them from shimmying up a pole or tree trunks. Shaped like large cones, metal baffles are placed about 4 feet up from the base of the pole and prevent the squirrels from climbing up to the bird feeder. Again, make sure there is no alternate route for squirrels to try.

Place feeders in a clear area that offers no hiding places for prowling cats. If a feeder is set out at or near ground level or close to any such ground cover, fence it in with wire mesh 3 feet high to prevent sneak attacks.

Shelter

When not patrolling the garden for bugs or making use of the birdbath or feeders, your feathered garden helpers need a secure place to rest or roost for the night.

Cover. This is the second vital requirement fulfilled by landscape plants. Many plants that offer food also provide shelter. A stand of evergreens protects against wind, rain, and snow as well as predators, and at the same time offers seed-rich cones. Thick or low trees or shrubs afford the next best thing in avian comfort. Barberry, juniper, hawthorn, beech, maple, flowering crab apple, winterberry, highbush cranberry, Virginia creeper, and pasture rose all score high in this area. Privet or other hedgerow plants provide good cover and, if not too religiously trimmed, will grow thick enough to invite birds in, but be careful not to let them grow so thick as to keep birds out.

If you don't have trees or bushes around that may appeal to the birds' natural instinct to take cover, provide a hiding place by building a loose pile of branches and trimmings. Although this is not considered particularly attractive by most humans, birds will appreciate it for the safe haven it offers.

Nesting Sites. Birds also need the right place to build their nests and raise their young. Offering safe, attractive nesting sites is one of the surest ways to keep the birds you want around the garden. Often those that migrate, such as bluebirds and swallows, will return year after year once they have established their nesting territory.

Some of the most attractive nesting plants include thick-growing evergreens, hollies, dogwood, hawthorn, crabapple, mulberry, elderberry, apple, elm, ash, beech, birch, maple, red cedar, arrowwood, highbush cranberry, and winterberry. Many birds nest in hollows of dead trees, so leave old trees to stand whenever possible. These same cavity-nesting birds will often take advantage of birdhouses built to their dimensions.

Birdhouses

Bird	Attractions
Barn swallow	Provide water, and mud and straw for nesting materials. Nail up 6"x6" nesting shelves 8 to 12 feet high, under eaves or other protected areas.
Bluebird	Provide birdbath. Plant berry plants, mulberry, pyracantha, holly, dogwood, blueberry, viburnum, wild cherry, Virginia creeper. Provide 5"x5"x8" birdhouses with 1½" entry holes placed 6" above the floor. Place houses about 5 feet high to discourage sparrows, who prefer higher nesting sites.
Chickadee	Stock the bird feeder with suet, peanut butter, sunflower seeds, bread crumbs. Provide 4"x4"x8" birdhouses with 1⅛" holes 6" above the floor. Place birdhouses 6 to 15 feet high.
Kestrel	Provide 8"x8"x12" to 15" nest boxes, with a 3" hole for entry 9" to 12" above the floor. Secure it 10 to 30 feet above ground.
Kinglet	Will nest in conifers near northern gardens. Likes suet, peanuts, and cracked nuts at the bird feeder.
Mockingbird	Provide birdbath. Supply attractive landscaping, to include blackberry, crab apple, grape, pasture rose, holly, red cedar, pyracantha, cherry, dogwood, elderberry, manzanita, mulberry, privet, serviceberry, and Virginia creeper.
Owl	Prefers large trees, conifers, oak, or shade trees. Leave dead trees, and any with hollows. A grassy area will support prey and attract owls as a hunting site.
Owl, barn	Build nest boxes 10"x18"x15" to 18". Cut a 6" hole 4" from the floor. Secure the boxes 12 to 18 feet above ground.
Owl, saw-whet	Build nest boxes 6"x6"x10" with a 2½" entry 8 inches above the floor. Mount securely 12 to 20 feet above the ground in a quiet area.
Owl, screech	Build nest boxes 8"x8"x12" to 15" with a 3" hole 9" to 12" above the floor. Mount the box securely 10 to 30 feet high in a secluded area.
Phoebe	Erect nesting platforms 6" to 8" square. Put them 8 to 12 feet high, under an eave or similar protected area.

Bird	Attractions
Purple martin	Erect apartment-style houses after the first martins arrive, to discourage starlings. Houses may hold from ten to twenty 6"x6"x6" units. Place the 2½" entry 1 inch from the floor. Mount the house 15 to 20 feet above ground.
Titmouse	Enjoys suet, peanut butter, sunflower seeds, bread crumbs, even doughnuts and nuts. Landscape with elderberry, mulberry, wild strawberry, beech, pine, or oak. Provide 4"x 4"x8" birdhouses with 1¼" entries 6" above the floor. Place them 6 to 15 feet above the ground.
Warbler	Supply attractive landscaping. Mulberry and raspberry are favorite treats, while wild rose, barberry, currant, grapevine, privet hedge, alder, and elder also provide nesting sites.
Wren	Put up 4"x4"x6" birdhouses with 1-inch entries 1" to 6" from the floor. Mount them 6 to 10 feet high.

Birdhouses should be constructed according to the size of their intended occupants and positioned with their habits in mind. Some birds prefer their homes to be elevated. Purple martins also like an apartment setting more than individual birdhouses. Large multicompartment birdhouses, raised up to 20 feet on poles or placed on rooftops, are most attractive to these social swallows.

Other birds construct their nests in forks of trees, along cliffs or ledges, or at or near ground level, and some even *prefer* manmade shelter, such as outbuildings. Some of these conditions can be simulated with nesting shelves, either raised on poles or attached to trees or buildings. Ground nesters need the security of a thick-growing cover or brush pile.

Just as with human house-hunters, location in avian real estate is of prime importance. Birdhouses should be placed in the open but preferably near a windbreak and source of afternoon shade. Obviously you want to keep the birds near the plants that need their attention, and water and any supplemental food supplies should also be close by.

As with artificial birdbaths and feeders, birdhouses require additional human attention after they are put up. They should be cleaned out each fall to prevent an accumulation of filth or parasites. Occasional monitoring also alerts you to invasions by undesirables including house sparrows, starlings, or even wasps. Entrance holes not bigger than 1½ inches across will keep out the chunky starlings and house sparrows while still welcoming bluebirds and other nesters.

A final consideration in attempting to load your bug-plagued garden with feasting birds is that of the natural instinct of some birds to establish and protect exclusive territories. Especially at nesting time, some birds will not tolerate others in their vicinity and may drive them off. Robins, mockingbirds, bluebirds, crested flycatchers, and most other cavity nesters generally require a good deal of space. Starlings are disdainfully noted for running off the meeker, more beneficial birds. While particularly

Birdhouse Basics

While birdhouses are always available in garden centers, making your own has several advantages. First of all it's fun! Some people put a great deal of creative effort into designing and constructing wonderful houses or entire birdhouse towns. More practically, it will invariably be less expensive since you can use scrap lumber or even old wooden boxes for materials. Also, by building your own houses you can tailor them to the needs of the birds you prefer. When making birdhouses there are some simple guidelines to keep in mind.

1. Design the house for the occupant. Dimensions should meet the requirements of the birds for which it is intended.

2. Forget perches. They are more useful to undesirables.

3. Make the birdhouse appear as similar to a natural cavity as possible. Leave the insides rough. When building, consider using wood with bark still attached or hollowing out small logs. If you intend to paint or stain it, stay with subtle, natural shades. Birds will distrust anything that is obviously misplaced in the wild.

4. Drill ventilation holes near the roofline and drainage holes in the floor.

5. Use good hardware. Screws are more secure than nails. Avoid screw eyes for hanging. They loosen with time and could send the house and those in it crashing to the ground.

6. Make sure the roof is waterproof, and extend it over the entry hole for protection against wind and rain.

7. Design the house to be easy to clean. A bottom or side door, either on hinges or pivot screws, will make this necessary fall chore quick and easy.

vulnerable because of the size of entrance holes, purple martin houses can often be spared from the likes of claim-jumping starlings by taking the houses down for the winter and not returning them before the purple martins are sighted in the spring.

Keeping Your Guests in Line

Sometimes even invited guests can wear out their welcome in the garden. To prevent your birdy buddies from causing more problems than they solve, some simple preventative measures can be taken. To protect seeds or seedlings, string a length of fishing line along the row and at random crisscross intervals (see "gotcha lines" illustration p. 11). Individual seedlings can be covered with small cages of hardware cloth, wire mesh, screen, row cover material, or even plastic berry baskets. Other plants, especially fruit trees and berry bushes, may require the protection of bird netting, as explained in chapter 1.

Fair or Fowl?

Imagine a half dozen cackling hens intently going about their business in your garden. They peck, they scratch, they peck some more, and devour every snail, bug, and slug they can catch. They are also so kind as to deposit free samples of nitrogen-rich fertilizer throughout the garden. Sound good so far?

Unfortunately, there are few forces of nature better equipped to totally rearrange a garden than a few busy chickens. The pecking is by no means limited to bugs; they enjoy a tasty salad of tender greens as much as anyone. In fact, they will gleefully strip broccoli and some other plants of foliage until only bare nubs remain. The scratching, their way of unearthing hiding bugs or seeds, is constant. They scratch up seeds, seedlings, flowers, even established plants. Woe be to that nice fresh, fluffy layer of mulch you just put down around the raspberries because, well, the hens thought it would look better in the paths. Chickens also relish a good dust bath, leaving wallowed depressions in your carefully prepared beds.

Ducks such as the breed Muscovy that are not dependent on bodies of water are sometimes recommended as an alternative to chickens. They are not quite as adept at scratching with those webbed toes, but can still dishevel a fair amount of plantlife. Some folks swear by the odd-looking guinea fowl as garden protectors. But one look at their sturdy clawed feet may leave room for doubt as to how tidy they are in their work.

Managing Fowl

So what's the answer? Keep the foul fowl away from the garden and rely on some other means of bug control? Not necessarily. There are three safe, sensible ways to employ barnyard birds in the garden with good results. Four if you count just handing them the bugs

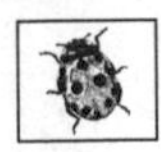

and slugs after you've gone to the trouble to handpick them yourself.

The first method is to put up barriers around the most vulnerable plants. Fences or cages of chicken wire will spare plants from attack. Of course, this also prevents the birds from getting to bugs that stay close to those plants.

Another useful idea is to release your fowl into the garden area first thing in the spring, prior to planting. Give them free rein to excavate any grubs, bugs, and slugs but round them back up in the coop come planting time. Make their job easier and more productive by tilling the soil to expose hiding larvae or pupae.

Lastly, consider designing your garden and bird areas to cooperate with each other. One way of doing this is to place the garden plot and the chicken run side by side, alternating their use each year. This way the hens get a full year to debug and fertilize the plot before it is planted.

An alternate plan is to fence a chicken run permanently alongside or even around the garden plot. This at least allows the birds a chance to nab any stray bugs.

Fly-by-Nights (Bats)

What could possibly be more cuddly and endearing than a bat? If the thought makes you shudder, please consider the following.

Yes, they are ugly, but they only work at night so it's not as if you have to *look* at them. During their shift, each will put away between 150 to 600 noxious flying insects per hour! Most notable on their menus are mosquitoes and the moths (adult forms) of some of the most destructive plant pests, including imported cabbageworms, cutworms, corn earworms, beetles, and many other nocturnal bugs.

They *do not*, despite paranoid folklore, fly at people or wildly entangle themselves in human hair. In fact, all bats, *including* the vampires of the American tropics, avoid *any* sort of close contact with humans. (Vampires, incidentally, do not *suck* blood, but lap it up after puncturing their usually nonhuman victims with their sharp fangs and injecting an anticoagulant that causes the blood to flow freely without clotting.) Many species, however, have adapted nicely to living near human haunts from rural farms to urban attics.

Hoary bats, 5½-inch-long yellowish gray bats with a "frosted" coat; red bats, 4½ inches long and red-brown colored; and several species of mouse-eared *(Myotis)* bats are common in many parts of the country, with the 3½-inch-long brown bat *(Myotis lucifugus)* being the most frequently sighted. They are harmless to humans and animals, as their tiny teeth are barely able even to pierce the skin.

All North American bats hunt insects in flight, often using their membraneous wings as a catchers' mitt, folding it around their victims and retrieving them with their teeth. With

Getting Rid of Unwanted Bats

As beneficial as our bats are, they can be a nuisance in an attic or other inappropriate place. Bright lights or recorded distress calls discourage them from entering to roost or worse yet, congregate, hibernate, or propagate. They gather in large groups, leaving a musty smell, droppings, and a grimy stain wherever they hang or enter. The only way to prevent them from entering is to seal all openings greater than ¼ inch with putty caulking, screen, or metal flashing.

the notable exception of rabies, which afflicts most mammals, they share no diseases directly with humans. *Histoplasmosis*, caused by the fungus *Histoplasma capsulatum*, is passed by spores through contaminated dust. Soils rich in bat and some bird droppings foster thriving colonies of the fungus.

Bats fly and hunt masterfully, even in total darkness, using that wondrous adaptation known as *echolocation*. Similar to sonar, this sensitive system works by using the bat's ability to send out sound waves of up to 48,000 cycles per second and instantly interpret them as they bounce back to him. Bats tend to be set in their foraging habits, following the same pattern and even flying the same path at the same altitude every night.

Encouraging Bats in the Garden

There is little you need to do to encourage area bats to harvest your garden bugs. Most will roost near a water supply in caves, dense trees, or miscellaneous hollows, venturing out less than a mile on their nightly flights.

Due to human interference in caves, many of the bats' natural roosting sites have been eliminated or made unacceptable to the bats. Numerous species live in caves at least part of the year, but without their natural habitat are forced to migrate or eventually die out. In an effort to help survivors adapt, you can put up a bat house and do both man and bat a favor. Sound eccentric? Hardly. The practice has been established in Europe for well over 60 years as a simple, practical solution to both the bats' need for housing and the peoples' need for nocturnal bug control.

Bat Houses

Build your own bat house, as shown in the diagram, of *untreated* 1x10 and 1x12 boards, keeping all rough surfaces on the inside. Cut 1⁄16- to ⅛-inch-wide horizontal grooves along partitions every ½ inch or so to enable the bats to get a secure foothold while roosting. Attach the house securely 10 to 20 feet above the ground to a tree or building so that the entrance

is unobstructed. Bats enter from the opening underneath. Help to maintain the high temperature (around 90 degrees F.) preferred by bats by first sealing all cracks and then positioning the house so that it catches the morning sun. Cover it with dark, heat-retaining shingles and make the house tall enough to allow the bats to move up and down within the structure to find the most comfortable temperature. For complete plans, write to Bat Conservation International, listed in Appendix 4.

Bat houses are available in some mail-order catalogs, nurseries, and garden centers. An outside night-light, mounted at least 20 feet high on a pole or tree, will draw clouds of bugs. Once discovered, this will become a major attraction to the bats in your area.

Interior of a bat house

Rat Patrol

Dogs

Problems with deer, woodchucks, or squirrels? Just tie Ol' Blue out back and he'll run 'em off. Wanna bet?

In the first place, tying up a dog is not only unkind, it is unsafe. Whether you live on a 300-acre farm or a 40'x60' lot, any number of unforeseen things can happen to a tied dog, from strangulation to an attack from another animal (or man). Left this way, he is totally vulnerable and helpless, which brings us to the second problem. The other animals, after a period of time, figure this out. It is not unusual to have deer nibbling just yards away from the end of a tied dog's chain! Wild things survive on smarts, both instinctive and learned, and it doesn't take most long to figure out that, for some reason, the dog can't get to them.

OK, so turn the hound loose. Maybe. But not *in* the garden. Rare is the canine who can resist the sweet smell and rich texture of your freshly turned garden soil. More common is the mutt who gives it a few fresh turns of his own. Perhaps unfortunately for us all, the time is past when neighborhood dogs can be allowed to roam free. Obviously they are not as vulnerable or helpless this way, but they can go out and *look* for trouble instead of waiting for it to come to them!

Ideally, a dog will do the most good as a garden sentry when he has free access to the garden area but not the

garden plants, and is also confined to a safe area. A dog-proof fence around the garden and another outside the first create a dog run around the garden that allows him to take on all comers without taking out the plants.

An alternative to this is to construct a portable kennel and move it to different spots in or around the garden every few days. Savvy as they are, most wild things are still wary enough to find this unpredictable presence something to avoid.

If your dog doesn't present a lethal threat to your crops, you may consider letting him have the free run of the garden every now and then and possibly resorting to plant cages or fencing around individual plants or beds. While this is a lot of trouble to protect plants from the one who is supposed to protect them from something else, bear in mind that once you have your setup in place it will pretty much take care of itself. And Blue doesn't necessarily have to stalk the garden *every* night. On his off nights his scent will linger to challenge any nosy beasts.

A few words of caution regarding garden guard dogs. If your dog is tied, change his location frequently, using a dog chain or vinyl-coated dog tie rather than a chewable rope, and a buckle-type collar. Never tie a dog to a slip (choke-chain type) collar, as he could strangle. And don't allow Ol' Blue free rein to roam. His garden post may soon be abandoned for more adventurous callings, and his safety and your legal liability depend on keeping him in bounds.

Cats

Some gardeners swear by their tabby garden stalkers. True, a good mouser may keep the garden free of rodents and birds (including beneficial birds). But the trade-off is that he will also use the most inconvenient places as his personal litter box, frequently digging up transplants in the process. The freshest earth is always the most inviting. Helpful reptiles and amphibians may also fall prey.

To tempt your kitty to spend more time near the garden, transplant catnip — several plants of good size — in hopes of having a few survivors. And leave a water dish and an occasional treat in a food dish nearby.

Ferrets

Whether or not you appreciate the ferret for the delightful companion animal it can be if handled properly, you may

be surprised to know that it is a naturally fierce hunter. When first introduced to the United States in the mid-1800s, it was as a "working animal." Ships, warehouses, and farms were stocked with the determined little predators to rid them of rats and other varmints. In Europe, and until the 1940s in much of the United States, "ferreting" referred to a day of hunting, usually for rabbits, whereby the ferret flushed the prey from its underground hiding place to be snagged in a net at the exit or picked off by a sharpshooter hunter, dogs, or even trained hawks. Though ferreting of this sort is now outlawed in most places, there may still be a place for the practical application of a pet ferret's instinctive hunting abilities.

Native to North Africa and genetically identical to the European polecat and the Asiatic Steppe polecat, ferrets are also related to minks, weasels, and the fun-loving otters. Likewise, they are agile, energetic, and naturally playful and affectionate. These qualities make for entertaining pets. When properly handled, they can be trained for such things as riding on your shoulder, walking on a leash, coming when called, and, of course, hunting.

Females, called jills, are the most useful hunters as they are usually more ambitious and much smaller than the males. This enables them to enter and maneuver in underground burrows more freely. At maturity they may be as small as 8 ounces, or up to 1½ pounds in weight, while males, called hobs, average 2½ to 3½ pounds but can grow as large as 4½ pounds.

Domestic ferrets resemble furry Slinky toys with long, lithe bodies and short, muscular legs. There are two coat variations, sable and white.

Management

Kept in clean, secure runs or cages, ferrets are fastidious animals, who will leave their messes in a single corner of their facilities. Though they possess scent glands not unlike those of skunks (another relative), they use them only when threatened, injured, or mating.

Old-time ferreters advise feeding a diet of fresh meat, preferably whole carcasses, such as rodents or rabbits. Their digestive systems are built for a high-protein, low-fiber diet. They can be kept healthy on commercial pet foods. However, any gardener plagued with rodents or rabbits may find a practical resource to supplement his furry friend's diet.

If you're training ferrets to work for you, they should first be very tame and gentle (to you). Gaining trust is easiest with babies acquired at about eight weeks of age, but older ferrets can also be won over with deliberate affection and firm kindness. By the age of four months they are ready to hunt such critters as rabbits, considered among the least vicious in the fighting-back department.

See the bibliography for references that will be of further assistance.

The Ferret at Work

Ferrets aren't much for digging, but once deposited near the entrance to a tunnel they will explore every nook and cranny. Though this may have frustrated the ferreter of old, it accomplishes a valuable task for the home gardener wanting to clear out the local garden competition. For while Jill is investigating she is leaving her scent throughout the tunnels, making them very discomforting to the residents. And should she discover those residents, she will either drive them out or kill them.

The major concern with dropping your rambunctious little pal down a gopher hole is wondering whether you will ever see her again. Some hunting ferrets develop the habit of killing their prey and then laying up with it, eating their fill and taking a nice, long, cozy nap. This is a very natural behavior to a ferret, and a worry to ferret owners. You don't really *know* if she's asleep or if she has found yet another tunnel or even an exit!

Retrieving a Ferret

Making noise on the surface may help to wake her if she is asleep. Sealing the exits to the tunnel until the next morning, when the ferret will be thirsty enough to come up looking for water, is another old tactic. Some other methods include sending a second ferret, with a line or an electronic "ferret locator" attached to find the first ferret, and then digging them both out with a shovel. Most recommended though is simply to sit and wait. She may still be working down there, and when she is finished, most likely she will follow her own scent back to the entry hole where she began.

Preparation may help to prevent the problem in the first place. Don't send a famished ferret into a den full of fat gophers. Make sure she has a snack before going to work. It will only take the edge off her hunger, not her killer instinct. Train the little imp to come when called, using her name, a whistle, or a squeaky pet toy. They love the squealing sound of these toys, which resembles the cries of their prey. While they may ignore you in the heat of the battle, they will come romping up to you a little later when they are ready for play, a drink, or a nap.

Ground Floor

Snakes

Also known as "those crawly, wiggly things," snakes are more often irrationally feared than reasonably respected. Many are reclusive and try to escape when disturbed rather than bite or attack. Only 20 of the 117 species found in the United States are poisonous. The vast majority are at least somewhat beneficial, consuming bugs, slugs, rodents, and even other snakes, among other things.

Most hunt for live food, devouring it whole. They kill either by constricting — literally squeezing the life out of their victim — or by holding it

fast with teeth or coils and swallowing it alive.

Snakes are cold-blooded, and thus able to regulate their body temperature only by moving to a warmer or cooler location. Though leg-less, they manage to move about quickly and quietly enough to capture their unsuspecting prey. Some are remarkably beautiful, like elaborate strands of colored beads, while others are utilitarian in color and pattern. All have the ability to unhinge their jaws to swallow prey several times larger than their heads. Most have comparatively dainty appetites and can survive without food for extended periods. This is true during winter hiber- nation as well as in times of scarce food supplies.

If you encounter a snake unfamiliar to you, it is best to keep a polite distance. While all snakes can bite, some are more prone to than others, and a relative few can inject poison venom through their fangs. Snakes native to the United States can be identified as poisonous if:

1. There are rings of red, yellow, and black along the body with the red next to the yellow (coral snakes).

2. The snake has a rattle.

3. There is a pit between the nostrils and the eyes.

4. The underside scales from the vent (waste outlet) back toward the tail run in a single row of wide plates, as do those on the belly.

5. The pupils are elliptical, rather than round like those of harmless snakes.

Several species can be a real help to the gardener, if not outright pets. Easily accustomed to handling, king snakes, bull snakes, and rosy and rubber boas may grow from 6 to 8 feet long but are among the safest snakes around. They will eat everything from bugs and slugs to gophers and other varmints. King snakes are exceptionally unfussy eaters, even lunching on other snakes, including poisonous ones. Rat snakes will eliminate their share of small animals as well as birds and eggs, an unfortunate taste indulged by more than a few large snakes. Brown snakes, green snakes, garters, and many other species will indulge in insects and slugs as well as our precious earthworms.

Hosting Snakes

If you are lucky enough to have a resident bull snake, don't be alarmed by his loud, snorting "hissy fits" if he's startled. He's bluffing. Instead, indulge him, or any of his beneficial brethren, with some amenities. A shallow dish of water will be welcomed on hot days and so will a cool, shaded hideout. Your slithering accomplice should find a comfy gopher hole to relax in! Snakes depend on warmth to maintain their activity, becoming sluggish if too cool. A dark, flat surface will invite them to crawl aboard and soak up some sun. If you turn loose a pet snake to patrol for you, this is the ideal place to recapture him, as he will probably be found there in the early morning or evening.

Turtles

Both wood turtles and box turtles may find their way into your garden. They may come in search of your low-growing strawberries, blackberries, or tomatoes or they may have found your garden to have one of the nicest slug patches around. If turtles invite themselves into your plot, protecting a few vulnerable plants is a better than fair trade for the slugs, snails, and insects these steadfast urchins consume.

Even though these turtles are primarily land dwellers, hot or dry summer weather will send them in search of a cool, wet place to rest. They are but one of many types of beneficial critters that will make for a very good return on the investment of a garden pool or pond. In fact, if the pool has a mud bottom, turtles even spend the winter hibernating beneath the murky depths. More fun for all concerned, though, is to bring them inside for the winter and enjoy them in a terrarium.

Toads

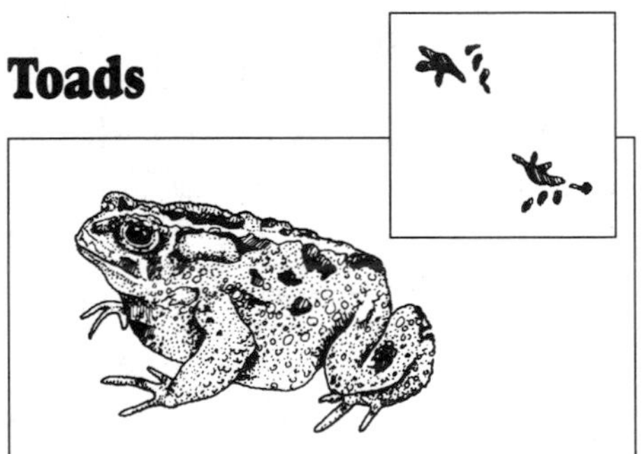

Imagine a quiet night in the sanctuary of your garden. A beetle lands on the lowest leaf of an eggplant a couple of inches from a lumpy, brown, inconspicuous dirt clod. The beetle's feast is interrupted as he suddenly vanishes! Hey! Did that dirt clod just smack his lips?

Unattractive though he may seem to some, the toad is so well camouflaged in his garden domain that often you won't realize you are looking directly at him. More likely, though, you won't see the toad because he seeks out a dark, damp hiding place by day and only gets down to business — the business of eating — after dark.

The toad uses his lightning-quick tongue to lash out at chow a full 2 inches away. The prey is glued to the sticky appendage and instantly reeled into his mouth.

Sadly mistrusted and misunderstood, the toad may well be the very best friend any gardener could ask for. Sportsman that he is, he goes only after live, moving game, from cutworms, armyworms, and other caterpillars to bugs, beetles, weevils, sowbugs, snails, and slugs. Nearly 90 percent of his diet is garden pests. In a single gardening season, one hungry toad can polish off more than 10,000 pests. Given a life span of at least several years, that's a lot of debugging.

Of the eighteen species of toads known to inhabit various parts of North America, all have diets considered to be beneficial to man. They are harmless, casting no evil spells or warts even onto the most superstitious people. They do, however, exude a noxious substance through their skin if attacked that seriously irritates mu-

A Garden Pond

If you are not lucky enough to have a pond on your property, you can improve the environment of present or potential pest predators by installing one. This is not as monstrous a project as it may sound. A small permanent body of water, no more than 3 or 4 feet square and a foot or two deep, will serve as a watering hole and/or breeding ground for birds, toads, turtles, insects, and more.

In building your very own garden pond, follow a few basic rules to maximize its effectiveness.

Locate the pond in an out-of-the-way corner if possible. This helps prevent it from being more popular with kids and pets than it is with the toads and other intended wildlife.

Be sure it is partially shaded for the comfort of frogs and turtles but receives enough sunlight to encourage adequate plant growth. Let some grasses and native water plants grow in and around the pond to provide cover and make it as inviting as the real thing. Stock the pond with water lilies or other ornamentals as well as a few fish and other aquatic life to make it all the more enjoyable for the gardener. Design your pond with a sloping bottom to make it easier for your visitors to climb in and out, and to allow for easier emptying and cleaning.

For more information on ponds, see Garden Way Bulletin A-123, *Creating Your Own Water Garden*, or A-19, *Build a Pond for Food and Fun*.

cous membranes. Watch how quickly any dog who gulps at one spits it back out! Be sure to wash your hands after handling toads, and keep them away from your eyes and mouth. One species, the giant toad, *Bufo marinus*, native to south Florida and southern Texas, releases a substance so potent that it has, on occasion, proven fatal to creatures that have bitten one.

Besides overzealous pets, toads have to contend with skunks, snakes, and some large birds. Except for leaving a bad taste in the mouth of his attacker, the toad's only other means of defense is to hide out. He can change his coloration somewhat to blend in with his surroundings, developing spots and stripes to camouflage himself in the shadows beneath foliage.

Toads do not drink through their mouths. Instead, they soak up moisture through their skin. Water is also mandatory to this amphibian's life cycle as a place for mama toad to deposit her 5000 to 25,000 eggs. Hatching into tadpoles who change into tiny toads in forty to sixty days, they quickly make their way to dry ground.

Toads are cold-blooded, so their internal body temperature depends totally on the temperature of their immediate surroundings. When it gets too cold, the toad digs in, slows his bodily functions, and sleeps until things get more comfortable. During hot spells, he becomes sluggish and may visibly shrivel unless he finds suitably cool, moist shelter.

Hosting Toads

Toads' needs for moisture and shelter make it easy to play host to a bevy of them. Install a deluxe toad suite: a few shallow holes, partially covered with boards or stones, and a shallow, sloping water source. A ground-floor birdbath works fine, or better yet, install that garden pond.

Rather than sitting back and waiting for the toads to find this idyllic setting, you can recruit a few in the spring by checking ditches or other sources of standing water for squiggly tadpoles.

Check under boards or other such hiding places for adults. Keep them in a shallow dish of water if you don't have a pond.

Decollate Snails

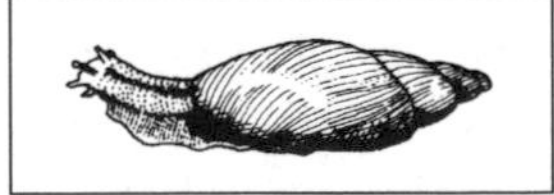

Under cover of darkness, the predator goes to work. He slips from his daytime hiding place just under the soil surface and begins to stalk his territory for game. Suddenly, he catches wind of his prey and the chase is on. He thunders the full 4 inches across a garden bed timber and with a mighty leap (or rather a gooey slide), assaults his victim. Thousands of sharp teeth rasp the flesh from a defeated helix (garden snail) as the deadly decollate enjoys his meal. Later he will resume his relentless search of the garden, killing again and again until ultimately he rids his garden home of the pesky brown garden snails. After that he will placidly roam the garden floor, seeking decaying organic matter and doing his part to help the composting effort.

These killer snails grow up to 2½ inches long and sport conical shells, unlike the smaller, brown garden snails who develop circular shells. Like the garden snails, they seek cool, moist refuge, especially in hot weather. But since they actually burrow into the soil, their presence is harder to detect than that of their seedling-seeking prey. Freezing weather also finds them digging for cover.

Snail eggs and the smaller hatchlings are the decollates' preferred prey, as grown snails can more readily escape or survive attacks. Very little feeding on growing plants has ever been observed, and it is believed that the decollates tend to nibble only at plants or damaged plant parts that are stressed to the point of showing signs of death or decay. With few exceptions, healthy, established plants — those with several pairs of true leaves

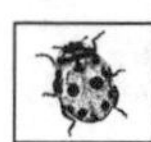

— are very rarely touched by these carnivores.

Decollates have been reported to feed, tentatively at least, on *Dichondra*, baby tears, and violets, and on occasion to sample germinating seeds. While this can be stopped with standard snail deterrents, it is most easily prevented by supplying the hunters with bits of dead plant matter. Once they have reduced the numbers of brown snails, decollates will have to hunt more and more to find them, and they'll require some plant matter if no prey is found.

Releasing Decollates

Originating in North Africa, decollate snails were introduced to the United States in the early nineteenth century, probably along with the brown snails shipped over to establish escargot "farms." They have found their way into many southern states as well as California. Available commercially, they are currently only approved for release in eight southern California counties. Not being a native species, the decollates have no known enemies, so government studies are ongoing to determine whether they can become problems in themselves. In almost all known cases of localized established decollate populations, they have minded their manners nicely and dined almost exclusively on escargot and rotting vegetation.

These beneficial snails are best released into a well-watered ground cover of low-growing plants. Don't release into freshly planted beds or in any areas where poison snail baits have been recently used as they are just as vulnerable as their unwanted kin. Though it may take a couple of years for these slow-paced hunters to reduce the garden snail population, you will eventually have a harder time finding a brown snail than the reclusive decollates.

Beneficial Insects

Oh, what a beautiful sight a healthy, productive garden crawling with insects can be. But how to achieve this success, and what makes it a victory rather than a crushing defeat?

A garden full of bugs is a boon instead of a bust when many of those bugs are beneficial insects — those that attack the bad guy bugs that attack our crops. How you can achieve such a lofty goal is at once very simple and very demanding.

Enticing Beneficial Insects

The number-one demand of beneficial insects is that you use no poisonous chemicals. Pesticide use is easily the primary reason that there are not more beneficial bugs at work today. Other requirements of beneficial bugs vary with the individual species, whether they be predator or parasite, but some general principles benefit all.

Diversify. Plant many different types of plants, particularly flowers and herbs. These supply beneficials with nectar and pollen necessary to many adult forms, as well as rest stops and breeding grounds.

Especially attractive are umbelliferous flowers, those with many tiny flowers arranged in tight umbels, such as members of the carrot family, dill, parsley, angelica, fennel, or the weed Queen Anne's lace. Daisies, strawflowers, goldenrod, yarrow, petunias, cosmos, zinnias, nasturtiums, marigolds, and sunflowers also draw beneficials. Weeds including lamb's-quarters, wild mustard, dandelion, nettle, pigweed, and knotweed are also important to beneficial insects. Many small-flowering herbs, including garden sage, thyme, oregano, lavender, catnip and other mints, rosemary, carroway, anise, coriander, sweet marjoram, and tansy (not ragwort) attract beneficial bugs.

Intercrop. Mix up your plantings so that plants that draw beneficials are located among those that need their protection.

Humidify. Many beneficials are tiny and lose their precious body moisture quickly. They require a habitat humid enough to prevent dehydration and keep them active. This can be established by placing plants close together to create a shaded, moist microenvironment. Misting or constant drip irrigation will also contribute to raising moisture levels.

Releasing Beneficial Insects

If you plan to capture or buy and release bugs not native to your garden, be certain that you have targeted your pest problems. Though many predators have a wide array of hosts, some are quite specific, and if their hosts are not present they must either relocate or die. Time the release of beneficials so that there is a sustainable level of feed (for both adults and larvae — nectar as well as pests). At times you may need to feed them sugar water or products such as Bug Chow. Manufacturers of commercial products claim these enhance the bugs' reproductivity and performance. Temper the number of beneficials you release with the level of your infestation problems. Too few predators won't be able to control the number of pests, while too many may produce competition that could result in other beneficials winding up as dinner.

Suppliers of commercially available predators or parasites often recommend repeat or staggered releases to best take advantage of the hosts' life cycles.

Insect Categories

There are two categories of beneficial insects that operate in two different ways. They may be *host specific*, which means they relentlessly seek out the one (or few) pests their livelihoods depend on; or they may be more *generalized*, using a variety of pests for

their needs. The means by which they eradicate our pests may be through either straightforward *predation*, whereby the beneficial hunts down the vermin and devours it, or *parasitic*, whereby the adult form lays eggs on or in the host's body and the emerging larvae destroy the pest from the inside out. Parasites are more apt to be host specific, and the adults more likely to be nectar or pollen eaters than the predatory larval forms. Host-specific beneficials will zero in on a problem pest immediately whereas the more general feeders will attack whatever is handy. Your individual pest problems should indicate which would be the more useful in your situation.

Unfortunately, nature doesn't give a rip as to which insects *we* prefer in our gardens. Survival for many depends on a diverse diet, which may at times include other beneficial insects. Be sure you are releasing a solution to a problem or you may find yourself with one form of beneficial ridding your garden of other forms.

Spiders

Had Little Miss Muffet been a gardener, her reaction to a visiting spider may have been considerably different. Granted, spiders do give a lot of people the creeps, perhaps because they dart out of the most unexpected places, perhaps because they seem to be ever lurking in dark corners, or maybe it's the images of grasping, tangled cobwebs from old movies that haunts some of us. True, many spiders do prefer a close, shadowed retreat, such as the base of low flowers or ground covers. Ageratum, asters, petunias, polygonum, sweet allysum, hypercium, and many others will provide safe haven for spiders to live, breed, and hunt. But to understand what a garden spider can do for you is to appreciate a friend you may never have known you had.

General Characteristics

Most spiders have good vision and well-developed senses of hearing and smell. Web builders especially have an exquisite sense of touch. Those long hairy legs do more than skitter across flower beds; they also carry the organs for hearing, smell, and feeling.

All spiders have tiny mouths and must liquefy their food before sucking it up. They all live by catching and eating prey, and most are none too fussy about what said prey may be. Insects are their diet staple. Unfortunately, they make no allowances for what we consider other beneficial insects. Some are avid hunters who attack and paralyze their victims with a poisonous bite. Some are active by day and others stalk the night. Many are artists as well as bug exterminators. Intricately designed silk spiderwebs trap hapless insects, and the weaver emerges from his hiding place to finish them off and wrap them in silk for safe keeping.

Hunting spiders burn much more energy and eliminate more bugs than

those that sit around minding the webs. They're found throughout the United States. Some to watch for are wolf, jumping, lynx, and crab spiders.

Wolf spiders are from ¼ to 1½ inches in length, hairy gray or brown, with eight eyes arranged on their heads. Mother wolf spiders may be seen packing scads of tiny baby spiders around just after they hatch. Wolf spiders are great hunters who swiftly run down their prey, or even burrow after it if need be.

Jumping spiders rarely exceed ½ inch in size but are no less superb hunters. These brightly colored predators rely on their excellent vision to help locate prey and can leap upon it in an instant.

Lynx spiders, common in the South, use their bright green camouflage coloring to sneak up on their quarry in broad daylight.

Crab spiders lay in wait to ambush their prey. They may be white or yellow, depending somewhat on their surroundings, and may change back and forth.

Aside from the fascinating orbs created by "ordinary" garden spiders, these silk spinners devise many other traps. Trap doors, nets, tangled masses of the stuff, and trap draglines are all among the spider arsenal. Silk is also used for creating egg cases and wrapping prey. At least seven different types of silk are made and used by spiders.

Generally, spiders live for only about a year, adults overwintering in protected places. Besides squeamish humans they have other natural enemies to contend with, from birds and toads to relentless wasps, who are believed to kill nearly 99 percent of all female wolf spiders.

Beetles

Though many beetles are bad news in the garden, a few have earned our appreciation. From the large ungainly ground beetles to the much adored ladybug (ladybird beetles), or ferocious soldier or tiger beetles, some of these bugs make dependable allies.

Ground Beetles

Lurking just beneath the soil surface a dark, shiny, heavily armored knight awaits. He is a ground beetle. Growing to a mere 1 inch in length, these black beetles are fierce predators of slugs, snails, and many pest larvae. They work the night shift, when their prey is most active. If disturbed during the day, they use their long legs to hurry to a safe hiding place. Adults lay eggs in the soil, producing just one generation per year.

Another ground beetle, known as the fiery searcher *(Calosoma scrutator)*, is similar in habit and appearance. This one exudes a caustic substance that burns on contract. If ever you handle one, wear gloves. They search out and devour caterpillars and other soft-bodied larvae.

These beetles, or similar species, are found throughout North Ameri-

ca. Collect some to overwinter. A jar with a couple inches of soil from the garden and some garden scraps should tide them over until spring. Then release them into your plot. Be sure to provide some sort of cover, such as a few flat rocks or boards.

Ladybugs

These cute little gals may well be responsible for the entire concept of biological pest control. Not only are they credited with the early reclamation of the California citrus industry from the cottonycushion scale, but they are nearly universally recognized by gardeners and accepted by even the faint of heart (bugwise).

Perhaps the abilities of ladybugs as a garden panacea have been exaggerated. Their appetites are limited mostly to aphids, scale, mites, mealybugs, whiteflies, and the eggs of some other insects. Though unquestionably helpful as predators, they alone can't keep most serious pest infestations at bay.

Ladybugs are less than ¼ inch long, rounded, bright orange to red, with several black spots (the exact number depends on the variety). White markings dot the thorax (distinguishing them from the similar Mexican bean beetle), and they have a black head and legs. The larvae are even more voracious eaters than the adults, known to knock off around forty aphids in an hour. In about twenty days from hatching, the larvae pupate to emerge as the ever-popular ladybug or ladybird beetles.

Some species of ladybug can be found almost anywhere in North America. Curiously, in the West especially, adults migrate to hibernate, spending winter in the mountains. Scores of them will collect in a sheltered spot to spend the winter together. In the spring they return to other areas.

Releasing Ladybugs. Ladybugs native to your garden are a gift; those that you buy and transplant may be a disappointment. Ladybugs are purchased and released in the spring. They have been dormant in hibernation all winter, and the first thing their instincts tell them to do is migrate. You open the container and away they go, eventually to settle in someone else's garden.

There are a few precautions you can take. First, don't release the beetles too early in the season. Be sure there are aphids or some other food for them to eat, in enough numbers to keep them from having to look elsewhere for sustenance. If necessary they can be kept dormant in the refrigerator until conditions are more favorable.

Second, don't release them too early in the day. If released at sundown they are more apt to rest overnight and begin feeding in the morning. Never handle them roughly, for they may fly off when agitated. Instead, gently place them near the plants that need their attention with a popsicle stick, cotton swab, or other tool.

Warm weather also stirs their drive to migrate. Water the area before releasing the ladybugs and provide them with mulch, which creates a cool, damp, inviting place for them to adjust.

If the ladybugs have done their job too well, they may face a shortage of food. Rather than letting them fly off in search of a decent meal, provide them with a free lunch. Squirt sugar water (1 part sugar to 4 parts water) on a few low leaves. Also, take advantage of naturally attractive plants — butterfly weed, angelica, marigold, and yarrow — which attract them to the garden.

Soldier Beetles

These beetles are often said to resemble burned-out fireflies. One type, the downy leather-wing *(Podabrus tomentosus)*, is dark with a whitish head and thorax. As the name implies, they appear to be covered with fine, downy white hairs. Adults grow to ½ inch long and feed on aphids. They are found throughout most of the United States and in southern Canada. Another soldier beetle, the Pennsylvania leather-wing *(Chauliognathus pennsylvanicus)*, is limited to eastern North America. They are golden with black markings and are also about ½ inch long. These feed on grasshopper eggs, cucumber beetles, and an array of caterpillars.

Tiger Beetles

While this species is found in the West, similar species occur throughout North America. They are metallic blue-green and grow up to an inch long. Both the adults and spiney, humped, curved larvae prey on a variety of small insects and spiders.

Bugs

Ambush Bugs

Hiding behind that innocent flower blossom is an odd-looking though ruthlessly efficient hunter. When mites, scales, or thrips happen along his path, the ambush bug lives up to his name, and pounce! One less pest. Though only ⅜ inch long, he will sometimes take on wasps or bees and other beneficial insects.

Assassin Bugs

While not all that common in home gardens, hundreds of different species of assassins are found throughout the United States and Canada. Some species are native to woodlands. If you live in the vicinity, you may notice evidence of the assassins's work. Empty shells of bugs, sucked dry and then discarded, are the only remains of those slain by this gruesome killer. Many a caterpillar, aphid, Mexican bean beetle, Colorado potato beetle, Japanese beetle, leafhopper, hornworm, and honeybee have met their fate between the bristly front legs of a hungry assassin. Once within his

grasp, their insides are liquefied by digestive enzymes and sucked out through the killer's beak.

One-half inch long, either black or brown and built for business, assassin bugs have broad bodies, with large eyes, sturdy front legs, and a long piercing beak. The life cycle can take several years to complete, so many stages of the bug are present at once.

If you find a couple of assassins in the garden, the best management practice is to let them be. They will tell you that themselves, for if molested, they bite, and it can bring a wince to the most seasoned hands. Sunflowers attract assassins (and other beneficial insects).

Big-eyed Bugs

This helpful predator scans Western gardens, searching for leafhoppers, aphids, Mexican bean beetles, and the eggs of various insects. The mere ¼-inch long grayish beige, oval-shaped big-eyed bug is native to much of western North America. He boasts oversize "bug eyes" for which he is named. These bugs supplement their diets with various weeds and may be attracted to a patch of wild plants and flowers.

Damsel Bugs or Damsel Flies

Still another predator that stalks ground covers and other low plants is the damsel bug. Don't let the innocent-sounding name or their demure appearance mislead you. These bugs are well-versed killers. With long, slender hindlegs and powerful, grasping forelegs, the dark, streamlined damsels grow to only ¼ inch long. Size is no handicap, however, as they put away their share of mites, aphids, leafhoppers, larvae, and other small plant pests. Some species are found throughout North America.

Soldier Bugs

Brown ½-inch-long bugs, with snouts half as long as their bodies, stalk the stalks of your broccoli in search of cabbage loopers and imported cabbageworms. They also have an appetite for Mexican bean beetles and many other harmful insects. These soldier bugs spear their prey with their specialized snouts, inject digestive enzymes into its body, and slurp up the predigested contents. The mercenary larvae are just as ruthless killers as the adults, starting to hunt just days after hatching. They range throughout North America.

Flies

Syrphid or Hover Flies

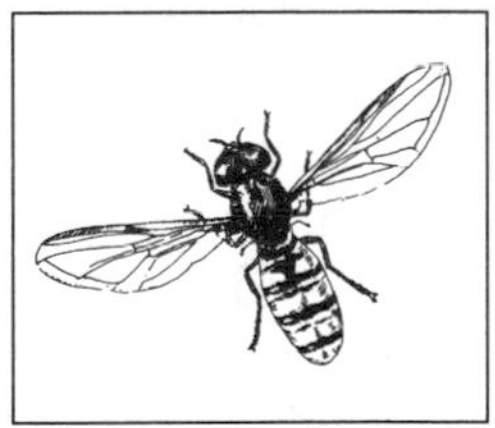

Adult hover flies, with their striped abdomens, resemble wasps. They hover before flowers, buzzing loudly as they sip nectar, but unlike their look-alikes offer no threat of a sting. Green or tan, the wormlike larvae of these flies are gung ho aphid eaters. A single larva can put away 1000 aphids before changing into an adult. Adult female hover flies can contribute about 100 eggs each to your gardening effort. Besides aphids, any small, soft-bodied insects such as mealybugs, thrips, or leafhoppers may find themselves on the hover fly's menu.

These flies are also important as pollinators. They favor cosmos, coreopsis, gloriosa daisies, dwarf morning-glories, marigolds, spearmint, baby-blue-eyes, and the herb meadowfoam. An assortment of these should draw some of the nearly 1000 species of hover flies found throughout North America to your plot.

Robber Flies

A loud buzz and an acrobatic aerial swoop, and snap — another airborne pest knocked from the sky. Robber flies are up to ¾ inch long, powerful, and ugly. These hairy-faced gray hunters take down a variety of flying insects, from beetles and butterflies to leafhoppers and grasshoppers, as well as a few unlucky beneficials. While adults are launching their winged attack, the white larvae are worming their way into the eggs and grubs of pests under the soil surface.

With many species found throughout North America (most east of the Rocky Mountains in the United States and Canada), a constant supply of flowering plants should keep a few at work in your garden.

Tachinid Flies

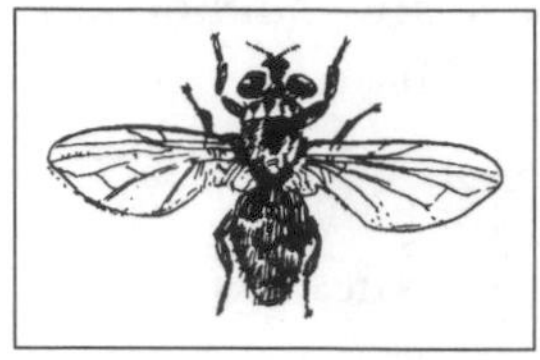

The tachinid flies often resemble black houseflies, but are occasionally found in shades of yellow, red, or brown. These bristly little flies are often seen around leaves and flowers, where they feed on nectar or the honeydew secreted by certain insect pests. Nearly 1300 different species exist throughout North America, and among them are probably *the* most important pest-control parasites.

The larvae of these flies invade and excavate the bodies of their hosts. Some are deposited as live maggots within the host's body by the mother fly; others are laid as eggs on foliage or on the body of the host. The larvae feed on many beetles, bugs, caterpillars, and grasshoppers. The list includes European corn borers, cutworms, armyworms, and Japanese and Mexican bean beetles. Adults are drawn to buckwheat, and a small patch should ensure a welcome population of tachinid flies.

Green Lacewing

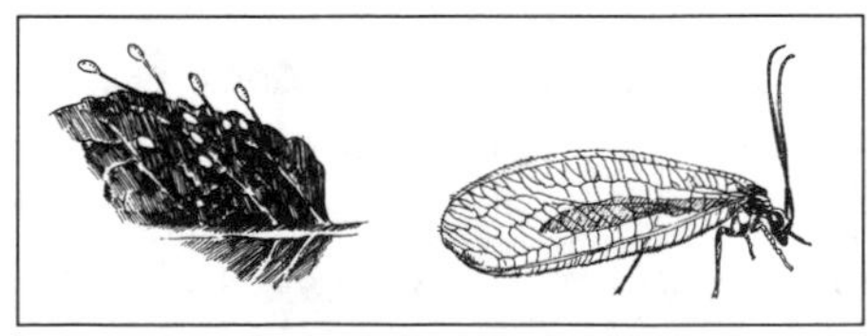

A delicate, fragile-looking, slender green insect, the adult lacewing feed-

ing on pollen or nectar gives no clue as to the voracious appetite of its young, also known as aphid lions. But this hungry larva is one of the best garden predators in existence for aphids, spider mites, mealybugs, leafhoppers, thrips, or even corn earworm and other caterpillar eggs.

Various species are native throughout North America and can be lured to the garden by planting a variety of flowering plants such as angelica, red cosmos, coreopsis, tansy, or goldenrod. They also appreciate the wild Queen Anne's lace, a weed you may learn to tolerate in modest numbers. Adults also feed on honeydew and prey on the bugs that produce it. Though considered somewhat more stable than ladybugs, lacewings still require sufficient food, in the form of pollen-bearing plants for adults and prey as well as accessible water, or they will leave in search of it.

Releasing Lacewings. Lacewings can be purchased by mail order as eggs, larvae, or pupae. Eggs usually hatch within hours of delivery into gray and brown larvae with large jaws. The hungry kids immediately start to look around for something to eat. If nothing else is available, they will start in on each other. In the wild, the females lay individual eggs on separate silk-spun stalks, quite likely to prevent her children from devouring one another. Protect your investment by releasing the larvae as soon as they hatch. Place them directly on the plants that need their attention. They are wingless but active searchers, and will disperse themselves quickly in their search for food.

Unlike ladybugs, lacewings *should not* be refrigerated. Keep them at room temperature. If you don't set them out immediately, keep a close eye on the bottom of the container for hatchlings, as the larvae will instinctively crawl downward looking for food.

Praying Mantis

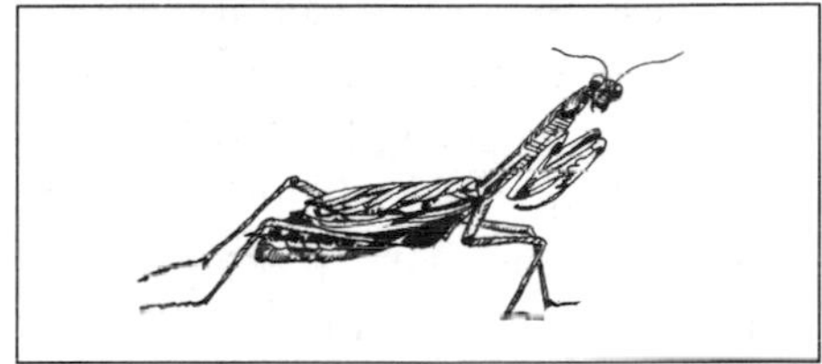

Next to the beloved ladybug, the praying mantis is perhaps the most recognizable insect predator. Their large size, up to 5 inches in length, and strange appearance make them fascinating to watch. They come in shades of dull brown to green, and are long and slender with strong, enlarged front legs designed for grasping prey.

Known to be included in their dietary repertoire are aphids, various beetles and bugs, leafhoppers, flies, caterpillars, butterflies, and sadly, beneficials such as bees and wasps. They even prey on each other. The larger they grow the more likely they are to take on bigger game, not excluding small vertebrates such as salamanders or frogs, or even a fiesty shrew. Even so, they are not especially aggressive hunters. They prefer to

wait patiently for whatever comes their way.

The pious-looking mantis waits, her forelegs poised before her reverently. As a likely-looking meal approaches, she grabs it with her powerful, spiney forearms. Dinner begins with a bite to the back of the victim's neck, which paralyzes it, ending any struggle. Our lady proceeds to eat her prey as it dies.

Releasing Mantises. Native mantises are cold-hardy and found through most of the United States and Canada. The eggs and newly hatched larvae are vulnerable to birds and ants — each takes its toll on mantid populations. Eggs are laid in masses in foamy-looking egg cases, which are glued to twigs or stems of plants such as goldenrod. These cases can be collected in the fall and refrigerated over the winter, or transplanted into the garden to overwinter. When you place them in the garden, hang them as close as possible to the position in which they were found.

Some folks advocate prehatching the eggs in jars, but the cannibalistic nature of the young makes this a tricky proposition.

To lure natives to your garden, plant cosmos or cultivate raspberry canes. Mail-order mantises are available. Often these are Chinese mantises, which while acclaimed to be more predaceous are also less cold-tolerant and in many areas cannot overwinter without human intervention.

Vendors tend to overrate the mantis as a pest control. Its diverse diet and lack of hunting prowess make it much less effective than many of its more inconspicuous counterparts.

Wasps

A vast array of wasps diligently scour even the tiniest garden plot in search of insect pests. Some eliminate their victims by outright attack and devour them on the spot. Others parasitize prey: the emerging larvae hollow out victims from the inside. Some to be aware of are the predatory wasps (the kinds that sting) and the parasitic trichogramma, braconid, chalcid, and ichneumon wasps (the kinds that don't).

Trichogramma Wasps

Found throughout North America, the trichogramma wasps are tiny pest-control agents. Several species are known to parasitize more than 200 different pests, including cabbage loopers and cutworms among other caterpillars and insects. Using her specialized ovipositer, the wasp lays her eggs *inside* the body of the host, effectively preventing the development of one more pest and releasing as many as twenty-five new wasps from one parasitized victim.

These tiny wasps, like other para-

sitic wasps, are harmless to people or animals. They are so small, barely 1/32 inch long, that when their miniscule eggs are sold, thousands arrive on a 1-inch square card that resembles a piece of fine sandpaper. *Trichogramma pretiosum* is the species most commonly sold for control of garden pests.

Braconid Wasps

Picture, if you will, a large, fat, lumbering tomato hornworm perched halfway up a tomato plant stalk. You're just about to pluck this munching menace when you notice something a little bizarre. Though he is chomping contentedly on your prize Better Boy, this hornworm is one you will definitely leave alone. His plump body is covered with tiny silken cocoons, the pupal stages of one species of braconid wasp.

Several species of braconid wasps exist. Some are very specific in the hosts they use, others victimize a range of insects. Those cocoons attached to the hornworm are the aftermath of the wasps having completed their larval stage inside its body. Not only do they ultimately cause the demise of that one hornworm, but more importantly, that particular hornworm serves as the launching site for many more of these beneficial parasites. Other species zero in on cabbageworms and other pest species of moths.

The various kinds are found throughout North America. They range from yellowish to red or black in color and from a mere 1/10 inch up to 1/4 inch in size. They possess wicked-looking ovipositors, which resemble an exaggerated, long, curving stinger. But fear not, for this weapon is used solely for depositing eggs upon or inside the host.

The adults feed on nectar and can be drawn by small, single-blossomed wildflowers or flowering herbs. Provide a varied assortment to ensure blooms throughout the season.

Chalcid Wasps

Chalcid wasps are effective parasites against aphids, scale, mealybugs, and the larvae of many flying insects, such as beetles, moths, and butterflies. Found throughout North America, they are extremely sensitive to environmental factors such as temperature, humidity, and even dusty air. The level or control they can provide depends on favorable conditions.

They are also very small, about 1/32 inch long, with proportionately tiny wings and enormous eyes. Some are black and others a golden color.

Like the other parasitic wasps, the adults require small-blossomed, single-blooming flowers for nectar. Including these in your gardenscape will help to attract these wasps.

Ichneumon Wasps

Though there are many species, on average they are streamlined, dark wasps with clear wings and long antennae. An oversized ovipositor is used only for inserting eggs into (or near) a host. Adults feed on host larvae as well as pollen and nectar. Along with their carnivorous larvae, they are effective parasites against many caterpillars. Ichneumon wasps are found throughout North America.

Predatory Wasps

Not all wasps are tiny or easily overlooked. Some, such as the mud daubers and paper, or social, wasps can make themselves painfully obvious. These wasps hunt for insect prey, attacking and stinging to paralyze the victim. Caterpillars, spiders, and many other insects are considered fair game. The adults take back portions of their kill to share with the rest of the colony. Those same stingers are used, not infrequently, to remind us humans that we are not the only workers tending the garden. In addition to giving the occasional pointed reminder, they also make themselves known by loud buzzing when they work. Their size, some over an inch long, and their bright, contrasting yellow or white and black markings make them hard to miss.

Mud daubers are solitary wasps; they do not form colonies like the paper wasps. Instead, females lay eggs in individual cells that each plasters together with mud. They provide each cell in the nest with a paralyzed insect to nourish the larvae as they hatch and grow. Mud daubers are nearly harmless to people, as they are not easily provoked to sting, but are serious enemies to insects.

More familiar to many of us are the **paper, or social, wasps.** These include the various species of hornets and yellow jackets, all of which are insect predators. They range in size from ½ inch to an inch or more in length, and, unlike the solitary mud dauber, they create large, highly organized colonies, which they fiercely defend. Workers from these colonies, designated as foragers, venture out to hunt and bring home food for the entire nest. Treat any foraging wasps with quiet respect and you should be able to work side by side.

Adults also require pollen and are particularly fond of flowers from the daisy family. Oxeye daisies, strawflowers, black-eyed Susan, and even goldenrod and yarrow will draw predatory wasps to your garden. Ripe fruits and berries are also irresistible to them.

At least a dozen different species of predatory wasps can be found almost anywhere in the United States.

Other Beneficial Bugs

New forms of predatory and parasitic bugs are being discovered and experimented with every day. There may well never be an end to the possibilities, as insects on both sides of the bug wars continue to adapt and change.

Three more that are fairly new weapons in the biogardener's defense arsenal are *Encarsia formosa*, beneficial nematodes, and predatory mites.

Encarsia formosa

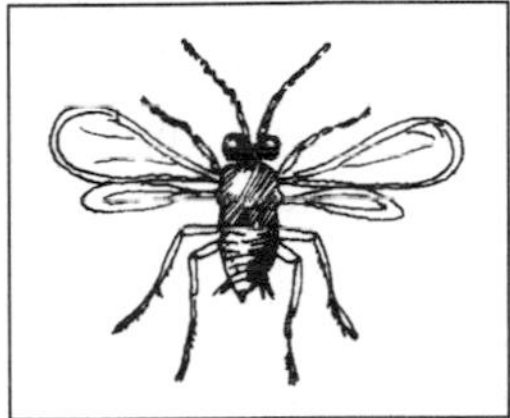

Most often recommended for greenhouse whitefly control, this tiny wasp is native to most of North America and can be established in home gardens. Adults are only about 1/40 inch long. Almost every one is a female, capable of producing more females without bothering with a male. They do best in temperatures over 70 degrees F., and what they *do* best is consume whiteflies. Nothing but.

Once they have done in up to 90 percent of the pest's population their own numbers will decline if not given a little help. If used inside a greenhouse, lower the temperature below 70 degrees F. and remove any whitefly traps. (You may want to leave one in place to monitor whitefly numbers.) A few whiteflies can't do any real damage, and are essential to the survival of the parasites. Place a few leaves infested with whiteflies and the parasites next to a rose geranium plant. Substances given off by the geranium cause the metabolism of both species to slow. Many people have had success overwintering the parasites in this way, then releasing them into the greenhouse or garden the following spring.

Nematodes

Nematodes. Not too long ago, any gardener familiar with these unseen creatures could tell you that nothing good could possibly follow that word. Insidious, destructive, and relentless, it's precisely those same lovely qualities that make *beneficial* nematodes so endearing.

Almost any insect pest that spends any time at all on or beneath the ground is vulnerable to attack by the tiny insect parasites *Neoplectana carpocapsae* and *Heterorhabditis heliothidis*. In the soil, these nematodes hunt down borers, root weevils, cutworms, beetle larvae, cabbage root maggots, wireworms, and much more. At the surface, juvenile nematodes are known to stand on their tails and wiggle around trying to hitch a ride (and a host) from any passing bug. They enter their host's body and begin to (shudder!) drink their blood. In so doing they release a bacteria, *Xenorhabdus nematophilus*, which breaks down the blood into simpler substances that the nematodes can digest. Alone, the bacteria pose no threat to insects, but require the action of the nematodes to finish them off. The bacteria and nematodes are symbiotic; without the bacterial action the nematodes are harmless and vice versa. Parasitized insects die within about twenty-four hours. Meanwhile, inside the host's body, the nematodes reproduce to re-

lease new generations of the infecting larvae.

Sold in the active juvenile stage, they are mixed with water and sprinkled along garden rows and at the base of plants. They must be kept moist to survive, and will keep in the refrigerator for up to two months.

Predatory Mites

Another bug not usually considered to be on our side is the mite. But at least four species of the genus *Persimilis* are more than willing to feast on red or two-spotted spider mites. They are extremely sensitive to temperature and humidity and are marketed for use indoors rather than outdoors. However, if temperatures in your area don't fall below 40 degrees F. during the growing season and humidity is not too low, you may wish to consider these little guys if you have a problem with their cousins.

Appendix 1

Plants and Their Pests

Here is a list of common garden plants and a sampling of *some* of the critters you may be up against when growing them.

Fruits and Vegetables

	Insect Pests	Non-insect Pests
Beans	Aphids, flea beetles, Mexican bean beetles, cucumber beetles, European corn borers, stink bugs, harlequin bugs, corn earworms, cutworms, other caterpillars, mealybugs, mites, whiteflies	Rabbits, deer, woodchucks
Beets	Aphids, flea beetles, cucumber beetles, European corn borers, cabbage loopers and other caterpillars, leafhoppers, leaf miners, root maggots, thrips, weevils, wireworms	Rabbits
Blueberries	Flea beetles and other beetles, caterpillars, leafhoppers, leaf miners, mites, scales, thrips, weevils	Bears, birds including starlings, children, squirrels
Carrots	Flea beetles, caterpillars, carrot rust flies, leafhoppers, root aphids, onion thrips	Deer, gophers, woodchucks
Celery	Aphids, Japanese beetles, borers, bugs, caterpillars including cabbage loopers, carrot rust flies, leafhoppers, mites, root maggots, thrips, carrot weevils	—
Cole crops (broccoli, brussels sprouts, cabbage, cauliflower, collards, kale)	Aphids, flea beetles, cucumber beetles, bugs including harlequin and stink bugs, cabbage loopers, corn earworms, cutworms, imported cabbageworms, cabbage maggots, leaf miners, thrips, whiteflies	Deer, chickens, slugs and snails
Corn	Aphids, flea beetles, Japanese beetles, cucumber beetles, harlequin and stink bugs, caterpillars, European corn borers, corn earworms, corn rootworms, leafhoppers, thrips, wireworms	Birds including blackbirds and crows, bears, deer, ground squirrels, opossums, porcupines, raccoons, skunks, squirrels

	Insect Pests	Non-insect Pests
Cucumbers	Aphids, flea beetles, cucumber beetles, bugs including squash bugs and stink bugs, cutworms, squash vine borers, leafhoppers, mites, thrips, whiteflies	Ground squirrels (seeds)
Eggplant	Aphids, Colorado potato beetles, flea beetles, harlequin bugs, stink bugs, cutworms, hornworms, potato leafhoppers, leaf miners, mites, pepper maggots	—
Grapes	Aphids, flea beetles and grape beetles, harlequin and boxelder bugs, corn earworms, leafhoppers, cutworms, scales, thrips, whiteflies, wireworms	Bears, deer, starlings
Lettuce	Aphids, flea beetles, cabbage loopers and imported cabbageworms, centipedes, mites, vegetable weevils, whiteflies	Gophers, woodchucks
Melons	Aphids, flea beetles, cucumber beetles, squash vine borers, squash bugs, cabbage loopers and other caterpillars, beet leafhoppers, mites, whiteflies	Crows, coyotes, bears, ground squirrels (seeds), porcupines, raccoons, turtles
Onions	Blister beetles, cutworms, onion root maggots, leaf miners, thrips, vegetable weevils, wireworms	—
Peas	Aphids, flea beetles, cucumber beetles, stink bugs, cabbage loopers and other caterpillars, leafminers, whiteflies	Deer, rabbits, voles, woodchucks
Peppers	Aphids, Colorado potato beetles, flea beetles, blister beetles, stinkbugs, corn earworms, beet leafhoppers, leaf miners, mealybugs, mites, pepper maggots, cutworms, whiteflies	—

	Insect Pests	Non-insect Pests
Potatoes	Aphids, Colorado potato beetles, flea beetles, cucumber beetles, various bugs, cabbage loopers, cutworms, hornworms, European corn borers, crickets, leafhoppers, leaf miners, mealybugs, vegetable weevils, whiteflies	Gophers, voles
Radishes	Aphids, flea and blister beetles, harlequin bugs, cabbage loopers, imported cabbageworms, cabbage maggots, leaf miners, weevils, wireworms	—
Raspberries	Aphids, borers, caterpillars, mites, scales, whiteflies	Bears, children, porcupines (bark), rabbits (bark), squirrels
Spinach	Aphids, flea beetles, cabbage loopers, cutworms, beet leafhoppers, leaf miners, vegetable weevils	—
Squash	Aphids, cucumber beetles, squash bugs, corn earworms, beet leafhoppers, squash vine borers, thrips, whiteflies	Ground squirrels (seed), woodchucks
Strawberries	Aphids, several beetles and bugs, mealybugs, mites, cutworms, scales, thrips	Deer, armadillos, children, ground squirrels, rabbits, starlings, turtles
Tomatoes	Caterpillars including cutworms, hornworms, cabbage loopers, corn earworms, aphids, blister beetles, flea beetles, spotted cucumber beetles, Colorado potato beetles, bugs including stink bugs, leafhoppers, leaf miners, pepper maggots, thrips, weevils	Ground squirrels, opossums, turtles
Turnips	Aphids, flea beetles, blister beetles, harlequin and other bugs, cabbage loopers, cutworms, imported cabbageworms, cabbage maggots, leaf miners, weevils, thrips	Slugs

Flowers

	Insect Pests	Non-insect Pests
Asters	Aphids, blister beetles, leafhoppers, stalk borers, tarnished plant bugs	—
Azaleas	Lacebugs, leaf miners, scale, stem borers	—
Begonias	Aphids, flower thrips, mealybugs, mites	Slugs, snails
Carnations	Aphids, cabbage loopers, (variegated) cutworms, flower thrips, mealybugs, mites	Slugs, snails
Chrysanthemums	Aphids, (clinging) cutworms, corn earworms, four-lined plant bugs, lacebugs, leaf miners, nematodes, spittle bugs, thrips, yellow woolybears, caterpillars	—
Columbine	Aphids, borers, leaf miners, mealybugs, stink bugs	—
Dahlias	Billbugs, European corn borers, potato leafhoppers, stalk borers, striped cucumber beetles, tarnished plant bugs	—
Delphiniums	Aphids, cutworms, flower thrips, four-lined plant bugs, mites, potato leafhoppers, stalk borers	Slugs, snails
Geraniums	Aphids, corn earworms, mealybugs, mites, termites, whiteflies	Slugs, snails
Gladiolus	Aphids, borers, cutworms, mites, tarnished plant bugs, thrips	—
Impatiens	—	Rabbits, slugs, snails
Iris	Iris borers, mites, nematodes, thrips, weevils	Slugs, snails

	Insect Pests	Non-insect Pests
Marigolds	Spider mites	Slugs, snails
Nasturtiums	(Bean) aphids, cabbage loopers, cabbageworms, corn earworms, (serpentine) leaf miners, lygus bugs, mites	—
Pansies	(Viola) cutworms, (potato) flea beetles, mealybug, mites, nematodes, sawflies, wireworms	Rabbits, slugs, snails
Peonies	Flower thrips, rose chafers	—
Poppies	Aphids, corn earworms, four-lined plant bugs, leafhoppers, lygus bugs, mealybugs, rose chafers	—
Roses	Aphids, carpenter ants, corn earnworms, earwigs, fuller rose beetles, harlequin bugs, Japanese beetles, leafhoppers, leaf rollers, red spider mites, root-knot nematodes, rose chafers, rose curculio, rose midge, rose scale, stem borers	Deer, slugs, snails
Snapdragons	Aphids, cabbage loopers, corn earworms, four-lined plant bugs, lygus bugs, nematodes, spider mites, stink bugs	Slugs, snails
Tulips	Aphids, millipedes, spider mites, wireworms	Gophers, mice, rabbits, squirrels
Violets	Aphids, flea beetles, gall midge, mealybugs, sawflies, yellow woolybears	Slugs, snails
Zinnias	Aphids, blister beetles, flea beetles, flower thrips, Japanese beetles, mealybugs, spotted cucumber beetles, stalk borers, whiteflies	—
Various Seeds	Seed corn maggots	Birds, mice, rats, voles, ground squirrels

Appendix 2
About Traps

When cultural and more polite tactics fail, animal garden intruders must sometimes be removed. Several types of traps can be used in the home garden. Live traps and box traps are the most humane and the easiest to use. They are designed to catch the offender and hold him until the garden warden arrives. Inmates may be executed or removed to a suitable, though distant, habitat and released on parole.

One advantage of live trapping is that you do not *have* to harm the animal. The trap serves as a cage for transportation. If a wire mesh trap is used, cover it with an old blanket or burlap bag to minimize the stress on the captive. If you capture a critter other than the offender, say your neighbor's poodle, Sneezy, you can release the innocent party with little more than an apology. No harm done.

Live traps require little technical skill to set up and catch something. You don't run the risk of endangering yourself or others while using them. However, you will be faced with a frightened pair of eyes and a frantic wild animal that you must deal with. Contact your local Extension Service or wildlife authorities for their recommendations.

Traps must be set to be as unobtrusive as possible. Wild things are naturally leery of strange-looking contraptions that suddenly appear in their territories. Cover the trap lightly with dirt and place bait so that the animal will place its foot on the trigger as it goes for the goody. Allow animals to steal the bait a few times; they will become familiar with the trap and lose their fear of it. Since varmints that are raiding your garden have become somewhat accustomed to your scent, you don't have to be absolutely sterile in handling the traps. However, try to minimize that repulsive human odor. Wear cotton gloves when testing the working parts or setting the trap. Some even recommend boiling or holding the trap in a flame.

Regardless of the type of traps used, there are some general rules that will help make your efforts successful.

1. Know what you are after. Identify damage and signs, and use bait appropriate to your particular vandal. Check with wildlife authorities to be sure it is legal to trap the critter.

2. Place traps in or just to the side of animal runways. If these are not easily identifiable, place traps between the animal's den or habitat and the garden.

3. Set up as many traps at once as is reasonable. The more of a pest problem you have, the more you should set out. Animals will become trap shy if they see their own suffering in them.

4. Set traps so that nothing but the working parts move. A trap that rocks or tips when a curious coon tries to rob it from the side will spook the animals.

5. Be certain that the working parts operate properly. Test, oil, and repair if necessary. File or cover any sharp edges in live traps.

6. Make it look natural. Cover the floor or area with dirt and grass. Cover live traps with a canvas to create a dark, cozy atmosphere inside.

7. Make it attractive to the critters. Spread animal scent. Use baits that are smelly and not available in the wild. Coons stuffed on corn still can't resist the temptation of an after-dinner sardine. You may have to go an extra step to get the critter's attention. Place feathers, crumpled balls of shiny foil, or bright Christmas ornaments nearby. Lay a scentline by squirting fish oil, chicken drippings, or broth from a squirt bottle.

8. Eliminate the negative. Place traps in a quiet area. Keep lights off and pets out of the area.

9. Check traps daily. Twice a day is better. Dispose of or release the catch as soon as possible.

10. Release any nontarget animals immediately, unharmed, and report any that may be tagged or banded to wildlife arthorities.

Commercial traps may be rented, borrowed from some wildlife agencies, or purchased from several companies. Plans for homemade traps follow in Appendix 3.

Appendix 3

Live Traps for Mammals

The information in this table was contributed by James L. Byford of the University of Tennessee.

Species	Bait	Live Trap Size (Inches)	Other
Chipmunk	Nuts, peanut butter, bread, shelled corn, unroasted peanuts, rolled oats, apple cubes, sunflower seeds	5x5x18	Set traps near trails or dens.
Coyote	Weiners, canned dog food	30x30x70	none
Dog	Weiners, canned dog food, bacon, smoked ham scraps	30x30x70	none
House cat	Fish, meat, cat food	11x11x36	none
Mouse	Cheese, bread, oatmeal, peanut butter, nuts, gumdrops, raisins, scorched bacon (most human foods are readily accepted)	3x3x10	none

APPENDIX 3

Species	Bait	Live Trap Size (Inches)	Other
Opossum	Vegetables, apple slices, sardines, scrap meat, canned dog food, chicken entrails, fish	11x11x36	none
Rabbit	Vegetables, cabbage, carrots, lettuce, bread	7x7x30	Enclosed box trap does not have to be baited. If baited, lead the rabbit over the trip pan by placing several small pieces of bait in front of the trap and at 3- or 4-inch intervals on into the trap.
Raccoon	Fish (fresh or canned), fresh corn, scrap meat, canned dog food, sardines, chicken, whole fresh egg over sardines, bacon	13x13x42	Fish oil or commercial raccoon lure are very good baits.
Rat	Bloody meat scraps, peanut butter, cheese, gum drops (most human foods are readily accepted)	5x5x18	Place traps along walks, behind objects, along sills, head boards and rafters.
Skunk	Chicken heads or entrails, fish (fresh or canned), scrap meat, canned dog or cat food, sardines, dead mouse, whole fresh egg over sardines, bacon	7x7x30	Skunks won't spray if trap is covered with burlap bag to darken it before transporting.
Squirrel	Nuts, peanut butter, whole peanuts, rolled oats, bread, shelled corn, pumpkin or sunflower seed, dried prunes	7x7x30	Set traps along paths frequently used by squirrels — tree bases, feeding stations, rooftops, etc.

Species	Bait	Live Trap Size (Inches)	Other
Woodchuck	Lettuce, peas or beans, corn, apples, carrots, other fruits, cabbage	11x11x36	none

Build Your Own Live Trap

Plans for live traps are often available at your state or county Extension Service.

The trap pictured below uses a 9-inch dowel of ½-inch circumference. Attach bait to the bottom of the dowel, which extends into the trap, firmly enough so that the animal must pull hard enough to trip the trigger mechanism.

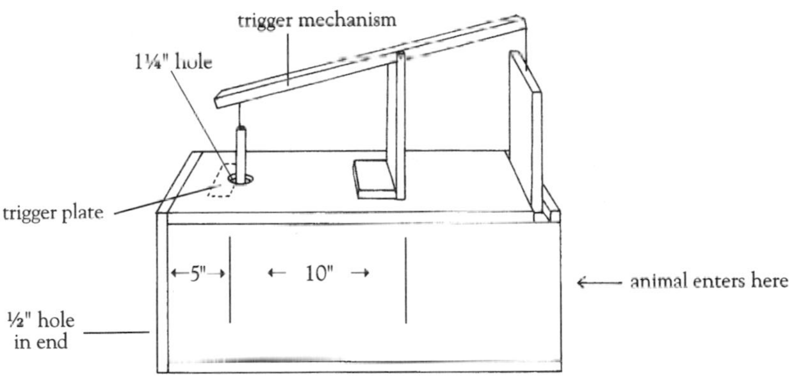

Courtesy of Washington Dept. of Game

Appendix 4

Mail-order Suppliers

Catalogs Offering a Variety of Pest-Control Products*

The Alsto Company
P.O. Box 1267
Galesburg, IL 61401

Henry Field's Heritage Gardens
1 Meadow Ridge Rd.
Shenandoah, IA 51601-0700

Gardener's Supply
128 Intervale Rd.
Burlington, VT 05401

Gardens Alive!
Natural Gardening Research Center
Hwy. 48
P.O. Box 149
Sunman, IN 47041

Gurney's
110 Capitol St.
Yankton, SD 57079

Harmony Farm Supply
3244 Gravenstein Hwy North
Sebastopol, CA 95472

H. G. Hastings
P.O. Box 115535
Atlanta, GA 30310-8535

Johnny's Selected Seed
Foss Hill Rd.
Albion, ME 04910

Mellinger's
2310 W. South Range Rd.
North Lima, OH 44452-9731

Modern Farm
1825 Big Horn Ave.
Cody, WY 82414

Natural Gardening Co.
17 San Anselmo Ave.
San Anselmo, CA 94960

The Necessary Catalogue
P.O. Box 603
New Castle, VA 24127

Walt Nicke's Garden Talk
P.O. Box 433
Topsfield, MA 01983

Peaceful Valley Farm Supply
P.O. Box 2209
Grass Valley, CA 95945

Plow & Hearth
P.O. Box 830
Orange, VA 22960

Seventh Generation
49 Hercules Dr.
Colchester, VT 05446-1672

Solutions
P.O. Box 6878
Portland, OR 97228-6878

Smith & Hawken
25 Corte Madera
Mill Valley, CA 94941

Unique Insect Control
5504 Sperry Dr.
Citrus Heights, CA 95621

*A number of these companies offer botanical insecticide and beneficial insects, as well as wildlife controls

Scare Eye Balloons

Rid-A-Bird Inc.
P.O. Box 436
Wilton, IA 52778

Netting

Orchard Supply Co. of
Sacramento
P.O. Box 956
Sacramento, CA 95805

Animal Repellents, Inc.
P.O. Box 999
Griffin, GA 30224

Distress Calls

Applied Electronics Corp.
3003 County Line Rd.
Little Rock, AR 72201

Signal Broadcasting Co.
2314 Broadway St.
Denver, CO 80205

Exploders

Alexander-Tagg Industries
395 Jacksonville Rd.
Warminster, PA 18794

Flashing Lights

Bird-X
325 W. Huron St.
Chicago, IL 60610

Tripp-Lite Manufacturing
Co.
500 N. Orleans
Chicago, IL 60610

Other Noise

Tomko Enterprises
Route 58, RD #2
P.O. Box 937-A
Riverhead, NY 11901
("Clapper" device with
timer)

Sticky Substance

Tanglefoot Co.
314 Straight Ave. SW
Grand Rapids, MI 49504

Velsicol Chemical Co.
341 E. Ohio St.
Chicago, IL 60611

Refined Coal Tar Repellent

Borderland Products Inc.
P.O. Box 366
Buffalo, NY 14240

Gopher Plant Seeds

Clyde Robin Seed Co.
23010 Lake Forest Dr.,
Suite D321
Laguna Hills, CA 92653

Gopher Traps

Z. A. Macabee Gopher
Trap Co.
110 Loma Alta Ave.
Los Gatos, CA 95030

Guardian Trap Co.
P.O. Box 1935
San Leandro, CA 94577

Joseph B. Cook
11508 Keith Dr.
Whittier, CA 90606

Woodstream Corp.
Lititz, PA 17543

Rodent Traps

Kness Manufacturing Co.
Hwy. 5 South
Albia, IA 52351

Woodstream Corp.
Lititz, PA 17543

Joseph B. Cook
11508 Keith Drive
Whittier, CA 90606

Ultrasound

The Monadnock Co.
P.O. Box 189
Dedham, MA 02026

Glue Boards

Available Exterminators
and Mnfg.
P.O. Box 137
Brooklyn, NY 11236

J. T. Eaton & Co.
1393 Highland Rd.
Twinsburg, OH 44087

Tanglefoot Co.
314 Straight Ave. SW
Grand Rapids, MI 49504

Ferret Scent

Bio-Pest Control
Box 401347
Brooklyn, NY 11240

Mole Traps

Woodstream Corp.
Lititz, PA 17543

Nash Mole Trap Co.
5716 East S Ave.
Vicksburg, MI 49097-9990

Live Traps

Pioneer Wildlife Traps
2909 NE Alberta St.
Portland, OR 97211

Tomahawk Live Trap Co.
P.O. Box 323
Tomahawk, WI 54487

Woodstream Corp.
Lititz, PA 17543

H. J. Spencer & Sons
P.O. Box 131
Gainesville, FL 32602

Mammal Repellents

Bio-Pest Control
Box 401347
Brooklyn, NY 11240

Deer Repellents

J. C. Ehrlich Chemical Co.
State College Laboratories
840 William Ln.
Reading, PA 19612

McLaughlin Gormley King Co.
712 15th Ave. NE
Minneapolis, MN 55413

Decollate Snails

Rincon-Vitova Insectaries
P.O. Box 95
Oak View, CA 93022

Foothill Agricultural Research, Inc.
3126 Tarlor Avenue
Corona, CA 91720

Slug and Snail Traps

Cedar Pete, Inc.
PO Box 969
Mt. Shasta, CA 96067
(Snailproof)

Brucker Snail Barrier Co.
9369 Wilshire Blvd.
Beverly Hills, CA 90210
(Snail-Barr)

W. A. Rapp & Son, Inc.
2031 S. Eastwood St.
Santa Ana, CA 92705
(The Garden Sentry Trap)

Other Products

IGENE Biotechnology, Inc.
9110 Red Branch Rd.
Columbia, MD 21045-2097
(Clandosan)

Maag Agrochemicals Inc.
5699 Kings Hwy
P.O. Box 6430
Vero Beach, FL 32961-6430
(Fire Ant Baits)

Bat Conservation International
P.O. Box 162603
Austin, TX 78716-2603
(Bat houses, plans)

Further Reading

Adler, Bill Jr. *Outwitting Squirrels*. Chicago: Chicago Review Press, 1988.

Bonney, Richard E. *Hive Management*. Pownal, Vt.: Garden Way Publishing, 1991.

Bull, John and Edith. *Birds of North America*. New York: MacMillan Press, 1989.

Carr, Anna. *Rodale's Color Handbook of Garden Insects*. Emmaus, Pa.: Rodale Press, 1987.

Coon, Nelson. *Using Wild and Wayside Plants*. New York: Dover Press, 1980.

Dennis, John V. *The Wildlife Gardener*. New York: Alfred A. Knopf, 1985.

Ernst, Ruth Shaw. *The Naturalist Garden*. Emmaus, Pa.: Rodale Press, 1987.

Goode, John. *Turtles, Tortoises, and Terrapins*. New York: Charles Scribner's Sons, 1971.

Harrison, Kit and George. *America's Favorite Backyard Birds*. New York: Simon & Schuster, 1989.

Headstrom Richard. *Suburban Wildlife*. New York: Prentice Hall Press, 1984.

Headstrom, Richard. *Whose Track Is It?* Ives, Washburn, Inc., 1971.

Johnsgard, Paul A. *North American Owls*. Washington, DC: Smithsonian Institution Press, 1988.

Mahnken, Jan. *Hosting the Birds*. Pownal, Vt.: Garden Way Publishing, 1989.

Mehrtens, John M. *Living Snakes of the World*. Fallbrook, Ca.: Sterling Publishing Co., Inc., 1987.

Novick, Alvin. *The World of Bats*. New York: Holt, Rinehart and Winston, 1969.

Philbrick, Helen and John. *The Bug Book*. Pownal, Vt.: Garden Way Publishing, 1975.

Riotte, Louise. *Carrots Love Tomatoes: Secrets of Companion Planting for Successful Gardening*. Pownal, Vt.: Garden Way Publishing, 1975.

Smith, Hobart and Brodie, Edmund D. Jr. *Reptiles of North America*. San Marino, Ca.: Golden Press, 1982.

Smith, Hobart M. *Snakes as Pets*. Neptune, NJ: TFH Publication, 1980.

Smith, Miranda and Carr, Anna. *Garden Insect, Disease and Weed Identification Guide*. Emmaus, Pa.: Rodale Press, 1988.

Stokes, Donald. *The Bird Feeder Book*. Boston, Ma.: Little, Brown and Co., 1987.

Stokes, Donald and Lillian. *A Guide to Animal Tracking and Behavior*. Boston: Little, Brown and Company, 1987.

Tomkins, Enoch and Griffith, Roger M. *Practical Beekeeping*. Pownal, Vt: Garden Way Publishing, 1977.

Tyler, Hamilton. *Organic Gardening without Poisons*. New York: Van Nostrand Reinhold Co., 1970.

Tyning, Thomas F. *A Guide to Amphibians and Reptiles* (Stokes Nature Guides). Boston: Little, Brown and Company, 1990.

Vivian, John. *Building Fences of Wood, Stone, Metal, and Plants*. Charlotte, Vt.: Williamson Press, 1987.

Wellstead, Graham. *Ferrets and Ferretting*. Neptune, NJ: TFH Publications, 1989.

Yepson, Roger Jr., ed. *Encyclopedia of Natural Insect and Disease Control*. Emmaus, Pa.: Rodale Press, 1984.

Index

A

Alcohol spray, 140
Alfalfa, 21, 40, 41, 50, 59, 153
Alligator, 84
Almond, 77
Alternative food, 13, 18, 41, 60
Aluminum flashing wrap, 34
Aluminum foil mulch, 103
Ambush bug, 182
Amdro, 132-33
Ammonia, 34, 67
Anise, 104
Ant. *See specific types*
Aphid, 102-5
Apple, 103
Apricot, 77
Armadillo, 132
Asparagus, 142
Assassin bug, 104, 182-83
Aster, 137
Aster yellows, 136
Azalea, 77

B

Baby powder. *See* Talcum powder
Badger, 25, 29
Baffle, 37-38, 162
Bag cover, 10, 13, 65
Barn swallow, 163
Basil, 77, 127
Basil spray, 108
Bat, 123, 132, 167-69
Beans, 40, 77, 103, 110, 114, 120, 122, 124, 128, 137, 140, 141, 145, 150, 153
Bear, 35, 43-46, 84
Beer, 80
Beet, 106, 128, 137, 139, 150
Beetle, 8, 15, 132, 180-82
Beetlejuice, 108, 110
Beetles, 105-14. *See also specific types*
Beets, 103, 110
Berries, 17, 30, 37, 45, 148. *See also specific types*
Big-eyed bug, 104, 183
Bio-control, 104, 108, 112, 114, 119, 121, 123, 125-26, 127, 132, 135, 138, 144, 151, 152, 153
Birdbath, 158-59
Bird feed, 159-62
Birdhouses, 163-66
Birds, 5-18, 113, 155. *See also specific types*
  acquiring and managing, 156-67
  beaks, 157-58
Bird scare reflecting tape, 9
Blackberries, 8
Blackbird, 5, 6 11, 125
Black pepper mixture, 60
Black salsify, 134
Blood meal, 37, 41, 51, 60, 64
Blueberries, 5, 15, 17, 45, 139, 148
Bluebird, 163
Blue jay, 18, 125
Bobcat, 35, 42
Boiling water, 132
Bone tar oil, 51
Borage, 112, 127
Borers, 115-16. *See also specific types*
Boric acid, 128
Botanical insecticide, 97-100
Braconid wasp, 127, 187
Brassica, 124, 142
Brewer's blackbird, 6-11
Broccoli, 103, 106, 117, 120, 143, 150
Brussels sprouts, 103, 117, 143
Bt injection, 116
Bt spray, 97, 121, 127
Buckwheat, 153
Bug bounty, 74

Bug juice, 95-96, 121
Bugs, 117-19, 138, 182-83. *See also specific types*
Bulb, 37
Burrowing. *See Tunneling*
Buttermilk spray, 140

C

Cabbage, 103, 106, 114, 117, 120, 139, 141, 143, 150, 153
Cabbage looper, 119-21
Cabbageworm, 119-21
Cage covers, 10, 13, 16, 24, 37
Cages, 49, 61, 71, 93, 166. *See also specific types*
Calendula, 142
Cantaloupe, 48
Cardboard collar, 125
Cardinal, 17-18
Carnation, 120
Carrot, 22, 40, 133, 141, 145, 150, 153
Carrot rust fly, 133-34
Castor oil, 28
Castor-oil plant, 22, 51
Cat, 25, 29, 34, 37, 38, 69-71, 84, 155, 170
Caterpillar, 119-26. *See also specific types*
Cat hair, 37
Catnip, 70, 107, 108, 152
Cauliflower, 103, 106, 117, 120, 143, 150
Cedar bough spray, 108
Celeriac, 133
Celery, 120, 128, 133, 137, 150
Chalcid wasp, 104, 187
Chard, 77, 103, 139
Cherries, 8, 15, 17
Chickadee, 163
hicken, 72, 166-67
dren and gardens, 72-74
powder, 60
nk, 35-38
04, 140
mum, 139
Cigarette plant, 77
Citrus, 131
Citrus rinds, 80
Clandosan, 142
Clover, 40, 41, 135, 153
Codling moth, 8
Cole crop, 106, 120. *See also specific types*
Collard, 114, 117
Colorado potato beetle, 107-8
Columbine, 139
Common grackle, 6-11
Companion planting, 8, 92, 104, 110, 114, 116, 118-19, 120, 125, 142, 144
Compost, 45, 57, 77, 86-87, 131
Copper sheet, 78
Coriander, 104, 108, 134
Corn, 5, 8, 13, 17, 18, 30, 37, 45, 50, 57, 63, 66, 72, 77, 110, 111, 122, 124, 128, 131, 140, 153
Corn earworm, 8, 121-123
Cornmeal, 126
Cornmeal and dry cement, 35
Corn oil spray, 115, 142
Cosmos, 110
Cotton, 122, 150
Cover crops, 139, 153
Cow, 72
Cowbird, 6-11
Coyote, 25, 29, 35, 46-49, 65, 84
Crab spider, 180
Creosote, 51
Crocodile, 84
Crop cover, 107, 108, 110, 116, 118, 119, 120, 127, 134, 138, 144
Crop rotation, 91, 103, 108, 110, 118, 121, 127, 139, 142, 150
Crotalaria, 142
Crow, 5, 11-14
Cucumber, 37, 109, 115, 118, 141, 145, 153
Cucumber beetle, 109-10
Cucurbit, 110
Curly top, 136
Currents, 17
Cutworm, 8, 15, 123-26

D

Daffodil, 22, 34, 77
Dahlia, 110, 128, 137
Daisy, 110
Damsel bug, 123, 183
Damsel fly, 183
Dead nettle, 108
Decollate snail, 79, 176-77
Decoy, 9, 18, 61
Deer, 49-56
  plants not eaten, 52
Delphinium, 77
Deodorant soap, 51
Diatomaceous earth, 81, 99, 105, 138, 144, 146, 151
Dill, 127, 133, 150
Distress calls, 16, 18, 168
Dog, 29, 34, 37, 42, 48, 52, 61, 65, 69-71, 84, 169-70
Dog hair, 23, 37, 51, 60
Donkey, 48
Dormant oil spray, 95, 104
Drainage, 153
Droppings, 63
Drought, 114
Dry ice, 26, 38, 42
Duck, 72, 79, 166-67
Dusts, 79, 94-95. *See also specific*
types
Dusty miller, 60

E

Earthworm, 27
Earwig, 127-28, 132
Eggplant, 106, 110, 122, 127, 137, 140
Elcar, 123
Elderberry cuttings, 23
Encarsia formosa, 152, 189
English sparrow, 123

Epsom salts spray, 108
Exclusion, 10-11, 13-14, 16, 23, 28-29, 41-42, 48-49, 57, 71, 78, 104, 107, 108, 110, 112, 114, 116, 125, 131

F

Farm animals, 72
Fencing, 24, 28-29, 31, 34, 41-42, 48-49, 53-56, 57, 60-61, 64, 71, 72, 74, 78-79, 80-81
  deer fence, 53
  electric deer fence, 54-55
  flat out, 56
  Minnesota Zaps electric fence, 46, 54-55
  mystery fence, 53
  New Hampshire three-wire, 54-55
  Penn State, 54-55
  slug fence, 79
  tripod slant, 53-54
Fennel, 78, 133
Ferret, 25, 34-35, 61, 170-72
Ferret scent, 23, 34
Fescue, 142
Fire ant, 123, 129-33
Fish heads, 51
Fish spray, 60
Flax, 108
Flea beetle, 105-7
Flooding, 25
Floodlight, 64
Flowers, 37, 40, 72, 120, 140. *See also specific types*
Fly, 133-34, 138, 183-86. *See also specific types*
Foil, 18
Foil collar, 145
Food chain, 155
Fowl, 72
  acquiring and managing, 166-67
Fox, 25, 35, 38, 42, 65
Freesia, 77
Fruit, 13, 15, 30, 37, 50, 57, 82, 110, 111, 148, 150. *See also specific types*
Fuchsia, 77
Fungus, 108, 142

G

Garbage, 45, 67
Garden debris, 107
Garden pond, 175
Garlic, 22, 41, 60, 104, 108, 112, 120, 123, 125, 140
Garlic spray, 71, 96
Garter snake, 79
Geese, 72
Geranium, 112
Geranium stalk spray, 110
Ginger, 77, 78
Gladiola, 145
Glass bottles, 23, 28, 60
Goat, 72
Goldfinch, 17-18
Gopher, 19-26
Gopher plant, 77
Gopher spurge, 22
Gosling, 79
Gotcha line, 11, 14, 17, 18, 166
Grackle, 123
Grain, 13, 15, 50
Grapes, 15, 17, 45, 60, 77
Grass, 40, 111, 135
Grasshopper, 8, 15, 134-36
Green lacewing, 184-85
Greens, 17
Ground beetle, 108, 125, 180-81
Ground squirrel, 35-38
Grub, 27

H

Hair, 23. *See also specific types*
Hairy indigo, 142
Handpicking, 78, 112, 114, 116, 119, 120, 122-23, 125, 127
Hardware cloth wrap, 31, 61, 78, 166
Harlequin bug, 117-18
Hawk, 25, 29, 35, 38, 42
Hibiscus, 77
Holly, 77
Hollyhock, 128
Home brew slug beer, 80
Horse, 72
Horse hair, 79
Horseradish, 108, 117
Hot pepper mixture, 37, 41, 60, 64, 71
Hot pepper spray, 37, 41, 52, 79, 96, 136, 139
Hover fly, 183-84
Human hair, 23, 51, 60, 79
Humus, 86
Hyacinth, 34
Hyssop, 120

I

Ichneumon fly, 123
Ichneumon wasp, 188
Insects, 27, 85-153. *See also specific types*
  beneficial, 177-90
  identifying, 100-101
Interplanting. *See* Companion planting

J

Japanese beetle, 15, 110-13
Jerusalem cherry, 77
Jumping spider, 180

K

Kale, 114, 117, 120
Kestrel, 163
Kinglet, 163
Kitty litter, 23
Kohlrabi, 117, 120

L

Lacewing, 104, 123, 140, 152, 155, 184-85
Ladybug, 104, 140, 152, 155, 181-82

Lamb's quarters, 139, 140
Larkspur, 112
Leafhopper, 136-38
Leaf miner, 138-39
Leafy vegetables, 77. *See also specific types*
Legume, 40
Lettuce, 40, 59, 120, 128, 141, 150
Light flashes, 16, 18, 45, 52
Lime, 119, 123, 144
Lime juice spray, 79, 105
Limestone, 60, 78, 107
Livestock, 72-74
Livestock feed covering, 15-16, 45
Lizard, 84
Location of plants, 8, 9, 138
Locust, 134-36
Logic, 132
Lynx spider, 180
Lysol, 71

M

Magnesium, 152
Mantis, 135
Manure, 52
Marigold, 60, 77, 106, 108, 118, 127, 142, 152
Meadowlark, 125
Melon, 30, 37, 40, 45, 82-83, 109, 115, 118, 140, 148. *See also specific types*
Metal band, 37-38
Mexican bean beetle, 113-15
Migratory birds, 5
Milkweed, 103
Milky spore disease, 28, 112
Mineral oil, 123
Mint, 107, 120
Misting, 106
Mite, 132, 139-40
Mockingbird, 163
Mole, 26-30, 79, 123, 125
Mole plant, 28
Mothballs, 51
Motion as scare tactic, 9, 18
Mound building, 131-32
Mounding soil, 116
Mouse, 31-35
Mulberries, 48
Mulching, 77, 83, 108, 110, 119, 140, 144, 145
Mushroom, 37
Mustard, 117
Mustard greens, 114

N

Nasturtium, 104, 108, 118, 139, 152
Neem, 110
Neem oil, 98-99
Nematode, 126, 132, 135, 141-42, 144, 151, 153, 189-90
Nesting site control, 33, 148-49
Netting, 10, 16, 18, 64
Newspaper mulch, 23
Nicandra, 152
Nicotine, 97-98
Nicotine sulfate, 71
Nitrogen, 87
Noise, 10, 16, 18, 23, 45, 52, 64
Nuclear polyhedrosis, 123
Nuts, 111

O

Oats, 18
Okra, 122, 131
Onion, 41, 60, 108, 120, 123, 125, 134, 140, 143, 145, 150, 153
Onion mixture, 71
Opal basil, 127
Opossum, 56-58
Ornamentals, 103. *See also specific types*
Owl, 25, 29, 35, 38, 42, 65, 163

P

Paper wasp, 108
Parasite, 113, 121, 126, 135, 152
Parasite wasp, 108, 188
Parsley, 77, 120, 133, 150
Parsnip, 133, 150
Peach, 15
Pear, 48, 103
Peas, 40, 72, 103, 110, 119, 120, 122, 141, 145, 150, 153
Pennyroyal, 134
Pepper, 122, 127, 139
Peruvian lily, 77
Petunia, 104
pH balance, 88-89, 112
Pheasant, 17-18
Phoebe, 163
Phosphate, 87
Phosphorous, 88, 152
Pig, 72
Pinwheel, 18, 23
Piperonyl butoxide (PBO), 97
Plantain, 40
Plant coverings, 92-94
Plant food, 88
Plant juice, 96
Plastic streamers, 18, 64
Plum, 48, 77
Porcupine, 30-31
Potassium, 88
Potato, 22, 106, 108, 110, 120, 122, 127, 128, 131, 137, 139, 141, 145, 150, 153
Praying mantis, 185-86
Predators, 25, 29, 34-35, 38, 42, 56, 79-80, 84, 108, 114, 121
  acquiring and managing, 155-190
Predatory wasp, 188
Pumpkin, 77, 109, 115, 118
Purple martin, 164
Pyrethrum, 98, 110, 115, 116, 118, 132, 138, 145

R

Rabbit, 58-62
Racoon, 62-65, 84
Radish, 106, 116, 117, 118, 120, 143, 144, 150, 153
Raspberries, 17, 111
Rat, 31-35
Red mite, 135
Redwing blackbird, 6-11, 123
Repellents, 22-23, 28, 34, 37, 41, 51, 60, 63, 67, 70-71, 77-78, 104, 108, 122, 134, 140, 142, 152, 153. *See also specific types*
Resistant varieties, 92, 106, 116, 117, 119, 120, 122, 145
Rhododendron, 77
Rhubarb, 77, 103, 111, 137, 150
Robber fly, 184
Robin, 17-18, 125
Rock phosphate, 144
Rodenticide, 19
Rodents, 19-42, 135
Roosting control, 8, 15-16
Root maggot, 143-44
Rose, 50, 110, 139, 145
Rosemary, 77, 120, 134
Rotenone, 97, 105, 110, 113, 115, 116, 138, 145
Rotten eggs, 51
Row cover, 104, 114, 166
Rue, 71, 112
Rutabaga, 143, 153
Ryania, 98
Ryegrass, 142

S

Sabadilla, 98, 118
Sabadilla dust, 119, 139
Sage, 77, 120, 134
Saliva, 142
Sanitation, 33, 57
Scarecrow, 9, 18, 45, 64
Scare eye balloon, 10, 13, 16, 18
Scare tactics, 9-10, 13, 16, 18, 23, 45, 48, 52-53, 60-61. *See also specific types*
Scillia, 34
Screening, 37, 119, 166
Seedlings, 124, 128
Seeds, 15, 17, 37
  drying, 151
  exposed, 9
Sheep, 72
Shore birds, 84
Shrew, 79, 125
Skunk, 25, 29, 65-68, 84
Slug, 75-81
Slug juice, 79
Smartweed, 122
Snail, 27, 75-81, 176-77
Snake, 13, 25, 35, 38, 135, 172-73
Snap beans, 108
Soaking crops, 121
Soap spray, 95, 104, 118, 119, 138, 139, 140, 145, 152
Soil, 86-91
Solarization, 89-91
Soldier beetle, 123, 182
Soldier bug, 104, 183
Soybeans, 41, 50
Spider, 104, 132, 135, 179-80
Spinach, 103, 106, 120, 139, 150
Spray, 71, 79, 94-95. *See also specific types*
  guidelines, 99
Squash, 37, 40, 109, 115, 118, 119, 122, 141, 145
Squash bug, 118-19
Squash vine borer, 115-16
Squill, 22
Squirrel, 35-38
Starling, 5, 14-17
Sticky barrier, 131
Strawberries, 15, 37, 128, 131, 140, 141, 148
Stress ethylene, 86
Succulent plants, 40
Sulfur, 152
Sunflower, 8, 17, 77, 103, 122, 125
Swedish ivy, 77
Sweet pea, 110
Sweet potato, 153
Syrphid, 183-84

T

Tachinid fly, 108, 123, 128, 184
Talcum powder, 41, 51, 60, 64
Tankage, 51
Tansy, 108, 118, 120, 125
Tarpaper collar, 144
Tea, 96, 107, 108, 113, 123, 131
  rhubarb, 140
  from tobacco stems, 104
Thrasher, 17-18
Thrip, 144-46
Thyme, 120
Tiger beetle, 182
Tilling, 9, 103, 122, 125, 127, 135, 139, 153, 167
Timed planting, 8, 77, 91-92, 114, 116, 120, 139, 143
Timothy, 142
Titmouse, 164
Toad, 79, 108, 125, 135, 174-76
Tobacco, 127
Tomato, 37, 57, 82-83, 106, 110, 120, 122, 124, 127, 137, 140, 141, 145, 150, 153
Tomato hornworm, 126-27
Transplanting, 24-25, 77, 118, 124, 152
Trap crop, 51, 103, 112, 117, 122, 125, 127, 144, 152
Trapping, 25-26, 29-30, 31, 35, 38, 42, 46, 57-58, 61-62, 65, 67-68, 70, 80, 84, 104, 107, 110, 113, 119, 126, 128, 148, 152, 153
  blacklight, 123, 138
  hopperdozer, 135-36
  Japanese beetle trap, 112
Trees, 22, 30, 31, 34

Trellis, 82-83, 119, 131
Trichogramma wasp, 186-87
Tubers, 22
Tulip, 22
Tumbler, 37-38
Tunneling, 23-26, 27-30, 38, 40, 42, 131
Turkey, 166-67
Turnip, 106, 117, 120, 141, 143, 150, 153
Turnip spray, 115
Turtle, 79, 81-85, 174

U

Ultrasound, 23, 34, 37, 94
Urine, 52, 63

V

Vegetables, 50, 103, 150. *See also specific types*
Velvet beans, 142
Vinegar spray, 79
Vining crops, 64-65, 82, 115, 118, 137. *See also specific types*
Vole, 31-35

W

Warbler, 164
Wasp, 121, 123, 126, 127, 138, 146-49, 186-88. *See also specific types*
Watermelon, 13, 48, 63, 153
Weasel, 25, 42, 65
Weeding, 8, 125, 134, 135, 140, 145
Weed mat, 34
Weevil, 8, 149-51
Wheat bran dust, 108
Whirligig, 23, 28
Whitefly, 151-52
White mustard, 153
White winter radish, 77
Wildcat, 38
Windbreaks, 138
Windjug, 28
Wire mesh, 23-24, 166
Wireworm, 152-53
Wolf spider, 180
Wood ash, 60, 107, 110, 119, 144
Woodchuck, 38-42
Woodpecker, 123
Woody plants, 50
Wormwood, 77, 107, 134
Wren, 164

Y

Yellow jacket, 121, 146-49
  avoiding, 147

Z

Zinnia, 110, 128